Communication Magic

Exploring the Structure and Meaning of Language

L. Michael Hall, Ph.D.

Formerly *The Secrets of Magic*

Crown House Publishing
www.crownhouse.co.uk

First published in the UK by

Crown House Publishing Limited
Crown Buildings
Bancyfelin
Carmarthen
Wales
SA33 5ND
UK

www.crownhouse.co.uk

First published 2001.
Reprinted 2002.

British Library Cataloguing-in-Publication Data
A catalogue entry for this book is available
from the British Library.

ISBN 189983673X

Printed and bound in the UK by
The Cromwell Press
Trowbridge
Wiltshire

Table of Contents

Lists of Figures and Charts

Foreword

Touched by Magic

Once upon a time an Ugly Frog was Touched by Magic.
A Wizard waved her wand, said some words,
and then, presto … poof of smoke …
the ugly frog discovered that he was really …
A handsome Prince
with all the resources he needed
to live fully and vibrantly.
For you see, the magic of the words restored him
to his true identity and his true destiny
as it opened his eyes to all the rich resources within.
And so he went on his princely way, merrily,
totally Transformed and Thrilled…
and repeatedly Telling his story to all who would listen,
which began to cause him to *feel really curious*
about that magic.
"Just how did she do that anyway?"
"Is there any Method in her Magic?"
"If I could find the Structure in the Magic,
could I then learn to perform Magic like that?"
And these words echoed in his mind.
Now it came to pass in those days
that two modelers were also touched by Magic
and forthwith thereafter began to hold workshops
throughout the Kingdom on the Structure of Magic.
And so as the prince took his place in the workshop,
not even knowing the extent of his magic skills
having been Touched by Magic,
and so he *accessed his most ferocious learning state*
because he didn't want to miss any of
the secrets of magic.
So as he began to *breath deeply and fully*
with a calm relaxation in the growing excited anticipation
of become even more skilled as
a Neuro-Linguistic Magician…

Preface

Communication Magic describes the *magic* that we can perform with *language*. It describes the neurological effects of words, symbols, and ideas on our lives and emotions. It shows how mental phenomena which we can't see, hear, touch, taste, or smell can turn life into a living hell or into an experience of ecstasy and delight.

In *Communication Magic*, you will find a model, a cutting-edge model about communicating, thinking, experiencing, constructing realities, and influencing the realities of others. That makes this *a dangerous book*. Yet when you finish this book, you may not feel that you have just completed reading something dangerous. Yet it is. In the wrong hands, this model can supply the unscrupulous with the human technology for influence and persuasion by which to do immense harm.

Why take the chance of arming the unscrupulous and dishonest with the model and techniques here? Because by hook or crook (in other books, in trainings, by trial and error experience) they can find such techniques anyway. I have written this for defense against such. After all, *awareness* of the magic of language gives us a 'heads-up' about dangerous spins and manipulations.

On the surface, this book is about how to communicate more effectively, precisely, and even magically. It is a book about how to effectively use your unique gift of language in a way that *expands* your mental maps and enriches your life. This book highlights the dangers of impoverished language that limits and undermines success and happiness.

The Magic of Language Elegance

Everyday, in just about everything we engage in, we *use language.* We use language to get along with others, to engage in business, to negotiate, to persuade, to sell, to solve problems, to express our creativity, and for a thousand other activities. And, sometimes, languaging works in seemingly magical ways. Sometimes a single word can set off an argument, break loyal bonds, violate friends, and ignite legal proceeds. Sometimes a word can turn a person around, create a new sense of hope and meaning, and heal a wounded heart. Words work powerfully in these ways.

Languaging uniquely defines how we use symbols in our everyday experiences. The pervasiveness of language as well as the centrality of our *language skills* explains why our *use of language* so crucially determines our effectiveness, self-management, and happiness. This book focuses on these things and on how to use language with both the magic of precision and the magic of hypnosis. It's about developing greater skills in the persuasion arts. In this book, you will be invited into a mindful understanding of several things:

- How language affects the mind-body system
- How language can perform magic-like feats in nervous and immune systems
- How we navigate the territory of the world via the magical realm of words and ideas
- How the magic can curse and sabotage and turn life into a living hell
- How the magic can bless, empower and enable us to take charge of running our own brains.

At a deeper level, this book invites you to take a journey—a journey into the wild and wonderful realm of 'mind,' into neuro-linguistic and neuro-semantic reality where mind-body works as a system in response to *symbols*. That may sound complex. And certainly, from the point of view of a neuro-biologist or neuro-scientist, there are all kinds of complexities about this that we have not begun to fathom. Yet, how *language* actually affects our mind-body system on a day to day basis is simple. You can test it. Test it simply by trying out some of the patterns, using the secrets, and noticing whether it empowers you as a person, enhances your life, or doesn't create any magic for you.

The Magic Things You can Do with Language

Since language operates as one of the meta-processes above and beyond ('meta') primary experiences, there's all kinds of things that we can do with language.

Austin (1955) recognized the 'performative' role of words and described such in his classic William James Lecture at Harvard, *How To Do Things With Words.* For Austin, much of our language use involves performative language; "to say something is to do something, or in saying something we do something" (p. 108).

Church (1961) took that idea further,

> "Words do not have meanings, but functions. The 'meanings' assigned to words by dictionaries are abstractions drawn from the way words function in various contexts." (p. 217)

Though stated here in either/or terminology (for words have both meanings and functions), Church emphasizes the functional role of words. What are all the things we can do with language, with symbols, verbal and non-verbal? What are some of the things *you* do with words every day as you move through the world?

Gather information
Understand another's perspective
Seek clarification when confused
Bond with another person
Dis-bond with another
Express endearment to another
Reinforce behaviors and responses
Extinguish behaviors and responses
Create patterns of persuasion
Experience a catharsis of emotion
Confess faults and problems
Take responsibility for myself
Shift responsibility away from myself
Update mental maps about reality
Hypnotize people into various states
Engage a person about something
Disclose various depths of things
Soothe, nourish, and comfort
Joke, create humor, jar consciousness
Learn something new
Inform another
Influence people
De-hypnotize
Unload emotional stress
Validate, affirm
Advocate a position
Problem solve
Formulate a problem
Apologize for hurts
Negotiate an arrangement
Confuse someone
Insinuate
Swear
Universalize a problem
Show off
Meta-communicate
Express intentions

Re-Visiting the Secrets of 'Magic'

We will begin with a very powerful and profound *model* of language called The *'Meta-Model.'* This model was first developed and popularized by a linguist (Dr. John Grinder) and a student of mathematics and computers (Richard Bandler). They conceived it as they over-heard two therapeutic wizards *use language in magical ways* to expand and enrich the lives of their clients.

We will start there, but we will not stay there. We will look at how the *Meta-Model* grew and developed over the years, how it evolved and changed. We will explore how it moved beyond the confines of psychotherapy into business, management, coaching, persuasion, parenting, and a hundred other arenas. We will also examine some of the future possibilities of this model.

When Bandler and Grinder first listened to Fritz Perls (founder of Gestalt Therapy) and then to Virginia Satir (founder of Family Systems Therapy) they noticed magical transformations that occurred through just talking. But they also heard something else. They listened to the *language* in a special way—in terms its *structure and form.* They noticed that the magic had structure.

That got them thinking.

> "Could the magic be nestled inside the structure of the words?"
>
> "Could the marvelous transformations arise, not from the *theories* that Perls or Satir proposed, but from the *unique ways* they *talked?"*

Taking their cue from this wild idea, they modeled the linguistic forms and published their findings in two books, *The Structure of Magic, Volumes I and II* (1975, 1976). As a linguist, John Grinder had already written a book on the linguistic forms and structures of Transformational Grammar (1974), a book, by the way, which is remarkably similar to *The Structure of Magic.*

I didn't encounter the Meta-Model of Language until the late 1980s when I trained with Richard Bandler. I then used it to reproduce the genius of Perls and Satir in my own psychotherapeutic practice. That lead me to write my doctoral dissertation on languaging, to become an NLP trainer, and to co-found the field of Neuro-Semantics.

Communication Magic not only surveys the Meta-Model, it also *updates* it. We will first revisit the original model and then we will observe how it has grown and evolved. Later I will suggest additional pieces to the model from General Semantics and Cognitive Psychology.

The Magic of Becoming the Boss of Your Words

As we adventure into the magic of our own neuro-linguistics, we will examine the Meta-Model and work with the profound simplicity of that model. In fact, this may fool you. I didn't realize the profundity hidden inside this language model when I first encountered the Meta-Model.

Actually, when I first read about the Meta-Model, I really didn't think that much of it. I liked it. Sure, I thought it had some merit for enabling me to speak more precisely. But it didn't ring any bells for me. Having studied the biblical languages (Koine Greek, Hebrew, Latin) as well as Transformational Grammar and General Semantics, the Meta-Model did not leave a very good first impression.

"Yes, I know that stuff; nothing really new."

Today I stand amazed that a person can hold a magic wand in his or her hands *and not know it!*

I got my attitude adjustment about the Meta-Model during my training with Richard Bandler. I heard Richard say, almost in an off-the-cuff manner, something to the effect that everything in NLP, every model, every technique, and every distinction that makes a difference arises from the Meta-Model.

"Oh really?"

He commented that *not* to know the Meta-Model inside out, backwards and forwards, and to understand it as *a model for modeling* subjective experiences would effectively prevent one from ever becoming truly proficient (let alone a master) with the *technologies of magic* in the field of NLP.

That caught my attention. I knew the power of NLP in creating profound transformation, but I had not fully appreciated its foundation in language, in linguistics. That mental frame then gave birth to numerous questions:

- How does he think that the simple model of the Meta-Model could be *that* powerful?
- What does he know about the Meta-Model that I must have missed?
- How does the Meta-Model play so crucial a role in modeling human experiences?

When I first began entertaining such questions I didn't know the answers. So I returned to the Meta-Model, to *The Structure of Magic,* and to freshly discovering the secrets of magic.

Later, after I found the secrets, I began exploring for more and additional expressions of such neuro-linguistic magic. That led me back to Alfred Korzybski who founded General Semantics, then to Cognitive Psychology, Cognitive Linguistics, and to a multitude of other fields, authors, and models. Eventually I wrote my dissertation on how language works in seemingly magical ways (*Languaging,* 1996).

As we journey back to *revisit magic,* set your mind to avoid making the mistake that I initially made when I discounted the profoundness of the Meta-Model because it seemed so simple on the surface. There are secrets of magic within. Let them haunt you, seduce you, and pull on the strings of your heart and mind until they reveal their secrets to you. By all means, don't miss the profound nature of the simplicity of the magic that lies before you in the pages of this book. Truly you hold a magic wand in your hands that provides for you significant keys to *the secret* of magic.

The Magic Hidden Within

The reason for revisiting the magic discovered 25 years ago is not merely for historical interest about its source. I have another agenda. I want to *update* the Meta-Model. In this book you will find a *new extended version of the Meta-Model,* one written not only for therapists, but for everybody who wants to use language in magical and persuasive ways.

I have not written about the structure of magic only to improve science and sanity, but also to *use* it in our everyday speaking and writing. If you have a magic wand, you might as well use it, mightn't you? So given that, here are a few caveats as warning ahead of time regarding some of the unique languaging practices in this book.

You will discover, in the following pages, that I have incorporated numerous linguistic devices from General Semantics. When you first come upon them, they may strike you as weird. Magic is like that. Alfred Korzybski (1933/1994) developed these as linguistic mechanisms to help promote a more non-Aristotelian language system and orientation. His aim in doing so was to promote "Science and Sanity." These *extensional devices* include 'etc', an emphasis on verbs, eliminating 'to be' verbs, using quotation marks, and hyphening terms.

I've sprinkled the magic of '*etc.*' frequently within this text. I did that on purpose, not as a bad linguistic habit! Let this extensional device remind you that "I have not said all," that "I could have said a great deal more." This helps to avoid the *absolutism* in assuming that a given statement utters the last word about something. Let the magic of '*etc.*' evoke curiosity and thoughtfulness in you as you read. Let it cue your brain to begin wondering about all the things that have been left out.

I've also used the magic of *verbs.* Verbs get things done! And, given the *dynamic universe of processes* that we live in, verbs allow us to map the world more accurately. Verbs give us the magic of a functional, behavioral, and dynamic language; it replaces the old static Aristotelian world-view and language forms. Expect to find 'emote' and 'emoting' for the thing-like term 'emotions,' 'somatizing' for experiencing psychosomatic results (i.e., headaches, stomach aches, ulcers, etc.).

There's magic in saying 'is,' and yet, for the most part, it is an unsane type of magic. It solidifies things. It freezes things in time and space, it identifies, etc. The General Semantics device of E-Prime seeks to *prime* (or eliminate) from English all forms of 'is,' especially the *'is' of identity* ("He is a failure") and the *'is' of predication* ("She is rude"). Originally, I wrote the first edition of this book using E-Prime. Many didn't like it, 'too weird' they said.

Putting quotation marks around words enables us to call special attention to terms whose magic can easily be misunderstood. I typically will write 'mind' to avoid the false-to-fact understanding that 'mind' can exist and operate apart from 'body.' The quotation marks call attention to the use of a word and invite consideration lest it evokes some semantic damage.

I've also sprinkled dashes here and there to caution about the black magic of 'elementalism.' Treating a single *element* of a process may allow us to talk about it, but that's the trick. We can only talk about it. It does not truly exist by itself. It can't. Semantic damage occurs when we forget that the element *only exists in thought and language,* and not in reality. We can talk about 'mind,' conceptually, *as if* it exists apart from 'body.' We speak about 'space' as if it exists apart from 'time.' But that's just talk. The magic of sprinkling little dashes here and there keeps the world connected: 'the time-space continuum,' 'the mind-body organism,' 'neuro-semantic' reality, etc.

Ready for Magic

Are you ready for *a touch of magic?* Would you like to *touch* the people in your life with the magic of precision, clarity, or resourcefulness? Language skills can give you that power. Language skill and understanding puts a magic wand in your hands so that you can communicate more effectively and clearly. It allows you to use the magic of precision to match the messages you're sending with those that your hearer receives. It endows you with the magic of induction or trance so that you can communicate in ways that invite your listeners to step into new conceptual worlds. It allows you to become a marvelous storyteller, hypnotist, and persuader. It puts into your hands the skills and tools for detracting high quality information from the people who are trying to get their messages over, but who don't know the secrets, principles, or structure of magic.

Magic lies at your fingertips. It lies in the language that you use to think, to imagine, to hope and dream, to formulate and solve problems, to express yourself, to bond with others, to make your dreams come true.

May your journey into magic—into the magical model that we call the Meta-Model—enrich your use of this magic wand.

L. Michael Hall

Acknowledgments

The original inspiration for this work came from the two geniuses that began NLP, *John Grinder* and *Richard Bandler.* They charted the way in 1973–1976 as they made the *Meta-Model* explicit in their original ground-breaking volumes of *The Structure of Magic.*

In *Robert Dilts* I found brilliant developments of NLP and the Meta-Model, especially his volumes, *The Roots of NLP* (1983) and *Applications of NLP* (1983). *Alfred Korzybski's* development of General Semantics and his masterpiece *Science and Sanity* obviously informs so much of what follows, as does *George Lakoff's* work in Generative Semantics and Cognitive Linguistics.

Bobby G. Bodenhamer, with whom I have been co-writing since 1996, provided encouragement, insights, and challenges. He challenged me to make the writing clearer and more practical and he designed many of the charts of the Meta-Model and the *Mind-Lines Model.*

Charles Faulkner kept me on my toes via numerous emails and challenges that he made about some of my assertions about the Meta-Model. I have long appreciated his scholarship in Cognitive Linguistics, metaphors, etc. Though we differ in some conclusions, he has sharpened my thinking.

Others have played a significant role in this work: *Katrina Patterson,* NLP trainer and editor, and *Debra Lederer,* author and trainer. *Joe Munshaw* and *Nelson Zink,* NLP Trainers in the USA. While I have challenged some of their ideas, they have certainly offered me several new perspectives. Peter Kean, NLP Trainer, supplied me with some historical information about the early Meta-Model. Other writers on whom this work depends: Lewis and Frank Pucelik's creative and insightful work, *Magic Demystified* (1982), Joseph O'Connor and John Seymour's description of the Meta-Model in *Introducing Neuro-Linguistic Programming* (1990).

A special thanks to publisher *Dr. Martin Roberts* who has provided constant editorial insight and encouragement throughout. When I get lost in the trees of the details I can always depend upon Martin for the larger perspective that he always provides.

L. Michael Hall

Part I

Becoming a Word Magician in Communicating

Chapter 1

The Discovery of Magic

"They are methods which give an onlooker
the impression of magic
if he be not himself initiated or
equally skilled in the mechanism."
H. Vailinger, 1924

"*Magic is hidden* in the language we speak.
The webs that you can tie and untie are at your command if only you pay attention to what you already have (language) and the structure of the incantations for growth..."
Bandler and Grinder, 1975, p. 19

The Story

It all began a long time ago (in the early 1970s) when a curious guy stumbled upon a therapeutic magician. This magician could do things that seemed like *magic* with his words in his conversations with clients. As the curious guy listened to the audio-tapes and transcribed them, he played around mimicking the language patterns of Fritz Perls. Later, as he continued the play in other contexts and with some of his college students, he found that he could actually replicate the magic of Gestalt Therapy. That surprised people, but not as much as it surprised him. It mystified him.

This is magical! How does this work?

To explore this, he contacted one of his professors, a young professor of linguistics, to help him figure out how *mere words* and simply expressing them in special ways could have that kind of magical effect. Thus the journey began.

Soon they found another magician in the person of world renowned family systems founder, Virginia Satir, and they began playing around with the linguistic structure of her magic as well. And after that, they came upon yet another magician, a wizard who used words to hypnotize and to create altered realities, Milton Erickson, M.D.

It wasn't long afterwards that they put their findings down on paper, into a book, and then formulated it into a model. At first they called it 'the Meta-Model of language in therapy.' Eventually, it was shortened to *the Meta-Model.* From that model a new field arose, a field known today as NLP, *Neuro-Linguistic Programming.*

The magicians Bandler and Grinder modeled happened to work their magic in the context of *psychotherapy* and/or hypnotherapy. It was simply by speaking, by speaking in particular ways, that they facilitated *transformations* in the lives of men and women. This absolutely fascinated the modelers. It evoked many questions. And it was that fascination which drove them to understand more fully the very *structure* of this 'magic.'

> How do these communication geniuses use words so that they have such powerful effects?
>
> Does the magic of the transformations lie in the specific words they use, or in some special way that they utter the words, or in their supporting non-verbal communications?
>
> What explains this magic?
>
> Can we learn this magic?
>
> Can we learn to replicate this magic?

These curious modelers came from such backgrounds as linguistics, Transformational Grammar, General Semantics, computer programming, and mathematics. Yet, here was an entirely new field before them, the field of psychology. So they entered that field from an entirely different point of view, and without the training in the typical paradigms that then governed psychology.

This meant several things. First of all, it meant that they had no investment in the various psychological theories of the day (i.e., psychoanalysis, behaviorism, client-centered, humanism, etc.). They really didn't care about the theories. That was not their focus. As they looked at Gestalt Therapy, Family Systems Therapy, and Medical Hypnotherapy, they focused on what worked. They had seen these different therapies work. In varying degrees with different clients, they worked. They also assumed that *if* they all worked, there must be a structure that made them all work. This lead them to the idea that if they could find *the structure within, behind, and above* the processes, words, rituals, etc., they could learn the secrets of the magic, the structure of the magic, and could then pass them on to others. And so it came to pass.

NLP: Studying the Structure of Magic

Today we call the components of this *magic* (its structure, process, as well as the formulas and incantations), NLP. This refers to how we become formed, structured, or *'programmed,'* so to speak, in our very *neurology* by means of our *linguistics* (the languages of the 'mind').

- How does this 'programming' occur?
- How can we re-program human response patterns?
- How do our human neuro-linguistics operate?
- What principles, laws, and guidelines govern our neuro-linguistics?
- How does communicating relate to such programming?
- What processes best allow us to run our brain and neurology and take charge of our programming?

Re-Visiting Magic

It has now been a quarter of a century since the 1975 publication of *The Structure of Magic (Volume I)* written by Dr. John Grinder and his graduate student Richard Bandler. That was the first work and the foundational work in the field of NLP. It presented an unformulated version of the Meta-Model and organized the theoretical foundations for the cognitive behavioral nature of NLP.

Given this historical consciousness, we can now reflect on the history of the NLP movement and on NLP as a field and the community that has grown from it. Doing so allows us to ask such questions as:

- What has happened to the Magic Model which the two modelers discovered?
- What else do we now know about the structure of magic?
- How has the knowledge of that magic grown and developed?
- What forms and expressions has it taken?
- What other pathways and directions has it taken?
- What has happened in the field of linguistics from which the Meta-Model arose?

Magic Wizards of Psychology

Dr. John Grinder and Richard Bandler subtitled their original work, *"A Book About Language and Therapy."* Why the emphasis on *therapeutic* language? Because as they discovered the three therapeutic wizards (i.e., Fritz Perls, Virginia Satir, and Milton Erickson), and applied their skills of modeling to the language and non-language interventions of these wizards, they happened upon the very structure of their magic, incantations, and genius. Once they found that, it didn't take them long to develop their neuro-linguistic model about human functioning and about how human brains and bodies get 'programmed' (i.e., ordered, patterned, framed, structured). They quickly began extending applications of NLP to fields beyond therapy, to education, business, management, law, sports, health, medicine, sales, persuasion, etc.

Yet it all started with the wizards of psychology. First, it started with *Fritz Perls*, the founder of Gestalt Therapy. Richard so happened to have stumbled on Perls while working in the warehouse for *Science and Behavior Books*. Publisher Dr. Robert S. Spitzer had an unfinished manuscript from Fritz Perls and wanted to get it finished. That's when he invited Richard, only twenty-one at the time, to finish it. The second part of the book consisted of gestalt therapy sessions which Richard transcribed from teaching films of Fritz's. Shortly thereafter, Fritz Perls died. The book was published as *The Gestalt Approach and Eye Witness to Therapy* (1973). Dr. Spitzer wrote,

> "Again, Richard spent day after day wearing earphones while watching the films—making certain that the transcription was accurate. He came out of it talking and acting like Fritz Perls. I found myself accidentally calling him Fritz on several occasions." (1992, p. 41)

Soon thereafter, even though still a college student, he began teaching a class at the University of Southern California at Santa Cruz on Gestalt Therapy. In *The Wild Days,* McClendon (1989) noted that in those days the University granted this privilege to fourth year students. It was in this class, with Dr. Grinder as his supervising mentor, that they began using Gestalt empty chair technique and other processes which would later become formats for NLP mental patterns.

Richard apparently had a remarkable ability to imitate. When he was asked to audio-tape and transcribe a month-long workshop by Virginia Satir, Richard quickly developed many of Virginia's voice patterns and mannerisms. Virginia's work introduced him to the psychological and communication field of Family Systems and to the magic of Satir's language patterns and processes of family sculpturing.

Later, urged on by their neighbor, another professor at the University, the anthropologist Gregory Bateson, Richard and John were introduced to the work of *Milton Erickson,* M.D. who founded Ericksonian hypnotherapy.

As so many others had experienced these wizards as having skills and secrets that seemed leaps and bounds ahead of other therapists, so did Richard and John. They experienced their work as

> "... so amazing to watch that it moves us with powerful emotions, disbelief, and utter confusion. Just as with all wizards of the ages of the earth whose knowledge was treasured and passed down from sage to sage—losing and adding pieces but retaining a basic structure—so, too, does the magic of these therapeutic wizards also have structure." (Bandler and Grinder, 1975, p. xiii)

The Wild Idea—Magic has Structure!

Bandler and Grinder distinguished themselves from others who had studied these geniuses of communication and therapy by focusing exclusively on the *structure* of the magic.

They looked deeper than the surface expressions of sudden release of pain, shift of focus, transformation of emotion, and change of behavior. Beyond the complexity and richness of the processes, they looked for the ordering syntax of the component pieces that made the magic work.

So in their explorations, they applied the scientific attitude of "understanding human behavior by breaking it down into relatively separate areas of study..." (p. 1). This led them to model the form of the linguistic structures. As Bandler and Grinder set out to do this, they sought to uncover the structure of human behavior.

John's Transformational Grammar enabled him to think of the speech behaviors and gestures in terms of how they operated in a *rule governed way.* Already a contributor to the field of Transformational Grammar, John used the discovery of Noam Chomsky (1957) that had revolutionized linguistics. By the 1970s Chomsky's model had come to replace Skinner's behaviorism. So utilizing the principle of language acquisition and development as '*rule governed*' Grinder and Bandler set out to explore how words can operate in seemingly magical ways in human neurology forming 'personality,' skills, and human mental-and-emotional experiences. For them,

> "The nervous system which produces digital communication (e.g., language) is the same nervous system which generates the other forms of human behavior ... —analogical communication systems, dreams, etc." (ibid., p. 54)

So they approached these therapeutic wizards with the wild idea that they could learn the structure of their magic, and replicate it. They called this approach '*modeling.*' To pull this off, they also brought to this task a very specific attitude—one of passionate (or ferocious) curiosity and interest. About the 'magical quality' of Satir and Perls they wrote,

> "To deny this capacity or to simply label it *talent, intuition,* or *genius* is to limit one's own potential as a people-helper." (ibid., p. 6)

By way of contrast, they took the attitude that like other complex human activities, the persuasive influence of such language has structure, and that they therefore could find it and learn it. They could learn it given the appropriate resources and training.

Mapping the Map

Grinder and Bandler also used the *map-territory distinction* which they found in the work of Alfred Korzybski (1933/1994). "The map is not the territory" succinctly highlights that we do not operate upon the world directly, but indirectly through our maps (or models) of the world.

Herein lies the magic. The magic lies in the very structure and syntax of our words, pictures, sounds, sensations, smells, etc. Here they found the magic. Precisely because our maps or models of the world powerfully influence and govern all of our experiences, if we change the map, our experiences change. What we call transformation of personality, awareness, emotion, and the emergence of new skills and abilities, arise from our mental frames. Here is a secret of magic: our *maps* drive the *magic* of influence, persuasion, and transformation.

It was in this way that the therapeutic wizards (Perls, Satir, and Erickson) applied their magic to their clients. They did not change the everyday life experiences of the clients, they focused on changing their internal maps. They focused on changing not the clients' world, only the clients' *model* of the world. Therefore they used the map-territory interface as their guiding principle. Using the prosaic and non-magical *communication process,* they just talked to their clients. They engaged them in a description of their plight as they asked questions and invited them to try out some different ways to think about things.

Out of that encounter, something wonderful happened. Something foundational changed. Surprisingly, people often found themselves living in a different world, feeling different emotions. Sometimes the *talk* brought about what can only be described as magical transformations.

Even more incredible, Bandler and Grinder discovered that they could offer a precise description of the change in terms of the person's internal representations. This enabled them to grasp the structure of the magic.

After all, if the *mechanism of transformation* involves *altering representational maps* of the world, a person's mental frames or paradigms, then we will want to ask:

- What *tools* facilitate this change?
- What *mechanisms* govern the change?
- How is the change facilitated?

Bandler and Grinder again pointed to something very simple, namely, the *communication process*. The transformation occurs via the set of verbal and non-verbal tools available to all of us. From this they modeled Perls, Satir, and Erickson for "a specific set of tools that seem to us implicit in [their] actions" (p. 6). These include the following tools as communication techniques which they incorporated in the Magic Communication model of the Meta-Model. I have here phrased these as language and relational 'games.'

Linguistic Change Tools

- *The Precision Game:* Asking for linguistic specificity. When?, where?, to what extent?, with whom?, etc.
- *The Indexing Game:* Indexing time, place, event, and person referents: when?, where?, who?, how?, etc.
- *The Explicating Process Game:* How does it work? How do you know?
- *The Exposure Game:* Challenging the structure of words, phrases, sentences: What if you could? Who says? What else could it mean? What are you presupposing when you say that?
- *The Rapport Game:* Matching the words of a speaker to pace his or her reality map.

- *The Mismatching Game:* Using opposite words to invite an alteration in representation.
- *The 'Going Inside Your Mind' Game:* Sending minds on guided fantasies to new resources.
- *The Incongruity Comparison Game:* Examining para-messages at a higher level to detect congruity and/or incongruity.

Non-Linguistic Change Tools

- *The Pacing Game:* Matching another's physiology in rate and tempo of speech, breathing, posture, gesturing, volume, tone, eye accessing, etc. to create instant rapport.
- *The Leading Game:* Using rapport to influence another's physiology, state, accessing cues, etc.
- *The Re-Enactment Game:* Inviting a re-enactment of an experience for reprocessing and transformation.
- *The Framing Game:* Setting up benevolent double binds.
- *The Pavlovian Game:* Anchoring responses and states to develop new resources and choices.

These communication tools or games provide an overview of the heart of this book about the structure of meaning and magic. Playing such games enables us to work magic with our words and in our communicating.

Summary

- Words, sentences, stories, metaphors, and other linguistic expressions can and do *touch us with magic*. This makes communication incredibly important and powerful in our everyday lives.
- The *structure* of meaning and magic means that there is rhyme and reason to things. Things do make sense. They operate according to the principles or 'rules' of how language works.
- It also means that we can learn the magic and replicate it so that we can then touch our minds and hearts with it as well as the minds and hearts of others.

Chapter 2

Locating Linguistic Magic

Where is 'Magic'?

"The worlds we manage to get inside our heads
are mostly worlds of words."
Wendell C. Johnson

If the therapeutic experts did not perform *real* magic, only *influential* magic, if they were not really wizards, but highly skilled clinicians who had a marvelous way of using language, a way that could touch people with magic, then what is this *magic?*

What is its nature?
How does it work?
Where does it come from?
How are we to understand it?
How can we learn to replicate it?

The three communication experts somehow had developed the skills, models, and resources (conscious or unconscious) whereby they could profoundly and powerfully influence the hurting minds-and-hearts of the people with whom they communicated. As Bandler and Grinder explored this using linguistic and programming tools, they stumbled upon the *structure* of this 'communication magic.'

The Source of Communication Magic

Where does the 'magic' (or impression of magic) actually occur?

It occurs in our minds. It occurs inside our mind-body systems as the *mapping processes and maps* that we create. The 'magic' actually occurs in the *way we represent,* or frame, things. This makes the magic representational magic or frame magic and a function of how we communicate or frame things. The magic occurs *in the communication process* itself, in the interaction between message sender and receiver, and in the mind of the person who encodes and frames the world.

Vaihinger (1924) wrote about this half a century earlier.

> "[We] hardly notice that we are acting on a double stage—our own inner world ... and also an entirely different and external world." (p. 160)

He noted that we experience the inner world and then "objectify" it "as the world of sense-perception." Yet it only (and always) exists *as a map*—a way of *representing* the world. This led Bandler and Grinder to pen this statement of the cognitive nature of our lives:

> "Each of us creates a representation of the world in which we live—that is, we create a map or model which we use to generate our behavior. Our representation of the world determines to a large degree what our experience of the world will be, how we will perceive the world, what choices we will see available to us as we live in the world." (Bandler and Grinder, 1975, p. 7)

We recognize today this paradigm about human functioning as the field of cognitive-behavioral psychology. This means that our experiences are driven by ideas, schemes, and mental understandings. It means that we *construct* our image of reality and then use it as we would use a map. It means that *how* we know what we know (epistemology) involves mental mapping and framing. Korzybski (1933/1994) expressed this in his map-territory in *Science and Sanity*.

> "A map is not the territory it represents but, if correct, it has a similar structure to the territory, which accounts for its usefulness." (pp. 58–60)

Here lies a key secret to the magical powers and interventions of all wizards, therapeutic, managerial, parental, political, etc. Somehow, in some way, by various techniques, models, parables, myths, etc. *they effect a change in their hearer's neuro-linguistic maps.* And, given that we operate in the world and on the world via our maps, when we change a map, we experience transformational magic. Our lives change. They change because our thinking-feeling perceptions change. We develop new and more effective behaviors, in expanded skills, and in enriched perceptions. It's like a spell has been cast upon us. It's the spell of the changed map which transforms our internal world. Suddenly we are inside of a new matrix. Suddenly, like Dorothy we throw open the door, and behold, a whole new world lies before us.

"Toto, I don't think we are in Kansas anymore!"

When Conversation Becomes Magical

Jerry said that he wanted to become more successful as a supervisor, but that he felt stuck in the organization. He said this during a workshop when I began working with him.

Do you know what it would take to succeed in your business, Jerry?

"Sure, you have to kiss up to them. And that's one thing I will not do! That's why it seems so futile to continue, I'm not that kind of guy."

So let me see if I'm understanding you clearly, by kissing up you mean ... what?

"You know, just that you have to schmooze with the boss, be a 'Yes' man, have no personal convictions, never disagree, you know, brown nose."

Sounds like you work for a cruel tyrant—a Hitler! A neo-Nazi who deprives you of all freedoms of mind and body. Mercy! So you want to escape that torture?

"Well, it's not that bad. It's just that the bosses want things done *their* way. That's the galling part. As if I don't have a brain."

Yeah, I hate it when that happens! People should do things my way, not their way. Who do they think they are anyway, the boss or something?! I'm with you on this.

"That sounds funny when you put it that way."

Well, it's one way or the other; black-or-white, either/or; either you get to run the business or the boss does. There can't be any cooperation can there?

"Okay, I get the point. So what do you want me to do, just bend over and take it?"

Another great metaphor. First kissing up, then brown nosing, and now bending over. Do these metaphors enhance your thoughts about that nasty word, 'authority?'

"No, I guess they don't, but what am I supposed to do, just ..."

Yes? Just ... What?

"Ah, just ... Put up with their stupidity?"

So there are times when you disagree with a specific policy, plan, or procedure that goes on at work?

"Right."

Do you disagree all *the time with* everything, *or just some things?*

"Just some things ... If they would listen to me, I could help them cut overhead, increase production, and improve the quality of the customer service. I have lots of ideas."

Certainly sounds like you do. So what you really want, if I'm getting you, is to more effectively communicate with your boss or bosses so that they can really listen to you?

"Right. That's it!"

So how well do you model that for them, I mean, really listening to them ... and trying to understand them and their intentions?

"Not very well. I'm too frustrated, too angry. I see the stupid things they do and it boils my blood."

Great metaphor, "blood boiling!" And how do you get yourself into such a mad state, what do you say to yourself—oh, I bet you talk about "kissing up, their stupidity, if only they'd listen ..."

"Yeah."

And that does it? That gets your blood boiling?

"Yeah."

And how well do you listen when you're raging like that on the inside and turning up the boiler on your anger?

"Not very well."

When you become a boss one of these days, or own your own company, how would you like to communicate your ideas and plans to your employees and receive their insights about how to improve things?

"Well ... I suppose if we just listen and ask questions and explore things, but when I'm boss, I'll have the final word ..."

You heard that, didn't you?

"Yeah."

And?

"So I guess I need to develop more patience and less anger so that we can work together."

How will that allow you to have ideas, even great ideas, and share them, and not always have them acted on—if the boss gets the final word?

"I guess I'll just need to frame it that 'Hey, he's the boss.' And know that one day I'll get into that role of authority."

Will that work for you? As you think about it, do you feel aligned and congruent with thinking about it this way?

"Yes, I do. And actually it makes me feel more empowered and less dependent or needy for their approval."

Great.

The Nature of these 'Magic' Maps

Later Jerry told me that while our communication was magical, he didn't know why it should be. "After all, we just talked." Ah, the subtleness of the magic. If the magic lies in the mind and how we map things, then it occurs as we use language to re-map.

That we humans operate from an internal *map* of some sort has long been intuited by philosophers (Immanuel Kant, 1787) and psychologists (William James, 1890). Yet it was only in the twentieth century that researchers and theorists honed in more specifically on the nature of our internal maps.

Korzybski (1933/1994) developed his epistemological model regarding the working and processing of human neurological abstracting. In *Science and Sanity,* he published his *Structural Differential* model. His diagram illustrates the logical levels of abstracting which our neurology engages in. This model differentiates the *levels* of our abstracting maps not only from the territory, but also from each other. He analyzed how the human nervous system interacts with the world at various levels. He described how our sense receptors are designed to leave out many characteristics and to generalize about the data from the energy manifestations 'out there.' He showed how different levels of the brain create different kinds of mental maps about things, that the lower brain centers (thalamus) create a very different kind of map from the higher cortical levels.

Piaget (1926, 1936/1952) similarly referred to innate *schemas* (or structures) of the 'mind' in his study of the development of cognitive skills and how they developed over the human life-span. These are the structures by which we represent, reason with, integrate, and attach meaning to events.

Bartlett (1932) introduced the term *schema* into Behavioral Psychology to indicate the role of some kind of internal *intervening* mechanism (or map) between stimulus and response. He sought to explain human learning and responding in this way.

Kelly (1955) described our maps as our 'personal constructs' which we use to guide, govern, and determine internal experiencing, construction of meaning, emoting, etc.

Then came the cognitive revolution in psychology, dated from the work of George Miller, Ulrich Neisser, Bruner, *et al.* in 1956. The idea that our internal maps govern our experience had become well accepted and documented by this time. At this time also Chomsky (1957) delivered his death-blow to Skinner's Behaviorism in his analysis of language acquisition and his demonstration of the complete inadequacy of the association theories as an explanatory model about 'verbal behavior.'

The Magic in Your 'Mind'—in Your Mental Maps

> "Every person carries within his head a mental model of the world—a subjective representation of external reality. This model consists of tens upon tens of thousands of images. These may be as simple as a mental picture of clouds scudding across the sky. Or they may be abstracted inferences about the way things are organized in society. We may think of this mental model as a fantastic internal warehouse, an image emporium in which we store our inner portraits of Twiggy, Charles DeGaulle or Cassius Clay, along with such sweeping propositions as 'Man is basically good' or 'God is dead.'" (Alvin Toffler, *Future Shock*)

If our mental maps are that important and critical in our everyday experiences and our use of language, what actually comprises these internal *maps, schemas, constructs, etc.*? Obviously words and, just as obviously, pictures, sounds, sensations, smells, and tastes. Representational magic, again. Yet we do not literally have any of these things in our bio-electrical, bio-chemical brain. These are functions of the *mind,* not the brain.

Bateson (1972) asked a similar question. He asked it using the map-territory metaphor about the 'mind.'

> *"What actually gets mapped onto the map?"*

These terms (i.e., map, schema, paradigm) do not *literally* describe what goes on in the brain. We use them solely in a metaphorical way as we describe the neurological processing of 'information' in terms of representation. Yet even representation gets us no closer to anything literal. We only 'phenomenologically' have a sense of 'representation.' Bateson answered his own question this way,

> "What gets onto the map, in fact, *is difference* ... and what is a difference? ... It is certainly not a thing, or an event ... A difference is an abstract matter. ... The territory never gets in at all. The territory is *Ding an sich* [Thing in itself] and you can't do anything with it. Always the process of representation will filter it out so that the mental world is only maps of maps of maps, ad infinitum. All 'phenomena' are literally 'appearances.' ... what gets from territory to map is transforms of difference and these differences are elementary ideas." (1972, pp. 451–457)

Bandler and Grinder's NLP model simply goes with the phenomenological idea of *representation* as 'good enough' for the purposes they had in mind. What does this mean?

It means that even though we do not *literally* have pictures, sounds, sensations, etc. in our cortex, and even though we have no *literal* 'screen' in our head or 'mind' wherein we *re-present* to ourselves what we have seen, heard, and felt via our sense receptors—this *phenomenological 'sense'* of internal sights, sounds, sensations, and smells does work well enough to explain how we create the magic of representation and language *at that level.*

If we change our representations at the level of our sensed representations, our nervous system uses its out-of-conscious neurological processes so that we respond differently. We change. We feel different, act different, see the world in a different way, think different. These transformations in our behaviors and skills are set in motion by the alteration of our internal representations. This is the 'magic.'

Starting there, Bandler and Grinder presented "experience and perception as an active process" and analyzed the neurological, social, and individual constraints which play a significant role in our map-making (1975, pp. 8–20). In this analysis, they quoted scientific experiments that led them to conclude that

> "... our whole nervous system systematically distorts and deletes whole portions of the real world. This has the effect of reducing the range of possible human experiences as well as introducing differences between what is actually going on in the world and our experience of it. Our nervous system, then, initially determined genetically, constitutes the first set of filters which distinguish the world—the territory—from our representations of the world—the map." (p. 9)

Huxley (1954) had previously commented on "the reducing valve of the brain and nervous system." This allowed them to highlight several of the constraints that we face in our map-making. These include:

- The *neurological* constraints: the nature and structure of our sense receptors, the neurological structures in our nervous system, our embodiment in the kinds of bodies that we have, etc.
- The *social* constraints: those that arise from living in communities, the sociological, cultural, and societal beliefs, values, rituals, etc., and
- The *individual* constraints: those that uniquely distinguish us: family life, style of upbringing, values, beliefs, economics, etc.

Under the *social constraints* that affect our map-making, they relied upon various sociological and anthropological studies. Language itself, as well as all of the social filters of beliefs and ideas powerfully affect *what* we can perceive and *how* we generate internal representations. The social constraints involve cultural presuppositions coded in the language, the beliefs and values of the society, etc.

Korzybski noted the effect of a culture's language on the nervous system (especially all Aristotelian cultures) in "*the is of predication.*" That is, we *say* or assert (predicate) things about the world depending on our senses, nervous system, emotions, etc. For example, if we say, "The book is blue" we use a linguistic category (i.e., 'blue') which constrains our thinking and perceiving and may even become confused in thinking that the *name* that we give to the sensation that we experience via our rods and codes in interaction with certain parts of the light spectrum '*is*' the same as the sensation. Yet 'blueness' actually occurs as both our internal neurological experience and a socially conditioned response given in the English language system. 'Blue' refers to our mental category about 'color' within the frames of our culture and does not describe the territory.

Bandler and Grinder quoted Vaihinger on this:

> "All that is given to consciousness is sensation. By adding a Thing to which sensations are supposed to adhere as attributes, thought commits a very serious error. It hypostatizes sensation, which in the last analysis is only a process, as a subsistent attribute, and ascribes this *attribute* to a *thing* that either exists only in the complex of sensations itself, or has been simply added by thought to what has been sensed. ... Where is the *sweet* that is ascribed to the sugar? It exists only in the act of sensation ..." (Vaihinger, 1924, p. 167)

No wonder we end up with models of the world that differ so much from the world! Yet the difference does not end there. We also have to consider the *individual constraints* that influence each of us as we generate our own unique maps. We all experience a unique personal history, "no two life histories will ever be identical" (Bandler and Grinder, 1975, p. 12).

Each of these three constraints on our mapping works systemically. By that I mean that the *products* of each domain re-enter the process to effect the functioning of the other domains. The beliefs and values that we develop individually and socially become perceptual filters at the neurological level (Meta-Programs, and frames of value and beliefs). They create our habits of thought, emotion, speech, perceiving, and relating. And these then, in turn, reinforce the cultural maps that we have received, thus confirming our 'reality.'

The Magic Tricks that We Map

So where are we? The magic occurs in our non-tangible 'minds' which emerge from all of the interactive stuff in our wet brains. Out of all of the neurological systems, levels of brain processing, the neural network of pathways, transmitters, neuro-peptides, etc., we experience 'consciousness' and how we form, frame, structure, and map our 'awarenesses' in our minds creates our mental maps that we then use for navigating reality. Right?

- Okay, so what can we say about these maps?
- What makes them magical or mundane?
- How do we construct them?
- What are the modeling processes involved?
- How can we re-construct them when they limit?

It's the nature of 'mind' to use 'maps' as we operate in the world, a map *of* reality. We have a map *of* reality that radically differs from the territory. None of us deals with reality as such—only 'reality' filtered and coded through representations, ideas, and beliefs. How do these mappings differ from the territory?

Our maps differ from the territory in that we have *deleted* lots of information. We do that to prevent ourselves from getting overwhelmed. Further, to cope with things, we have created *generalizations* to summarize and synthesize patterns. And in deleting and generalizing data, we thereby *distort* things according to our neurological, cultural, and individual constraints.

Inside, in our 'mind,' it's all a matrix of maps and frames. Some arise from the structure of our neurology; some from the social patterns that others have learned before us, and others from ideas that we've picked up.

By the very nature of our maps, we inevitably operate in the world and with each other from our schemas, paradigms, and frames of references, and these differ radically from the territory. Some of them enhance our life experiences, some of them severely limit us. Ultimately, it's all a magical trick—a trick that we've incorporated into our perceptual 'mind.'

When Our Magic Maps 'Problems'

Korzybski's statement, "the map is not the territory," offers a telling and suggestive metaphor. As our neurology 'abstracts' from the energy manifestations which impinge upon it and turns that energy into other forms of data, bio-electric and bio-chemical, this describes our first mapping. What we create within our neurology is not the same as the energy 'out there.' At best, it's a model *of* that energy. And if it works to get us around, then it's magical in that sense.

Similarly, *'The menu is not the meal.'* Recognizing a menu as 'a menu,' and distinct from the meal it references, is important if we want to make a good adjustment to restaurant eating, wouldn't you say? How well adjusted is the person who enters a restaurant and attempts to consume the menu? I don't think that his or her nervous system will tolerate that kind of a mistake for long!

Where do 'problems,' distresses, and conflicts arise?

Our *'problems'* actually arise primarily from the *discord* between our mental maps and the territory that we seek to reference and map. After all, we have places to go, people to visit, experiences to step into. So we need a map. 'Problems' arise when our maps do not guide us where we want to go. 'Problems' speak about our inability to navigate to the experiences, states, and feelings that we want. We call it a 'problem' when we can't figure out how to move to our desired goals and outcomes. 'Problems' are mostly problems with the mental 'maps' in our heads.

1) Inaccurate Maps
'Problems' arise, in part, because our menu *inaccurately* represents the meal. When the waiter brings us something very different from what we thought we ordered, the difference between our anticipation and our experience often shocks our system. Now we have a 'problem'—a gap between expectation and experience.

All of our mental mapping is inaccurate to some extent anyway. We cannot create a map that doesn't leave some things out, generalize other things, and distort others. We *have to* delete, generalize, and distort if we want to create a map. All maps suffer varying degrees of inaccuracy.

Inaccuracy, in and of itself, does not make a map worthless or unreliable. Some inaccuracies serve us very well. Mapping problems arise from having a false-to-fact map in a critical area, which, in turn, *disorients* us. Therefore it fails to provide us with a good guide.

- Is our map sufficiently accurate for where we want to go?
- Does our map correspond to a sufficient degree with the territory it represents?

2) Inadequate Maps
As with inaccuracy, all of our maps suffer varying degrees of inadequacies. In navigating geography, we have many different kinds of geographical maps, each one offering a different level of adequacy for a different kind of purpose and function. While a topographical map would be adequate for mountain climbing, it would not be adequate for driving around town.

Similarly, we have an inadequate map when we pick up the short version of a menu and only see three choices when the full menu includes hundreds of items. We could have had a much greater range of choices, yet the menu did not provide it.

- Is our map adequate to the task?
- What mapping do we need to map so that it adequately serves our needs?

3) Distorted Maps
Sometimes our maps simply get it all wrong: they leave out the very streets and roads we need; they link one road to another where none exists. On some maps someone pens in, "Fountain of Youth" as a joke. So off we go on a treasure hunt! Major map distortions occur in Aristotelian maps that confuse map and territory, that sort things in either/or categories, and that exclude middles.

- How distorted is this mental map?
- Does the distortion help or hurt?
- How can we straighten out the distortion?

Mapping for the Magic of Solutions

Given all this, we now know the nature of linguistic magic. What primarily governs our experiences? What determines how we perceive, think, feel, act, and relate?

> *Our maps. And more specifically, the quality and richness in our representations of the world.*

Linguistic magic depends upon having rich maps. Problems emerge when we have impoverished maps. Bandler and Grinder (1975) described this in the following words:

> "What we have found is not that the world is too limited or that there are no choices, but that these people [who come for therapy] block themselves from seeing those options and possibilities that are open to them since they are not available in their models of the world." (p. 13)

The richer our map, the more accurate, adequate, and useful our menu, the more choices. The more impoverished our model, the fewer choices. The richer and fuller our linguistic maps, the richer our mind.

This model of our mental map-making suggests something else crucial for becoming truly effective in communicating. It offers us a new and different attitude which enables us to handle more effectively the challenges of life and to develop more effective coping and mastering skills. The 'problems' we experience and feel arise from our maps.

If our lives, emotions, perceptions, understandings, etc. are functions of our mapping, then people *are* not bad, crazy, demonic, or sick. People are not broken. They just have some problematic, inadequate, stupid, and toxic maps. If we think or experience a person as broken, weird, sick, out-of-touch with reality, pathological, etc., we are seeing and focusing on the *result*, not the cause. Any given person's state is, after all, a function of his or her maps. This explains why we often experience magic just by talking, thinking, writing, etc. This explains why 'talk therapy' works.

This describes the *magic* that we can develop, experience, and use in all kinds of *communications*. If we know the structure of magic, the secrets for using it, and develop our skills with such, we will find our language patterns to be like using a magic wand.

The foundation for this lies in the fact that *the quality and richness of our maps* governs how we actually navigate the experiences of life. For this reason we say that people are always making the best choices they can. They do their best given their map of the world and given the constraints and limitations built into those maps. *With those maps,* we could do no better.

When someone misbehaves, when someone behaves in ugly, hurtful, pathological, and criminal ways—we need look no further than their governing maps for the cause. Maps induce states, and states govern perception and behavior. What can we experience from a person who has mapped revenge, hatefulness, racial superiority, etc. into his or her way of dealing with people? What can we expect from someone who maps suicide as the only choice in the presence of personal loss? What can we expect from someone who maps "Make the bastards pay!" as the way to cope with personal insult or contempt?

Such individuals, like us, only have the options available to them in their mental maps. If the only choices on their menu are baked, fried, or raw worms—that's the menu they have to choose from. Maps make sense, even if they do not make things better.

…ıse someone yells when upset, feels defensive when crit-
…ls guilty about feeling afraid, etc., these responses do not
…m 'crazy.' Such responses accurately reflect their model of the world. What such persons lack is a rich and resourceful model of the world, one that empowers and gives more resourceful responses.

> "... human beings' behavior, no matter how bizarre it may first appear to be, makes sense when it is seen in the context of the choices generated by their model." (ibid., p. 14)

What controls the quality and richness of our maps? Our ability to make high quality maps and to quality control our maps and mapping so that our manipulating of conceptual symbols produces truly enhancing maps.

Over-generalizing in our map-making creates limitations because it eliminates alternative choices for how we can respond in various situations. We typically over-generalize by making 'rules' for living which then fail to contextualize when and where to use them.

> "Don't touch hot stoves."
> "Rocky chairs are unstable."
> "Don't express feelings."

Over-generalizing sees things in all-or-nothing terms. This leads to creating limiting frames:

> "No one ever gives me a break."
> "The only way to get along with people is to do it to them before they do it to you."
> "You can't trust people."

We create limiting maps in quality and richness as we delete information and filter out representations, concepts, understandings, ideas, etc. that could enrich or make a difference in our perceiving and acting. So we move through the world without the empowering strategies that allow us to resolve conflicts respectfully, explore new options, invent new ideas, get over the past, etc. We discount things by bringing in various criteria so that we don't even notice.

As we manipulate symbols, we inevitably distort things. This can enrich our lives as in fantasy and creative imagination. It can also limit when we distort the world via beliefs about causation and meaning.

> "He *makes* me feel afraid by yelling at me."
> "When she doesn't look at me when I talk, I know she thinks I'm stupid."
> "I'll never get over that hurt!"
> "You just can't teach old dogs new tricks."

A higher level of 'problems' arise when we create maps biased against any contrary information. This essentially prevents us from updating our maps and staying current. When this happens, we're stuck at our current stage of development. Of course, that's valuable if we want 'peace and stability.' By inputting no new information, by not correcting incorrect mapping, and by assuming we know it all or enough, we can feel solid, secure, definite.

Yet we pay for this 'peace,' 'security,' and 'comfort' with a closed and rigid map in that every day it becomes more and more outdated and irrelevant. That's not exactly the best kind of guide to have in moving through an ever-changing environment. A rigid map like that will *not* serve us well. It will only make us closed to new information. It will limit our choices, and generate disempowering perspectives.

If we generate most of our 'problems' by our maps, the same applies for 'solutions.' *Re-mapping* allows us to develop ever-better guides for thinking, feeling, and acting. If our cognitive-emotive schemas wrongly orient us in the world of things, people, and tasks, then new levels of effectiveness come through restructuring our cognitions (e.g., our beliefs, values, understandings, paradigms, etc.). Adopting a new schema offers new ways of orienting ourselves in the world.

Bandler and Grinder discovered that this describes what the therapeutic wizards did.

> "They introduce changes in their clients' models which allow their clients more options in their behavior. What we see is that each of

> these wizards has a map or model for changing their clients' models of the world—i.e., a Meta-Model—which allows them to effectively expand and enrich their clients' models in some way that makes the clients' lives richer and more worth living." (ibid., p. 18)

Through years of working with hurting people who lacked rich and enhancing maps, the therapeutic wizards (i.e., Perls, Satir, and Erickson) developed a model about the linguistic patterns they heard in such persons. This model of their models (i.e., their meta-model) enabled them to know *what to go for*—what distinctions they were not making, what data they had deleted, what limitations they had mapped for them, etc.

Modeling 'Magic' Without *Using Transformational Grammar*

If you think you need to know Transformational Grammar to understand or use the Meta-Model, here's some good news. The Meta-Model is *not dependent* upon Transformational Grammar.

Yes, Transformational Grammar did launch the exploration that eventually became NLP. Dr. John Grinder brought to the original discoveries an extensive experience with the Chomskian model of linguistics called Transformational Grammar (TG). The year prior to the publication of the Meta-Model, he and Elgin (1974) published the *Guide to Transformational Grammar*, which has many of the Meta-Model formulations in it.

Using TG as a map about language, Grinder and Bandler sketched out the linguistic distinctions which seemed critically important in the communication experts they were modeling. This is how NLP inherited a lot of its jargon (i.e., TDS, complex equivalence, nominalizations, modals, etc.). Relying heavily on TG for their terminology and understandings about language, they assumed that NLP was based upon and dependent upon TG. They even included an extensive appendix in *The Structure of Magic* which they entitled, "A Brief Outline of Transformational Grammar" (Appendix A).

Yet neither NLP nor the Meta-Model needs TG to legitimize its theoretical foundations. Though TG left NLP with a jargon legacy, the magic of the Meta-Model does *not* depend upon TG. From TG NLP adopted the simple logical level system as it distinguished between Surface Structure statements and Deep Structure statements.

In the twenty-five years since its beginning, every writer, researcher, and developer of NLP has utilized and relied upon the distinction of *levels*. But not one has relied upon the Transformational Grammar model. Not one has even reproduced the Transformational Grammar Appendix.

Magic Demystified (1982), by Lewis and Pucelik, exemplifies the amount of dependence on TG that we find in most subsequent presentations. They devoted all of two paragraphs to "Transformational Grammar" (p. 73). What did they primarily focus on in those two paragraphs? The logical level distinctions:

> "A contemporary school of linguistics proposes a relationship between what is spoken or written by an individual and some deeper internal linguistic representation. The production of a sentence, the actual sound or written sequence of symbols and phrases, is called the *surface structure* (SS). The *deep structure* (DS) is also a system of symbols and phrases, but it is much more complex and abstract. The DS is the complete linguistic representation of a person's experience which might be considered the intent or thought behind the SS sentence."

What does this mean?

It means that while John Grinder originally used Transformational Grammar to give form to the original Meta-Model, the Meta-Model did *not* need TG. In fact, the Meta-Model quickly moved on from TG. That's because the Meta-Model is *not* a model about language *per se.* The Meta-Model is rather a model about:

> *how language works in and affects our neurological states of mind, emotion, perception, relationship, skills, etc.*

It's about *neuro-linguistic* processes and effects in a living person.

What the Meta-Model mostly took from TG was the idea of *logical levels.* Yet for that, we have the levels from Korzybski's General Semantics model, the Levels of Abstraction that he developed in his Structural Differential. This formulates the 'Levels of Thought' (or mind) that I used in designing the Meta-States model (Hall, 1995, 2000).

Besides, Transformational Grammar pretty much died in the late 1970s. Since the 1970s, Chomsky radically changed many facets of his original model. When he did, George Lakoff along with other linguistic scholars sought to push the TG model to its logical conclusions. That led them to initiate a field of *Generative Semantics.* But that didn't last for long. It soon became evident that it was a dead-end alley. Harris, in *The Linguistic Wars* (1993), described the people and the linguistic models that arose in the wake of the ending of the original TG model. Today Cognitive Grammar and Cognitive Linguistics have replaced the original Transformational Grammar model. (See Appendix A.)

What does any of this mean for understanding and using the modeling of linguistic magic for developing powerful and elegant communicating for persuasion and influence?

It means that you do *not* have to follow the same path that Bandler and Grinder took in discovering the model. TG gave birth to the original Meta-Model. It provided insights, understandings, and form for the first model. Yet the Meta-Model has grown. It has moved beyond its original foundations. Further, our focus here is on *embodied* language, not on formal linguistic processes, on how language works magically in our minds, bodies, emotions, and on neuro-linguistic and neuro-semantic processes.

That's why we will explore the work of Korzybski in coming chapters, rather than the work of Noam Chomsky. That's why we will look at General Semantics and the newer Cognitive Linguistics of Lakoff, Johnson, etc.

Summary

- There is neuro-semantic magic hidden in our words, language, and symbol systems. This *magic* bridges the gulf between the external world and our experience on the inside of the world.
- We do not deal with the world directly, we only deal with it through our neurological and linguistic transforms of the world, that is, our maps of the world. This means that *everything* in our lives (experience, skills, emotions, relationships, etc.) *depends upon our maps.*
- We can now use language as we would a magic wand. We can wave it over the way we, and others, map and thereby initiate powerful transformations. Frogs can be turned into princes.
- Our navigational maps govern our experiences. We need not evaluate these as 'right' or 'wrong,' but whether they enhance or limit us on our journeys.
- The Meta-Model gives us a map for thinking about our mental maps. It gives us a new way to listen to and detect maps as we communicate. It offers ways to question them in ways that elicit richer and more useful maps.
- As we do this to increase our resourcefulness, we make life more magical, powerful, and wonderful. Now, on with the journey.

Chapter 3

'Seeing' Magic as a Magician

Developing the Eyes and Heart of a Magician

There's magic all around us,
and for the having,
if only we learn to see it.
L. Michael Hall

Okay, so *magic* lies in the *language* we use. And every now and then we sense it. Every once in a while we experience it directly. Someone says something that melts our heart, that renews our vision, that excites our motivation, that arouses our ire. But *magic* in all of our language? Magic in all of our words, sentences, stories, metaphors, and linguistic expressions? We create *magic* that touches our lives and the lives of others all the time?

Yes. The communication magic of language both blesses and curses. It touches life with a positive and radiant transformation that powerfully enriches. The same magical wand can touch a life to cripple, hinder, and hex. It can turn life into a living hell. When we communicate, we can induce all kinds of things into the mind-body (neuro-linguistic) system for weal or woe. The mechanism is one, how we use it depends upon our awareness, intentions, and heart.

To access this magic of language and communication *we only have to learn to 'see,' to really see.* We have to develop the eyes of a magician. And to do that we have to rise up in our minds in order to recognize the mapping magic of our nervous system and brain. That's what this chapter is all about.

The magic of language involves the *reality constructions* we weave with our words. By various language systems (e.g., linguistics, mathematics, music, sensory representations, etc.) we *formulate* worlds and *call forth* dimensions of experiences. We weave our subjective webs with our incantations that we call stories, reasons, explanations, ideas, and gossip.

Do you *see* this? Do you *recognize* it when others talk? Do you *recall* it when you watch television? Does it *appear* to you when conversing with friends?

Typically it does not. We swim so much in the sea of language that it's easy to forget about the linguistic environment. Yet a magician sees. A magician knows. So, the more clarity we have about our neuro-linguistic mapping, the more we empower ourselves in working with neuro-linguistic magic to cast spells, to break old imprisoning incantations, and to invent new spells. The art of using communication elegantly and magically begins when we develop clarity about how we build our mental maps, what they are made of, how they work, what drives them, and how to alter them gracefully.

Clarity at a Higher Level

If communication elegance arises from our conceptual clarity about mental mapping, how words work, *how* we create our maps, the map-making processes we use, how this shows up in language as linguistic markers, and how we can re-map, then clarity governs us becoming powerfully skilled in handling this magic.

It all begins as we *step back* to think about the structure and secrets of magic. Stepping back allows us to *design engineer* the very structures in our lives. Then we can take conscious control over the cognitive maps we choose and use.

This *stepping back* and thinking *about* describes what we mean by the term 'meta.' *Meta* refers to moving up to a higher level of awareness, an awareness of our awarenesses. It is meta-cognition, that is, a thought *about* another thought. A meta-feeling is a feeling *about* another feeling. A meta-model is a model *about* a model. And since we use language and symbols as our model of the world, our way of mapping or representing the territory, when we step back to describe it, explain it, understand it, etc., we move up ('go meta') and develop our own meta-model about the mechanisms, structure, and secrets of magic. Then meta-magic occurs.

Understanding how our maps work (a cognitive map itself) and how we can alter and transform them equips us with the power of a magician. Recognition of and skill with the secrets of this magic empower us to become *magicians* over our own neuro-semantic realities.

We begin with our *map* of mapping (a meta-map) to raise our appreciation of the importance and value of a meta-model. If you don't know this, your power to be a magician with words will be severely limited. With a meta-model, you gain a higher level understanding about the whole mapping-process and how to manage it effectively.

This explains the power and wonder of the Meta-Model. It gives us the equivalent of a *magic wand* by which we can catch, break, and cast spells. All of this arises as we realize that communication magic has structure—a structure that we can learn and replicate.

To the uninitiated, it may seem that the moves (i.e., the sleight of mouth and sleight of mind maneuvers) of the therapeutic magicians happened 'magically,' 'out of the blue,' and without rhyme or reason. But no. *There is a method to the magic.* The method arises from its structure and there are secrets or principles that govern it.

See Neuro-Semantic Reality and Magic

Learning to use the communication magic model effectively will empower you to become a *magician* over your own neuro-semantic reality, as well as that of others.

"Neuro-semantic?"

'Semantic' refers to meaning or significance. In the last chapter I noted that *meaning* operates as an *inside* process, that it is not real externally, and that it does not exist inside words or symbols. Meaning arises and consists of the mental-emotional ideas that we associate with things. In subjective experiences (which are the only kind of experiences there are), when we link or connect one thing with another, we do so *inside* our nervous system. This creates *associative meaning.* Later when we map that associative meaning we create internal *contextual or frame meaning.* This becomes our frames of reference and frames of mind. It becomes our neuro-linguistic and neuro-semantic meanings.

> "What does any particular thing mean to you?"
> "What does 'insult' mean?"

It all depends upon the particular sights, sounds, sensations, etc. that you have associated with that term. "What does 'joy' mean?" Again, what have you connected, neurologically, to that word? "What qualifies as a pleasure to you?"

Meaning does not occur apart from, or independent of, human processing, representing, connecting, framing, and punctuating. We can't see, hear, feel, smell, or taste 'meaning' in the outside world. It does not exist there. It exists only and solely in the inside world, in the functioning of a human nervous system. Yes, we can express and record the connections, associations, and meanings externally. We can write them down, share them, and pass them on to the next generation. But that's just an external record of the internal activity.

When we get together collectively, we invent 'shared reality' that we call culture. We then build our society around those meanings. As we engage in similar kinds of internal representing, processing, framing, etc., we experience a shared reality with others. As we then incorporate such in our laws, buildings, environment, social mores, etc., we externalize our internal meanings.

Our neuro-semantics consist of the mapping that we have coded and programmed into our body and nervous system. We feel these neuro-semantics when we *react* (kinesthetically, emotionally, and mentally) to various triggers or stimuli. *Semantic reactions* refer to our reactions which have become automatic, unconscious, and habitual. By way of contrast, *semantic responses* refer to those responses which we make consciously, thoughtfully, and by choice—a much more human way to live.

Seeing the Nature of Our Maps

Given the gap between the territory and our maps as previously noted, it's evident that we *always* and *only* relate to the world via some cognitive model. Where we go, how we go, and the quality of the journey that we make in the world depends entirely upon *the quality of our maps.* That's where the magic lies. Yet every map inevitably leaves things out (deletion), sums up a lot of details into more global configurations (generalization), and radically changes things (distortion). These map-making processes affect the quality of the resulting maps we use for navigation.

To imagine, pretend, or believe that we operate upon the world apart from the abstracting of our nervous system *confuses* map and territory. Infants and small children think like that. Theirs is a primitive kind of thinking, magical thinking. The baby's cries *create* the milk, or so it seems. So the cry magically makes the milk appear. When young children want something very much, they feel that their very wish for it *is* their right to have it and *will* make it happen.

Korzybski described this kind of a simplistic reasoning and mapping as *Aristotelian.* Such primitive thinking and reasoning is pre-scientific thinking, and unsane. He noted that *identification* lies at the heart of such primitive and undifferentiating thinking.

Identification refers to *identifying* the territory with a map (with some term, name, or word that we use to reference the territory). If we forget that our symbol *is* not the referent, but only a symbol of it, we *identify* one thing with another and treat them as if 'the same' when they are not. Typically, infants, children, primitive people, and animals use their nervous systems in this way to confuse map and territory. They identify.

We can hear such identification in the word '*is.*' For them, the menu *is* the meal. The cry *is* the nursing breast and soothing milk. The bell *is* the meat and so evokes the response of the saliva glands.

When we move beyond the Aristotelian stage of development to the Non-Aristotelian we begin to recognize (and feel) the world as a world of differences. Then we can recognize and feel the difference between map and territory. We know that 'whatever we say a thing is, *it is not*.' Language maps *are* not the territory, only maps *of* the territory—symbolic representations.

Identity (or sameness) does not exist in the world of dynamic processes where everything is *different* at every next moment. Nothing is 'the same' as anything else. Nothing is even 'the same' itself over time. As only differences exist, we ought to recognize such in our mapping. If we don't, we fall into the deception of identifying, of failing to see differences, of confusing similarities with sameness.

The Magical Power of Detecting

Once we deeply incorporate this awareness into our mind and neurology, we gain a sense of distance from our maps. This allows us to be the master of the language, rather than its slave. If 'the map is *not* the territory,' then a map is just that—a map, a representation, a set of symbols. This meta-level understanding enables us to recognize them as *maps* and to have the mind of a magician that can do magic with language.

Rising up in our mind to this level of awareness and *going meta* to our models of the world allow us to evaluate them as a magician:

- Is this map useful?
- Is this map valuable?
- Does this map enhance life?
- How solid is this map, how locked in?
- How is it formatted and sustained?
- What are the leverage points to transform it?

From that higher perspective we can recognize all of our verbal maps as rule-governed and structural frames. The grammar of any given language system simply comprises the set of rules that describes the well-formed patterns in that language. Stepping back to reflect on our languages as maps gives us magic-like *powers of detection* about the characteristics that we have left out in our mapping, the generalizations that over-state things and leave out exceptions, and the ways we have distorted things.

Knowing that all of our thoughts and emotions, all of our beliefs, opinions, judgments, understandings, paradigms, etc. are 'just maps' also frees us from the blindness of dogmatism and releases us to explore the world afresh. It frees us from old semantic reactions, it endows us with a new degree of flexibility, and a willingness to use feedback to keep correcting and refining our maps. This promotes true science and sanity.

Given the importance of *going meta*, in our training as magicians, it serves us to practice stepping aside from our *thinking*, emoting, and internal experiencing to model more clearly the structure of language and how it works in our mind-body system.

Seeing 'the World' in Our Mind

Let's model 'thinking.' How do we 'think?' What are the modes, mechanisms, and processes that enable us to think?

We think using the basic *modes* (or modalities) of our *senses*. We think by using our *sensory senses* of sights, sounds, sensations, smells, tastes, etc., by *representing* them to ourselves. That is, at the most basic mental mapping that we do, we *present* to ourselves *again* (re-present) what we have seen, heard, felt, smelled, tasted, etc. In NLP, we designate this as the sensory, or representational, model (the three predominant senses of visual, auditory, and kinesthetic are summarized as 'the VAK model'). Through these basic modalities we 'think.' On the inside of our sense of 'mind,' we experience an audio-video movie of former experiences or imagined experiences. Yet even this is not literal, we only 'sense' the pictures, sights, sounds, voices, etc.

Yet we do not stop with such representations. We then step back from these sights and sounds and use arbitrary symbols to *stand for* the sensory movies. Words operate as a higher-level representation, a meta-representation system. Language enables us to streamline the contents of our mind, it allows us to classify things, categorize, and create abstract concepts. Our language formats our mental matrix of frames.

Using words enables us to *comment on* the things we see, hear, and feel. We use *sensory-based or descriptive words* to speak with clarity, precision, and specificity about the see, hear, feel referents. As symbols, they allow us to 'point to' empirical realities (at least at the macro-level). As the abstraction process does not cease there, we next move to yet another higher level to model those descriptive, empirical words with more abstract ones. This creates and introduces into language *evaluative words*.

Recognizing that we both 'think' and model (create mental maps) via our sensory modalities (the VAK), sensory-based language, and evaluative-based language—we can now employ these components of subjectivity to create an effective technology for empowering us in hearing language patterns. This will enable us to recognize the very structure of our maps.

How?

How do we do this? By simply paying attention to the internal representations as we hear (or use) language. We can then *directly track over from* words to pictures, sounds, movements, etc. on the 'screen of our mind.' This becomes a kind of *representational testing or tracking*. In doing this we use our sensory-based representations to track and test things. Bandler and Grinder (1975) offered this experience as an example.

> "Read the following sentence, then close your eyes and form a visual image of what the sentence represents. 'I'm afraid!' Now examine your image. It will include some visual representation of the client and some representation of the client's being afraid. Any detail beyond these two images was supplied by you." (p. 58)

Representational Tracking—Technology Fitting for a Magician

As a magician, play around with this trick of *representationally tracking* and see what happens. First, simply read the words below trying to make sense of them as you normally would.

"I've been struggling with depression, if you know what I mean. It just seems that lots of things get me down and I go into a depressive cycle, especially this time of year."

What did you get? What did you *track directly from those words* to your mental screen?

- What internal representations did you use?
- What do you see, hear, feel, smell, taste, etc. in the movie that you play in your mind?
- What referents past or future do you use?
- Where are you?
- Who is there or not there?

Notice also what state your reading puts you in. Did you read the passage sympathetically and go into a corresponding depressed state? Notice also what happens on 'the screen of your mind' when your mind takes those words and attempts to 'make sense' of them.

A confession. That was a very difficult passage to *representationally track*. In fact, it was impossible to track over to immediate see, hear, feel referents! If you had difficulty with that exercise, good. That means you were *not* seduced by the passage to hallucinate your own stuff and fill in the blanks. If you did create an internal movie, then the passage *got you!*

That's what language does. If you haven't risen up in your mind to take a magician's point of view and adopted the eyes of a magician about the map-like nature of words, then words all too often induce you into states. They hypnotize. They entrance. They invite you to *go inside your mind* and create 'sense' from your own experience. Then you don't 'hear' what people say, you use a few key words to re-access your internal worlds.

That's why it usually takes some practice to become truly conscious of the sensory modalities and how we use them in translating *words* back into *movies*. Most of us focus our awareness so much on *the content* of our thoughts that we lose awareness of their *structure*. This also explains our low capacity for performing neuro-linguistic magic. Without this awareness, we will not even *hear* the spells cast on us or the spells that we cast on others!

Conversely, by noticing *how* you represent words and the ideas and stories suggested by the words, you begin to become conscious of the internal pictures, words, sounds, and sensations you use in your own 'making sense' of language. Doing this brings your unconscious language processing into conscious awareness and gives you more choice about how to represent things.

When we're unaware that the magic that lies in the structure, our 'minds' simply bypass the *form* of our internal processing and rush onward to *content*. We focus more on content and tend to equate it to 'meaning.'

In the example, I used the nominalization (a verb turned into a noun) *'depression.'* Typically we all 'make sense' of terms like that lightning quick by using our own referent experiences and definitions *without even noticing* the lack of sensory-based information in the word and the sensory-based representations we access and invent as we process it. Did you?

'Depression' is the name of a class of thoughts, feelings, actions, etc. We use this label as a vague summation term for many possibilities. The term is an abstraction without any details. How different if we had written, "I've sat on the sofa watching television all day and did not feel like getting out for some exercise."

To the extent that we supply our own see-hear-feel referents without thinking about our own representing and processing of the term, we assume that the word has meaning in and of itself, and that we contribute nothing to the effect of the word on us. Not good. Not the mind of a magician. Often we will experience an induction by the term without knowing it. The term itself hypnotizes us. The magic that then occurs (probably gloomy dark magic in this case) will seem to have nothing to do with the words, we will jump to other conclusions. "I'm just not over X..." "I'm just a depressive kind of guy. It runs in my family."

Relating to language in this way is like driving a powerful sports car with blinders on. Not only do we not enjoy the ride, but we set ourselves up for disasters.

The Magic of Know-Nothing Questioning

Language use is not neutral. Korzybski in General Semantics suggested that, like driving a car, we should not turn speakers loose in society without a license to use language and speak. Just because we all automatically learn language and do so from childhood, does *not* mean that it's not a powerful neuro-linguistic mechanism.

To use language effectively, professionally, and persuasively, we need to know what we're doing with it, how it works, how it casts spells, how to break negative trances, and how to put a turbo jet in our language when we really want to go places.

If we don't adopt a *meta-view* of language and our languaging, we will not even think about a speaker's representations or what spells they invite. We will foolishly assume that meaning lies in the words and then move through life with a pseudo-understanding of people and things, suffer from continual mis-communications, project our own references and perceptual filters onto others, etc. All of this will then lead to unuseful hallucinating of meanings, blindly receiving hypnotic commands from others, and getting duped easily and regularly.

Conversely, our magician skills begin when we *carefully listen* to the actual words given and, using *only* those words, *construct a representation*. That leads to accurate listening. While it is not an easy skill to develop, everyone can develop it with practice.

Once we can accurately hear, we can begin the meta-modeling process. After we learn how to base our internal representations on *only* the words given, we can use what's missing in our representations for guiding our information-gathering questions.

We best meta-model when we operate from a *'Know Nothing'* frame of reference. This is the magician's stance. Assuming nothing enables us to explore curiously so that we obtain high quality information. We can explore as did the television detective Columbo, who asked searching questions that, on the surface, seemed innocent enough, but which ultimately enabled him to get to the real issues.

Representationally tracking words as symbols for referents over to our internal movie develops our awareness of how we represent words. This gives us the unique opportunity to explore our own consciousness regarding where our brain goes in response to words and to the references that we use. *Tracking to our mind's internal movie screen* enables us to develop a knack for asking high-quality questions and getting to the heart of another's meanings.

The technique that will *not* work in seeking to understand someone's model of the world is *advice giving.* When we talk with someone who has obviously deleted key information from his or her model of the world, key distinctions for how to do something, the very last thing that will work in influencing that person is advice giving. *Telling* someone what to do will typically fall into the gaps created by deletion in the person's model. The advice will typically not even make sense to the person. Why? Because the person's mental maps are not structured to receive it.

Our desire and tendency to give advice describes one of the central things that get in the way of our *accurate hearing.* When we decide we already know what another means, needs, should do, etc., we stop listening and, in fact, can no longer accurately listen. This is *not* the heart of a magician.

The power of exploring, questioning, and challenging with the Meta-Model makes the technique of giving advice look as old fashioned as a Model-T in the twenty-first century. Meta-Modeling enables us to *enter into* another person's model of the world and, by just asking questions, enrich that world of frames.

How does it work? The questioning itself facilitates the other person's *active involvement* in examining his or her maps and mapping processes. This gently challenges the neuro-linguistic processes and invites the person to expand understandings. The conversation itself takes the person *up a level* where he or she can run

Quality Control checks on the mapping. This lets the person change frames, reject and deframe old frames, give new meanings to things (reframe), etc. That's why we mostly use questions when we use the communication magic model. We call this questioning, *meta-modeling.* We ask questions that invite the person to 'go inside' to examine the very structure of the mapping and the referent experiences. This gives the other person a chance to re-map in more accurate, appropriate, and enhancing ways and to experience the new magic that arises.

Recognizing the Two Kinds of Magic

Earlier I mentioned that we have two basic categories for sorting linguistic patterns. This now gives us two different kinds of 'magical' things that we can do with language in our communications.

- *Sensory-based language* primarily describes see-hear-feel 'things' or objects in the external world. You can video-tape these referents. This kind of language gives us the powerful magic of precision and clarity.
- *Evaluative-based language,* by way of contrast, describes our attributions of value and meaning to various things, processes, and ideas. Of course, such language takes us to the realm of non-things (i.e., concepts, abstractions, relationships, and processes). These referents concern *mental* constructs, they deal with things inside the nervous system (i.e., understandings, beliefs, evaluations, etc.). This kind of language gives us the powerful magic by which we can inspire, en-trance, persuade, hypnotize, motivate, create higher frames, etc.

How do we tell the difference?

> *Representationally tracking and testing language enables us to distinguish between these different levels.*

Consider the statement, "You look angry." Can you representationally track those words to your mental screen? No, you can't. Whatever you fill-in about 'anger,' *you* invented it. It came from your model of the world, not from the language itself. This reveals the *non-sensory* nature of the term. The phrase does not describe anything about a person's looks, facial expressions, breathing, movement, sounds, voice, tone, etc. We cannot video-tape any of that.

The statement, "You look angry," expresses the *evaluations* of some speaker. It gives us a little glimpse of the speaker's understandings about some unspecified looks. What does 'anger' look, sound, or feel like in behavioral, facial, muscular, or action terms? About such we need to inquire. That's how we would Meta-Model the speaker.

> How do you know that's anger?
> What about the person's expressions suggests that to you?

Notice how different is the following sentence:

> "I notice that you have not made eye contact with me and have talked in a lower than usual volume."

This sensory based language provides an immediate referent. We can track those words onto a mental screen. By *describing,* rather than *evaluating,* the speaker has given me specific language that leads to understanding. The statement gives no interpretation of what those action words mean to the speaker.

Clarifying the linguistics and meanings that we hear empowers us to use language with more clarity, precision, and accuracy. This really helps when sharing meanings (i.e., evaluations, interpretations) because conceptual language inevitably involves evaluations.

By contrast, sensory-based language describes. A simple way to express ourselves without coming across with 'judgments' involves shifting to descriptive language. Descriptive language pushes fewer 'buttons.' So most people experience it as less offensive. This describes the magic of descriptive languaging for communicating with less abrasion.

> "I could hear you better if you didn't wave your index finger in my face."

Evaluative language typically pushes buttons because it judges and evaluates. This makes such language more provocative.

> "I can't hear you because you talk down to me and insult me with your superiority attitude."

When we language with evaluative statements, people typically feel that we are imposing our meanings on them or, if handled very gently, inviting them to try on new meanings which may enhance their lives. In the first case, people will typically respond with resistance, denial, opposition, rejection, etc. In the second, they will access a hypnotic state of suggestibility. We can perform all kinds of magic—both 'black magic' and 'white magic' by using evaluative language patterns.

Hypnotic magic occurs mostly with evaluative languaging. Non-sensory based language, lacking immediate referents, inherently invites people to go inside to make up their own referents. By not providing sensory-based referents, people develop an internal focus in order to construct mentally the referents in their meaning-making of the words. This invites them to 'hallucinate' about our communications and to enter into trance states.

> "Sally became depressed when Tad rejected her."

This statement provides no specific verbs and hence no details in our internal pictures, sounds, or feelings for the term 'rejected.' The statement invites us to supply those details. Yet whatever referents we access in our own unique 'making sense' of 'rejection' we create out of our history, experiences, learnings, etc. It's our stuff, not the speaker's.

Tad could have raised his voice with her, slapped her face, dated someone else, cussed her out, refused to write a letter of recommendation for a job, etc. Whatever initial references we thought (read 'imagined'), we generated from our own model of the world. This shows something very special. *It's the very nature of language to hypnotize.* In fact, all language hypnotizes in that it uses symbols that invite us to 'go inside,' access our own memory banks or reference structures, and use them to make sense of things. To the extent that we succeed in 'understanding,' we have entered into an altered state.

The mind and heart of a magician distinguishes these two categories of language. We can then understand why we find 'naming' actual existing *things* useful, but *naming* 'ideas' and 'concepts' unuseful. Naming (nominalizing) actions and verbs and concepts typically creates a fluffy sense of understanding while not really understanding.

Sensory-based names and terms appropriately name items to which we can point. What we can *point to,* we can agree on. The referent comes into sight. But 'naming' a way of conceptualizing or a process of interactions (a set of relatings) usually does not give us a specific referent. It doesn't give clearly defined referents. The referent is un-pointable to. And when we can't *point to the reference,* "This is what I'm talking about," there's a lot more room for confusion, misunderstanding, disagreement, etc. when we communicate.

For example, does the phrase 'the law of gravity' describe or evaluate? What do we have in this phrase? We have an abstraction or idea. We have a linguistic conclusion that someone has made from some observations.

We certainly can see an apple fall from a tree. We may also hear it, feel it, etc., but we cannot see, hear, feel, smell or taste 'the law of gravity.' Before Newton saw some specific apple fall, hundreds and thousands and millions of other people had similarly seen such an event. Yet Newton 'saw' more. He saw in the event an *idea,* a concept, and so he drew a conclusion. This occurred in his mind. In doing so he created a generalization about a relationship between objects and their movement downward to the surface of the planet. His idea related to the apple's falling and described the relationship between the apple and the ground. It described the *process* of the apple moving from one place to another. Yet the 'law' of gravity (or 'gravity') is not a 'thing' that exists apart from our nervous systems. Nor was it a piece of legislation that a group voted into existence. 'Law' here is a metaphor. Out there, only 'objects' in motion exist. This abstraction indicates a conception generated in our minds about such external objects and events.

As a model about the structure and form of language, the Meta-Model enables us to make more clearly these distinctions between the different levels of our mapping. In doing so, it enables us to move through the world with better maps, and with the skills and tools for constantly updating and improving our maps. It enables us to see with the eyes of a wizard and to develop a magician's heart.

Summary

- A *Meta*-Model refers to any model that's *meta* or *higher* than its subject. We go meta by moving up a level of awareness so that we can then think and feel *about* the previous level. This gives us the eyes and mind of a word magician. Without this perspective, we cannot control the magic.
- A Meta-Model of language enables us to become clear and insightful about the *model of language itself*—how it works, the mechanisms that drive it, and how to use it to enrich our everyday lives.
- Because we can do a great many things with language, there are numerous kinds of magical things we can do in communicating. As magicians, we can use the power of precision and accuracy as well as the magic of creating powerful meanings, inducing altered states, and setting higher frames.

Chapter 4

Expressions of Magic

Map Magic for Transformations

The magic of language lies in its *structure* and it is this that enables us to do some pretty magical things with words as we communicate. The *secrets* of how to use and work with this magic give us access to higher and more elegant communication skills. In the following chapters, we will review the language model that describes the form of neuro-linguistic magic as well as explore many of the principles that govern this *magic* in our lives. In doing so, we will identify the linguistic distinctions in our communications that open the door to the models that govern our lives. These distinctions inform us of the leverage points in the mind—leverage points for magic.

This will prepare us for *using the magic to transform our lives*. If there's transformational magic in the words that we use, in the mental maps that we develop, in the frames of mind that we cultivate, then knowing the structure and the secrets of that magic will improve and enrich our lives. This brings us to a set of application questions:

- What *magic* does this model allow us to perform?
- What *magic* can we perform on our own minds-and-emotions, and those of others?
- How can this linguistic magic enrich our communications, states, skills, expertise, etc.?
- What other benefits will this create?

To answer these questions we will explore some of the neuro-linguistic and neuro-semantic magic that we have found in the communication magic model. When Bandler and Grinder first experienced the wondrous magic-like cures that they saw and heard in Perls, Satir, and Erickson, they set out to model the structure in that communication excellence. Eventually, they were able to replicate it themselves, and teach others to do the same.

One of my objectives in doing this is to go beyond the mere replication of that expertise so that we can develop the *attitude* of a creative magician. Why? Because if we fully appreciate the power and wonder of language in our thinking, communicating, and relating, then we'll develop a very special attitude—one that will keep us alive and vital as we make a difference in the world.

"Hey! Where's the Magic?"

In the USA in the 1980s the Burger King hamburger chain ran a series of commercials wherein a 'little ole lady' kept asking, *"Where's the beef?"* She didn't want some tiny little shriveled up burnt burger that could get lost in a bun. She wanted 'the real thing.' But when she peered under the gigantic bun, she didn't find the real thing.

Similarly, in the fields of communication, coaching, therapy, consultation, personal empowerment, learning acceleration, etc. we often hear more offered than delivered. The P.R. sounds great. But the results indicate an over-sell. Consequently, all too often we find the helpings under the bun very sparse compared to the marketing.

"Where is the beef?" Or, as we ask here, "Where is the magic?"

The magic lies in the language, in the way we represent, format, structure, and frame our ideas. Since we do not deal with or interact with the territory directly, but as mediated by our maps, the magic lies in how we communicate and map things.

If the interface with the territory occurs in our map, then that's where we will find the *magic*. As we construct images, schemas, paradigms, or models of the world and *use them to navigate* as we move through life, the excellent ones put 'magic' in our hands. They form, mold, govern, direct, organize, modulate, and determine *our experiences* as we navigate the world. Our maps determine what we can see or not see, what we feel or don't feel, how we organize our skills (or fail to do so), how we portray to ourselves (and others) our options and choices in the world, the programs that we build for coping and adapting, etc.

No wonder our paradigmatic models of the world carry so much influence in our lives! They are our *interface* between the real world 'out there' and our subjective experience of that world. This means that the 'magic' occurs in knowing the leverage points for altering impoverishing maps.

In *The Structure of Magic,* Bandler and Grinder pointed to the linguistic markers as distinctions which indicate possible mapping problems. These can leave us with the lack of choices and so cast a black spell of un-resourcefulness on us. Via these linguistic markers (and other non-linguistic markers, *The Structure of Magic: Volume II*), we have a pathway into a human reality structure, i.e., our constructed model or matrix of the world. Moving along that pathway offers the opportunity to challenge most effectively impoverished maps and design new ones. We can facilitate a much more effective re-mapping that utilizes the principles and secrets of magic.

The process of using the Meta-Modeling distinctions to address and overcome ill-formed maps and semantic ineffectiveness gives us leverage points for transformation. Or, if we shift to a computer analogy for a moment, we could say that the linguistic markers, which indicate various qualities and codings of our mental maps, provide us with the *human programming language*. When we take our mental mapping into consideration, all of our experiences, perceptions, emotions, behaviors, psychosomatic illnesses, skills, etc. make sense. Also, the experiences and 'reality' of others begin to make sense. Whatever behaviors they produce make perfect sense *given their mapping.*

Even what we call 'dysfunctional' and pathological behavior makes perfect sense. When we start with a person's model of the world, how that person copes, responds, and navigates life makes structural sense. It may not work very well. The person may not get what he or she wants. It may even create lots of limitations and pain. Yet in terms of their reality model and the strategy that results from it, all of these responses make sense. That is, the *frame* governs the 'games' that the person plays. Further, if we modeled that person's way of thinking, reasoning, languaging, etc., we could replicate that 'way of being' and experiencing.

This understanding of the relationship between map and territory, between frame and game, between model of the world and experience of the world, reflects something the early NLP developers repeatedly asserted. *"People are not broken, they work perfectly well."*

The *broken model* of human psychology had it all wrong. Schizophrenics 'are' not broken, 'bad,' or 'crazy' in any ultimate sense, they simply operate from some different maps than the rest of us. Yet, the map that any given schizophrenic uses to move through the world *works.* It not only works to achieve the schizophrenic experience, it works regularly, methodically, and systematically. You can count on it working with consistency. In other words, there is *structure* to that particular madness. The 'black' magic that makes their lives a living hell makes perfect sense when we examine their frames of reference. Their frames, comprising the content of their ideas, beliefs, understandings, etc., determine their response.

Again, the map controls the magic. It always does. It does so due to the extent that human consciousness itself is a languaged consciousness. How we language ourselves, our world, others, how to cope, etc. governs how we then play the games of life.

'Magic' as Skills of Wonder

Sometimes we use the term 'magic' to refer to the absolutely amazing, incredible, and wonderful skills, abilities, and powers that we see exhibited in certain people. When we encounter a highly talented artist, scientist, musician, therapist, educator, or anyone performing at the expert or 'genius' level, we stand back and marvel in awe.

> "How can they perform with such high-level achievements?"
> "What explains their intuitive genius?"
> "They seem so gifted and so natural in what they can do!"

> "What a wizard to just know how to do this—in coming up with these new insights!"

Since all subjective experience operates from *structure* (or neuro-linguistic mapping), then all we need are the sufficient tools for modeling human excellence. If we have those, and if we spend the time to do so, we can discover the structure of the magical achievements. The domain of modeling excellence in NLP and Neuro-Semantics precisely involves these things. It involves finding the *internal strategies* that people use to perform seeming 'magical' feats. What are some of these feats? Some of the early models developed in this field include:

- Relating quickly and effectively with people, developing 'instant rapport' and emotional bonds.
- Persuading and influencing: identifying and using the leverage points when influencing, and doing so with integrity and ecology.
- Teaching, educating, and training with excellence: accelerating the learning process for high-level skills in comprehension, integration, implementation, etc.
- Innovating new products from the creation of new ideas and models: increasing creativity and flexibility.
- Creating new markets, creating new marketing processes, and developing more expertise in entrepreneurial adventures.
- Slimming to an optimal weight and maintaining it: reaching and sustaining a naturally slim and fit body.
- Parenting children with grace, love, and firmness to create healthy, vigorous, autonomous, cooperative, and well-balanced young adults.
- Managing people in business contexts: working with and through people effectively to reach larger outcomes, working as a team that validates the contributions of all participants.
- Inventing new models and ideas in physics, chemistry, engineering, etc.
- Etc.

The expertise within and behind these facets of life are *learned skills*, skills that we develop by learning how to use our neurological 'languages' (e.g., our VAK sensory-based languages and our conceptual linguistics). To function in any domain, as a gymnast, rock climber, pilot, diplomat, scholar, musician, hypnotist, writer, or whatever, necessitates that we order and structure our consciousness in a particular way.

When we establish the right frames in the right syntactical order for our mind-body system, we are empowered to perform the magical feats. Establishing the higher matrix of the mind with certain intentions allows us to align more easily our everyday attentions. Then, the higher intentions set the direction for our neuro-linguistic states and we experience expertise emerging in our experiences. The higher intentional frames along with the higher paradigms operate as a self-organizing attractor. Then we 'naturally' notice the particular qualities that enhance our skills and we filter out those that do not. At times, this can seem *magical*, and in a way it is. It is the structure of the particular magic that makes for a given expertise.

This process also involves a *semantic structuring*. We see this in how a gymnast, rock climber, cyclist, Olympic athlete, entrepreneur, etc., languages him or herself in terms of the beliefs, values, understandings, and identity frames that support and bring out the experience of that achievement.

Having worked for several years as a coach of boys' gymnastics, and as a coach and psychological consultant for a girls' competitive team, I have seen firsthand how the languaged distinctions involved in defining oneself as a gymnast slowly transform a young person. It's an amazing transformation. In the end, the gymnast has a mind-set that differs radically from the non-gymnast. Mere skill isn't enough. A young person also has to *semantically structure* his or her consciousness. To become a gymnast the person must form certain meta-level beliefs that support the intensely focused states. The person has to accept, validate, and experience certain Cause-Effect beliefs, Complex Equivalences, Identifications, etc. These include neuro-semantic constructions such as:

> "Practice, practice, practice will turn me into a champion."
> "Falling and even getting hurt is just part of the process that will put me at the top."
> "I have what it takes to become a highly skilled gymnast."

"Being a skilled gymnast is critically important; it's what I want most of all!"
"Focusing all my attention totally and completely on my routine gives me more control."
"I can see and feel my body going through the movements in my imagination."
"I need a coach to coach me through the exercises and routines that will move me to a higher level."

What seems *magical* to an outsider in terms of the external structure of the experience will typically just seem normal to the one inside the experience. Why? Partly because the experience of becoming an expert happens over time, bit by bit, frame by frame, experience by experience. It creeps up. The person's model of the world slowly evolves and transforms. As it does, it increasingly becomes the person's reality strategy so that it doesn't seem like anything special or magical. It's just the way things are.

Just prior to the first edition of this book, several Palestinian young men strapped on bombs, walked into a Jerusalem marketplace, and ignited the bombs. What many of us label as utterly strange and foreign 'black magic'—unable even to imagine *how* they could do such a thing (either to self or to the innocent victims), their comrades and associates praise them for the epitome of courage, loyalty, commitment (i.e., 'white magic'). Whether we see it as holy or hellish, the structure of such magic lies in the person's mapping processes—how the young men syntactically learned to structure their senses and how they semantically learned to language the 'reality' of what they were doing. Was it murder or bravery? Did they act to promote a sacred cause or to needlessly destroy human life? The matrix of all of the frames of their mind about honor, war, commitment, death, religion, etc. came together to enable them to do something beyond the imagination of most people. Living in an entirely different mental-and-emotional world, we stand aghast and unbelievingly ask, "How in the world could they do something like that?" "What got into them?"

Yet that last question, "What got into them?," misunderstands the nature of our neuro-semantic structures. Nothing *got* into them. Nothing *went* wrong. Nothing *misfired.* All of their belief frames, value frames, identity frames, outcome frames, etc. combined in a psycho-logical way to generate their skills.

Our skills and their magic arise from our symbolic or semantic structures. We map them into existence. They operate by a model. This now allows us, when we meet fantastic skills and expertise, to specify the structure and to create a model which describes how it works and how to replicate it in others.

'Magic' as Fast and Radical Transformations

We also use the word 'magic' in another way. In our map-making, we use it to refer to *a process that transforms something so quickly and radically* that it violates our expectations and assumptions. We look at a result which we can't figure out—not its structure, not its speed. The processes tapped into some leverage points of change that we know not of with the result that change seemed to occur *suddenly* and *inexplicably*. It seemed like magic. In such instances, the processes *shifted the person's paradigms* so completely that it ignited something new suddenly to emerge. As observers, we were left with no explanatory model. And without a way to understand or explain the processes, we were left in the dark. We say "I can't figure it out; it blows my mind." We feel stunned. Sometimes we feel overwhelmed.

> "I don't understand. How did you make my phobia just disappear? All you did was talk to her. What happened?"
> "Amazing! Suddenly I don't feel bad at all when I think of things that way."
> "It took years and years for her to get that way—how could she just change like that? Doesn't a person have to go through the pain for months before getting over something like that?"
> "When you watch her work with clients—it seems like she just reaches right into their insides, tweaks something and suddenly, they are re-born into a new world. I don't get it."

These statements illustrate the powerful effect that systemic knowledge can provide. When we know *where* to intervene in a system of interactive parts, and when we know *when* to do so, and *how* to utilize various mechanisms or processes in place within the system, the results seem like magic. Yet while knowing where to exercise a critical leverage point may appear as magic to an outsider, to the insider it seems like a little thing, a common sense thing.

The Magic of Resolving Old Phobias

NLP has a pattern called the 'Phobia Cure.' It provides a way to reprocess or reprogram neuro-linguistic structures. It makes it so that we do not have the 'Phobia Response' or frame as our default program. When you are let in on the secret of this process, it will seem very simple. You may even find it ridiculously simple. "Of course. Why didn't I think of that before?" Yet until you know the *secret* of that magic, 'curing' a phobia will seem hard, difficult, involved, even impossible. Some theoreticians will say it takes months even years to 'get over it' because it is just the symptom of much deeper problems and issues. Others will explain it as a function of neurological conditioning. For them it will take months of de-sensitization and re-conditioning. I used to think of it in these terms. But no more.

From a neuro-linguistic and neuro-semantic viewpoint, it's simply a matter of coding, of framing.

> "Simply use some process to invite the phobia-driven person to *step aside* from the representations so that he or she can *just notice* the old thoughts."

Sometimes we see this kind of *magic* with regard to mechanical things—cars, computers, televisions, VCRs, the latest electronic gadgets. Someone 'in the know' about engineering and structure simply taps on a seemingly insignificant part and in an instance the thing works just fine. They know the magic. They know the structure, the dynamics involved, the leverage points.

In a similar way, if we know the neuro-linguistic and neuro-semantic principles that govern human functioning, we also can perform magical things with people. When we are let in on the secret of our own design engineering (i.e., how to run our own brains), then suddenly the *structure of a phobia* no longer seems strange, foreboding, or incorrigible. The mystery disappears. Now it all makes sense.

When we know that 'to have a phobia,' whether we want to give one (!) or take one away from someone, we need to change the form and syntax of a person's internal representations and frames. This means that we can actually count on every phobia having a similar structure.

When a person thinks and represents a situation as fearful, that person will do so by *stepping into* the representations (remembered or imagined) and associate into it. This will cue the brain with danger and threat. The person will then feel as if *in* the situation. Cue the brain this way and the system will work as any healthy system will. The autonomic nervous system defenses will respond with the Fight/ Flight/ Freeze response to take care of the danger or threat. In one sense we can say, "It's magical." In another, we can say, "It's natural."

If that's the structure of *how to have a phobic reaction,* then *how to avoid* a phobic reaction will involve the opposite. If we simply change the coding from associated into the representations to dissociated from the representations, the phobia will go away. The person's sense of threat will immediately be reduced. So, we simply invite the person to *step back* from the representations. We set up a format that allows the person to take a meta-position of calm observing.

After we have elicited that neuro-linguistic state, we may even invite more of it. Step into an even calmer observing so that you observe yourself observing. Typically this is sufficient to prevent the person from stepping back into the horror movie. It also provides the individual with the ability to think *about* the fear, rather than the thinking *of* it. This spectator's viewpoint of the phobia creates for the person an expanded frame of reference. It allows the person to access other resources: calmness, relaxation, reality testing, etc. By *bringing these resources to bear* on the phobia, a person alters his or her model of the world. This changes everything.

So does playing 'the movie' to its end, and then on to a scene of comfort. As process instructions about *where* to send one's attention, namely, to a *scene of comfort,* this trains one *not* to stop at the scene of trauma, but to *go on*—move on to a more resourceful place. The trauma scene doesn't have to be the last word about your life.

In the magic of the 'Phobia Cure' in NLP, we next invite a person to take yet another step. "Step into that *comfort* scene at the end of your movie ... good. And just enjoy that sense of comfort." Often that's sufficient for resolving the trauma. But we can do more.

We can use the *comfort* feelings in a new and, perhaps, surprising way. We can have the person *step in fully* and then rewind the movie, to go backwards from the comfort to the beginning. By doing this in a fast rewind motion, while *inside* 'the movie,' we invite the person to experience an entirely different syntax. Before it was 'from the beginning of the pain to full blown traumatic fear and hurt.' Now we set up a different order. 'From comfort back to the beginning of the unpleasant experience.' Many with whom I've used this process have spoken about the comfort feelings *spreading backwards.*

Typically, running information backwards alters the meanings that we attribute to things. Read any sentence in this book backwards and notice what happens to the 'meaning' of the sentence. Backwards sequencing alters order, alters structure, and so alters meaning. In the 'Phobia Cure,' we invite the person to run their old movie backwards and to turn up the speed so that it happens in one or two seconds. And, they are to rewind the phobia movie from the inside. Talk about *altering consciousness!* That will do it.

Next we invite the person to repeat this process five or more times. Why? To run the neuro-pathways using these frames. As this habituates, the person's attention, feelings, and states all change. The person maps things in an entirely different way.

What a leverage point for transforming a phobic response! Who would ever have thought that such a simple procedure could have that kind of pervasive alteration?

Psychologists for decades had assumed an entirely different theoretical basis for the 'curing' of a phobia. First they postulated that people had become fixated on the phobic object as a transform from some other fear. So they sought to 'analyze' the repressed fear and chase it out into the open. The battle cry was, "Where Id is, let there be ego!" But the tricky nature of reflexivity made the search continue for years. Behaviorists eventually sped the process up so they could achieve a resolution in six months using a re-conditioning process of gradual de-sensitization by training a neurological response of relaxing in the face of a noxious or toxic element.

Today, the 'ten minute phobia cure' has been replicated thousands of times by thousands of practitioners. People shift from being able to reproduce the phobia response by just thinking about it to not being able to do it at all. Typically most find this so dramatic that they do not believe it at first. It violates our beliefs about change, about changing things quickly, and about what has to take place for a change to have truly occurred. It seems magical.

The Magic of the Achievement Frame

The neuro-linguistic and neuro-semantic models of human functioning (i.e., thinking-emoting, speaking, behaving, and relating) give us many of the *secrets* for understanding and installing new subjective structures. They provide us with the *magic* of marvelous skills and abilities. These include both the strategies of genius and the strategies of pathology.

In doing this, Bandler and Grinder established a *different attitude* from what we typically find in the field of psychology and psychotherapy. They did not look upon such subjective states as schizophrenia, multiple personalities, or phobias as inherently 'bad' or 'evil' experiences. They rather looked upon them as *human achievements.*

Using the *achievement frame* enabled them to explore afresh the structural and engineering facets of the structure of an experience. They asked, *"How does this experience work?"* Then, once they modeled it in terms of strategy, Meta-Programs, Meta-Model distinctions, physiology, Meta-States distinctions, etc., they began to ask various utilization questions:

- What can we use it for?
- When and where would we find it a valuable strategy?
- How could we fine-tune it to offer a useful skill?
- Where does the leverage point lie for transforming it?

Prior to this development, most practitioners in the fields of psychology and psychotherapy did *not* even have these questions. Their paradigm did *not* orient them to ask such questions. In fact, they tended to ask questions that began from the opposite assumption. Their paradigms about human functioning started from the idea that any and every pathology was 'bad.' This frame prevented them from even asking the utilization questions just quoted.

It took modelers from outside the old psychological paradigms to enter the arena of *human functioning* and to ask an entirely new set of questions. They had not been schooled to think of these experiences as 'bad' things. They started from a *different attitude*. They began from the assumption that these experiences, behaviors, skills, thinking patterns, etc. were achievements because the persons creating them could produce them regularly, methodically, and systemically. That suggested order and structure.

They began from the different attitude of engineering. *"How does this work?" "What are the mechanisms that govern this?"* They did not ask 'Why' questions ("Why are you this way?") so much as they asked 'How' questions. And these different questions led them in an entirely different direction.

In 1987, Richard Bandler worked with a young schizophrenic named Andy before a video-camera. Andy suffered from hallucinations. He heard people yelling at him, ordering him around, wanting him to do things, telling him that he was no good, etc. He presented typical paranoid schizophrenic symptoms.

According to Bandler, when he first met Andy he adopted a different attitude from the one held by the psychiatrists who were working with him. Rather than viewing schizophrenia as a bad thing, Richard viewed it as a *human achievement* and set that frame with Andy as they talked. This allowed him not to get caught up in the *content* of the schizophrenia. He focused on *how*: "How do you do this?" "How do you know you do this?" "What is it like?" "How do you know when to do it?"

In the questioning, Richard discovered that Andy hallucinated characters coming off the television and chasing him around. Richard asked, "What do you watch?"

It turned out that Andy was hallucinating the character "Mary," the Mary on the "Little House on the Prairie" TV series. She would come off the TV screen and chase him around the house and 'rag' on him with her little bitchy voice. Andy said that she was "a powerful person" and that she had a lot of control over him.

His paranoid schizophrenia began to make a lot of sense. If you have unpleasant characters coming off the television and chasing you around and insulting you, that would be fearful and seem like people are out to get you.

Richard said that the first thing that struck his mind upon hearing about a character coming off the TV and chasing him was, "This is a million dollar disorder!"

He didn't view it as a 'problem,' but as a skill, as an achievement. Andy was able to create and produce this internal experience regularly and methodically. That's a skill. But was it useful? How could it be useful? Did he have control of it? How much control?

Richard said that this wasn't pathology, it was a case of "bad taste in viewing." Thinking about it as a structure, he started thinking about other shows and channels, the Playboy channel, the Money channel, the History channel, etc.

> "We could teach this strategy to traveling salesmen so that they would never have to feel lonely again. But first, I want the strategy."

Richard then noticed a change in Andy's response. From a guy who had worked for years trying *not* to have this experience and problem, and who had experienced many therapists trying to get him *not* to have those hallucinations, he changed to a guy who responded to Richard's request for him to tell him *how* he did it with, "Well, maybe I'll tell you and maybe I won't."

This shows how *structure* dominates content. Yet getting hung up in content, especially in judging an experience 'good' or 'bad,' has blinded and continues to blind many theorists from even seeing, at the meta-level, the form of the mapping and how to use it effectively for change.

When Bandler and Grinder discovered the *structure* of the subjective experience of phobias, schizophrenia, or genius, it then became easy to work more directly with the structure of the strategies themselves. It now becomes easy to mess up a strategy so that it does not work in the way that it always has worked. It now becomes easy to transform the strategy so that it works in new ways.

Sometimes this can happen in just a matter of a few minutes as in the 'Phobia Cure' model. That model enables a person to recover from tormenting memories about past traumas. After all, 'memory' simply describes our ongoing coding of past events. Memory is what we are doing right now with former representations. When we change the internal representations of those events, and the meta-level frames of meanings given to them, we change the experience itself. The ongoing traumatization no longer works the way it has worked.

The ongoing discovery for the structure of magic continues today whenever we look upon the forms of human behavior, skills, and responses as accomplishments. When we start from this perspective and attitude, we can then go after the internal strategy by which it operates. This means learning to identify, articulate, and specify the strategies that empower people for effectiveness in all kinds of realms that express forms of personal genius (e.g. communicating and relating, selling and persuading, parenting and bonding, accessing states of creativity, etc.). In terms of working with maladaptive strategies that create pain and limitations, it involves a similar strategy analysis.

The Magic of Modeling

All of this returns us to the place where NLP began—*modeling*. This journey has brought us back to the modeling attitude that's succinctly summarized in the following:

- How does this process work?
- What internal structure governs the way this experience operates?
- What does a person represent first, then second, then third, etc.?
- What other qualities and factors play a crucial role in the formula of this piece of human excellence?
- If I took your place for a day so that you could have a day off from this problem, how would I do it?

The first work that formulated some of the basic modeling skills and distinctions appeared when Robert Dilts formulated the strategies model. Along with the original co-founders, Bandler and Grinder, Judith DeLozier, and Leslie Cameron-Bandler, he put together *NLP: The Study of the Structure of Subjective Experience, Volume I* (1980). This work summarized the strategy model by rehearsing the process of identifying the structure of subjectivity. The book provided a detailed description for how to identify strategies, unpack strategies, elicit strategies, etc.

There's *magic* in articulating the rule-governed structure of an experience. The strategy model began this by using the representational systems to detail the sensory steps in strategies. Since then, numerous works have followed which have presented specific strategies for excellence in sports, education, management, law, health, medicine, therapy, and many other fields thereby extending the idea of 'magic' (or human excellence that amazes and astonishes the uninitiated) far beyond the field of psychotherapy.

I'm not suggesting in this brief description that the magic of modeling only involves finding a strategy. Modeling involves much more than mere strategy elicitation and description. It involves building models out of multiple strategies, turning theoretical ideas into working models, testing and refining such models, exploring the literature in any given domain, etc. Yet the magic in modeling the excellence of human expertise does provide a way to accelerate the time it takes for expertise to progress.

Summary

- We can touch our lives, and the lives of others, with magic by empowering people to find and develop more resources. Becoming more resourceful in mind, emotion, and body enables us to achieve more things of value.
- To touch our lives with magic with NLP and NS, we have to access the most resourceful neuro-linguistic states. As we access the states that enable us to be at our best, we're able to be more creative, flexible, insightful, balanced, healthy, vigorous, etc.
- Magic emerges as we create the richest kind of maps for navigating reality. We then learn to handle effectively the magic of reframing the meanings that we attribute to things, people, events, and words. This, in turn, endows us with a sense of more choice and response-ability.

Part II

The Model for Communication Magic

Chapter 5

The Magic Model Part I: Deletions

"Men are apt to be much more influenced by words than by the actual facts of the surrounding reality."
Ivan Pavlov

- What does neuro-linguistic magic, the 'magic' that changes minds and emotions, that renews dreams and hopes, that formulates skills and talents, that structures genius, and that transforms business, relationships, etc. look like?
- If you wanted to touch someone with magic or receive the touch of magic, how would that process work?
- If you wanted to learn the model of that magic, what would you actually be learning?

With this chapter we begin our exploration and review of the *Communication Magic Model* that we call the Meta-Model. The extensiveness of the model has led me to divide it into four chapters (Chapters 5–8). I have divided the sections of the Meta-Model using the modeling categories of deletion, generalization, and distortion following Dilts's format.

Now that you have the mind, eyes, and heart of a magician (Chapter 3) to see and handle *language* as an expression of neuro-linguistic magic, you can play with the following *linguistic distinctions* as if each put into your hands a magic wand, can you not? Each and every *linguistic distinction* operates like a mapping structure, it isn't 'real' but just a map, just a symbol of the real. Knowing that, you can now use it to perform the 'magic' of inducing states knowing, as you do, that every *signal* from the linguistic symbols *induces* experiences—neuro-linguistic and neuro-semantic experiences.

You already know that Bandler and Grinder formulated the first expression of the *Communication Magic Model* using Transformational Grammar (TG) and applied it in the context of psychotherapy. This will show up at times in the next four chapters. Yet both were accidents to the model.

So relax comfortably in the knowledge that the Meta-Model is *not* about Transformational Grammar, and it is not about psychotherapy. Not at all!

This model is about the power of words to affect our neurology. It is about how the symbols we use in language and gesture affect our thinking, emoting, responding, construction of meaning, matrix of mind-frames, construction of 'personality,' skills, abilities, etc.

That makes it pretty important, wouldn't you say? While TG and psychotherapy are not *innate* to the model, many of the quotations included in what follows do allude to these subjects. As you detect some leftover aspects of TG, especially in the terminology, don't let that put you off, the Meta-Model has grown beyond both.

This chapter presents the first and simplest part of the Meta-Model, the linguistic distinctions involving *deletions*. I have put the deletion distinctions first because of their simplicity and because *you already have the magical intuitions regarding how to handle them.*

"I do?"

Yes, you do. We all do. All native speakers of a language do. It comes with the territory of language acquisition. You will tend to have most of the *intuitions* about the linguistic distinctions of generalizations too. In Chapter 7, however, you will wish to the high heavens that such intuitions came with the distortion distinctions! That's where your way of handling the *linguistic* distinctions may even seem counter-intuitive. There you will have to retrain your linguistic intuitions.

But not here. Here it will seem so simple, so intuitive, so "Give me a break! Of course!" Intuitively you will know most of the questions to ask about the deletions because you naturally have to do that to make sense, understand, and representationally track the words to a mental movie in your mind.

Organized by the Modeling Processes

Bandler and Grinder did not organize the linguistic distinctions in this communication model when they first wrote *The Structure of Magic (1975)*. The content was there, but it was haphazardly scattered throughout the book. Robert Dilts created the first (or one of the first) organizations of the Meta-Model. He took the three modeling processes and used them as formats for the linguistic structures. This allowed him to create a diagram of the model so that we could see it at a glance:

Figure 5.1: Diagram format of the Meta-Model

Linguistic Distinctions	Questions Explorations	Results Effects
Deletions...		
—	—	—
—		
Generalizations...		
—	—	—
—	—	—
Distortions...		
—	—	—
—	—	—

Since we all use these processes as we create our mental models in the first place, it makes sense to format the *Communication Magic Model* using these categories. We leave things out; we generalize; we distort. As we recognize this in our everyday linguistic expressions, these categories will facilitate our meta-level ability to recognize problematic mapping distinctions (i.e., give us the mind of a magician).

> "The processes by which people impoverish their representation of the world are the same processes by which they impoverish their expression of their representation of the world. The way that people have created pain for themselves involves these processes. Through them they have created an impoverished model. Our Meta-Model offers a specific way to challenge these same processes to enrich their model." (p. 46)

Figure 5.2: Linguistic Distinctions of Deletions

1. *Simple Deletions:* Characteristics left out
2. *Unspecified Referential Indices:* Unspecified nouns and verbs
3. *Comparative and Superlative Deletions:* Unspecified relations
4. *Unspecified Processes:* Adjectives modifying nouns.
5. *Unspecified Processes:* Adverbs modifying verbs

Deletion Magic

When we delete information, we leave things out and then only selectively pay attention to other dimensions of our experiences. This leads us to exclude and filter out elements. This works to our benefit to the extent that it saves us from being overwhelmed and over-loaded with stimuli. It works to our detriment to the extent that we delete critical data that are important to our resourcefulness.

Positively, we map via deletion to reduce the world to more manageable proportions. By it we create a reduced and more manageable version of reality. All deletions do not create problems. Well-formed deletions occur when we have sufficient redundancy in the immediate context. Without such redundancy, a model results that lacks the needed specificity for navigating the territory efficiently.

To become a professional communicator we need the ability to hear deletions in the language of people as they occur so that we can recover valuable information. The language that indicates the presence of *deletion* primarily involve *unspecified* verbs and nouns, references, and comparisons. In these, we look for expressions indicating missing information pieces that impoverish our mental model and lead to limited behavioral options. Generally, we will ask such meta-questions as:

- Is this representation complete?
- Is there anything missing in this description?
- What could fill in the gaps?
- If I made a mental video-tape from just these words, would I have a clear and detailed movie or would I find vague and unfocused areas?

1) Simple Deletions

As an example, consider the statement *"People scare me."* The word 'people' does not pick out anyone in particular for a reference. It leaves us without the critical information regarding *who specifically.* The surface expression has left out the referential index. The over-generalized class term, 'people,' sketches too broad a map for the listener. We need to index it more specifically. And almost everybody intuitively knows to ask:

"Who specifically scares you?"

Our design in asking this is to bring clarity to our map as well as the speaker's model of the world. As the person re-connects this generalization with the original experiences, the person produces a fuller expression, perhaps "My father scares me."

While this gives us a little more detail, it continues to be pretty ambiguous. We still don't know what to track over to our mental movie regarding what 'scares' means. How does he scare you? When? In what way? For how long?

Regarding deletions, almost everybody has a natural and intuitive sense about how to respond. We simply inquire about the details that have been left out.

"I was told not to do that when I worked on that report."

Told not to do what? By whom?

"I'm just confused about all of this."

About what?

"She's happy with renting this space."

Which business owner feels happy?

Every sentence contains deletions. Sometimes it doesn't make any difference, but frequently it does. Unspecified nouns which designate categories include lots of deletions: 'The people,' 'the government,' the 'geography class,' 'capitalists,' 'liberals,' etc.

2) Unspecified Referential Indices (Unspecified Nouns and Verbs)

As we discover that the speaker's *father* scares her, this gives us some of the key referents (i.e., the speaker and her father), while the unspecified verb ('scares') provides no clear image of the experiences, how they take place, when, where, etc. We still have lots of deleted information. This leads us to another natural intuitive question:

> "*How* does your father scare you?"

This question explores the unspecified verb. It invites the speaker to recover that deleted information. The surface expression offers us a *reduced version* of her full experience with her father. Frequently such impoverished models painfully limit our life, perceptions, choices, emotions, etc.

So with regard to verbs, inasmuch as every verb suffers from some degree of deletion, every verb presents only a certain degree of specificity. This gives us a direction for exploration as we probe verbs for how much clarity of image they convey.

> "Ask yourself whether the image presented by the verb in its sentence is clear enough for you to visualize the actual sequence of events being described."

For the linguistic distinction that we call 'unspecified verbs,' simply ask for more information and specificity of the action. *"How specifically did this occur?"*

This applies equally to nouns and pronouns, statements that have no immediate referent, or to any referent that we find unclear. When a speaker deletes an object, person, event, etc. while making a statement, we only need to inquire about it to challenge the unfocused statement for more precise information. This invites the speaker to re-map the referent experience with more or different words to provide a fuller linguistic expression.

"That's not important."

Important to whom? Important in what way? How do you know to evaluate it as unimportant?

"They always interfere with my work schedule."

I don't understand, who interferes and how do they do that?

Unspecific verbs only *generally* point out some referential activity but fail to offer enough specificity so that we can *representationally track* it to the screen in our mind. That's why we need the speaker to provide more indices of that reference. So we ask about when, where, how, whom, etc. to get more specific details.

Now because verbs in language describe processes, they represent the most dynamic part of a description. In terms of the audio-visual cinematic features of our internal movies, the nouns describe the objects and the verbs describe *what happens*, the movements, actions, etc. Without encoding verbs into our movies, we only represent a static list of the items on board in our mind. When we add verbs, the verbs transform our snapshots into movies. When we express ourselves with vague and unspecific verbs, this leaves us guessing *how* the process occurs and hallucinating the actions. With such hallucinations, we all engage in making up meanings rather than receiving those of the speaker.

To test unspecified verbs, make an image of the information given. Then ask yourself "Can I clearly visualize the actions, movements, and sequence of events?"

"He really frustrates me."

What does he actually do that frustrates you? How does he specifically frustrate you? When?

"She hurt me deeply."

How did she hurt you? In what way did she hurt you?

3) Comparative and Superlative Deletions (or, Unspecified Relations)

"He's a lot scarier."

This statement suggests a comparison, but does not specify the subject that the speaker compares. Intuitively, we know this. So we naturally inquire in order to fill in the details on our mental representational screen.

"Scarier than whom?"

Comparatives and superlatives typically show up in adjectives that end in *er* (e.g., faster, better), *est* (e.g., fastest, best), or *with more or less* (e.g., more interesting, less important).

We question this by asking:

"Compared to what?" "With respect to what?"

This pattern of speaking with over-generalized terms, terms that delete important distinctions, creates "an intensional orientation" (Korzybski). This means operating from the definitions in our heads rather than empirical facts out there. When we index the specific referents we clarify our mental map. This enables us to *extend* our meanings on out to the real world, and so creates 'an extensional orientation.' Bandler and Grinder actually noted this and built it into the Meta-Model. In the following quote, however, they (or some editor) mis-spelled intensional:

> "An extensional definition of a set is one which specifies what the members of the set are by simply listing (i.e. enumerating) them; an intentional [i.e., intensional] definition of a set is one which specifies what the members of the set are by giving a rule or procedure which sorts the world into members and non-members of the set. For example, the set of all humans over six feet in height who live in Ozona, Texas, can be given extentially [i.e., extensionally] by a list of the people, who, in fact, live in Ozona, Texas, and are taller than six feet, or intentionally [i.e., intensionally] by a procedure, for example:

(a) Go to the official directory of residents of Ozona, Texas.

(b) Find each person on the list and determine whether he is taller than two yardsticks placed end to end.

Korzybski (1933, Ch. 2) has an interesting discussion of this distinction. Notice that, in general, lists or a set specified extentionally [extensionally] have referential indices while sets intentionally [intensionally] given have no referential index." (1975, p. 56)

Structurally, we begin our representational tracking using nouns and verbs. Nouns locate the objects on our mental screen and verbs specify the movements and actions transpiring there. Next come the *relational-words* which give us relational descriptions, propositions, and functions. These words do not map out 'things,' but *concepts* (abstract meanings) regarding how the subjects and objects relate to other subjects and objects. When we have words like better, best, faster, good, evil, superior, before, after, during, etc., these are the words that provide the code for these relationships.

This means that when someone offers us a relational term which lacks specificity so that we cannot representationally track the term to generate a clear, precise, and understandable internal movie scenario, it's time to index that relational word. It's time to index it in terms of degree, extent, criteria, etc.

Someone says, *"I've never been more depressed."*

We reply, "On a scale from 1 to 10, how depressed have you ever felt? What degree of these down-feelings are you experiencing now? What facets of your thinking-feeling, behaving, etc. are you depressing right now?

Sometimes *what* a person deletes, or fails to specify, involves the standards by which he or she makes comparisons.

"She's the best cook."

The modifier 'best' alerts us to the unspecified relations in that term and invites us to index the comparative standard which the speaker has deleted.

Best in what way, under what circumstances, at what time?

"He's better at golf."

Better than whom?

4) Unspecified Processes—Adjectives Modifying Nouns

Bandler and Grinder added another form of deletion to the Meta-Model that has been deleted in most versions of this communication model. In *The Structure of Magic, Vol 1,* they speak about adjectives modifying nouns:

> "One of the ways in which Deep Structure process words may occur in Surface Structure is in the form of an adjective which modifies a noun. In order for this to happen, deletions must occur." (p. 62)

As an example, consider the expression, *"I don't like unclear people."* We have an adjective in the term 'unclear.' While the speaker has asserted his dislike of 'unclear people,' he has also deleted much of the context. What does 'unclear' refer to?

"Unclear to whom, about what, when, etc.?"

Consider these examples:

a) I laughed at the irritating man.
b) You always present stupid examples.
c) The unhappy letter surprised me.

In these examples, the speakers have deleted the process (and hence structure of) these adjectives. 'Unclear' (or lack of clarity), 'irritating,' 'stupid,' and 'unhappy,' refer to mental and emotional states. They leave out so much. Is it that some people are 'unclear' in their presentations or that I feel 'unclear' in my listening and interpreting? Am I 'irritated' by the man's behaviors, or is the man 'irritated?'

Not only have these processes become solidified in a single trait label, but the speaker has probably projected this evaluative state onto these stimuli. In example a) we have a man who, in some way, provided some stimulus to which the speaker thinks-and-feels irritated (first process). The speaker then projects his or her thoughts-and-feelings of irritation onto the man by labeling him with his state/judgment (second process).

As an aside, this languaging actually indicates a meta-level or meta-stating process. The evaluations ('irritating,' 'stupid,' 'unhappy') occur at a level *above* the referent (man, examples, letter). It therefore designates the speaker's *meta-state* evaluation from which he or she projects and imposes a judgment. Adjectives enable us to covertly meta-state in this way.

5) Unspecified Processes—Adverbs Modifying Verbs

In unspecified processes we have some process hidden by the use of an adverb that typically ends in *ly*. In other words, the *ly* adverb deletes the process and simultaneously solidifies the result by applying a 'state' word (word indicating a state of mind-body consciousness) to a verb. Consider these examples:

> *Unfortunately,* you forgot to call me on my birthday.
> I *quickly* left the argument.
> *Surprisingly,* my father lied about his drinking.
> She *slowly* started to cry.

The Meta-Model procedure for recovering the deleted material involves putting the phrase '*It is.*' in front of the former adverb. This converts or translates the ly-adverb.

> *It is unfortunate* that you forgot to call me on my birthday.
> *It is quick* that I left the argument.
> *It is surprising* my father lied about his drinking.
> *It is slow* that she started to cry.

These translations of the ly-adverb enable us to see more clearly what was deleted. The phrase, *"It is unfortunate..."* indicates the speaker's judgment, evaluation, and meta-state *about* the person 'forgetting to call' on his or her birthday. This provides another hidden or covert meta-stating structure. When a speaker announces, "*Unfortunately,* you forgot to call me on my birthday," it all sounds like an uncontestable fact. It's actually a *Lost Performative* (to be covered in the next chapter) of a judgment.

This reveals the modifier of the action (or verb) as a process itself is a quality or characteristic of the person's state. Sometimes it is a mental judgment ('unfortunately'), sometimes it refers to a way of doing something ('quickly,' 'slowly'), sometimes to a state of mind ('surprisingly'), etc.

Summary

- Part of the way all of our maps differ from the territory lies in what we have deleted and the characteristics we have left out. This necessary and inevitable facet of mapping often serves us very well.
- Deletions can also create limitations, problems, and mapping errors. The Meta-Model questions enable us to step back and to think about our mapping functions and to question the form and legitimacy of our mapping.
- By Meta-Modeling, we can touch our lives and the lives of others with magic as we ask questions that activate our mapping functions to develop richer maps.

Chapter 6

The Magic Model Part II: Generalizations

So what's your point?
Would you get to the bottomline?
Okay, okay, enough details, in just one sentence, what are you saying?

Ah, the call to generalize! When we make generalizations, we take pieces of an experience and use them to represent an *entire category*. When we do this, we mentally jump a logical level as we classify, abstract, and categorize the territory. What's the basis of our generalizing? Generalizing is founded in the very way our sense receptors and nervous system relate to the energy manifestations beyond themselves. As with deletions, we generalize to reduce the world to more manageable proportions.

Modeling the world through generalizations, however, frequently leaves us with impoverished maps. For this reason, we need to recognize our generalizations and run quality checks on them.

"Does this generalization make life more productive and empowering?"

When we generalize, we create something new for the mind. We create rules and programs for living, relating, communicating, etc. We create beliefs, principles, concepts, values, paradigms, and all kinds of meta-level phenomena. Yet generalizations can, and often do, outlive their usefulness. While the following rules probably could have been very useful for someone raised in a dysfunctional home, they are to the same extent unuseful and problematic for living a full and vital life.

"Don't express feelings."

"Don't disagree with Dad."

"Don't point out incongruencies in parents."

"Be seen, but not heard."

When we run a reality test or an ecology check on such rules, it's easy to see that they are not productive or healthy if we want to fulfil our dreams. It's for this reason that we need regularly to check and re-evaluate the generalizations in our maps.

Under the category of *generalization,* the Meta-Model specifies linguistic structures by which we create rules, classes, classifications, and abstractions. These can enrich or impoverish. Though we inevitably create generalizations to create empowering ideas, insights, beliefs, etc., they just as frequently impoverish through a loss of detail and richness. When that happens, we are left without the ability to make the crucial distinctions. Whenever we generalize to new abstractions (i.e., concepts, beliefs, understandings, etc.) we leave characteristics out.

"You just can't trust people, they do you dirty."

"Learning isn't fun; it's hard and gets you nowhere."

"Change is hard; you can't change your personality."

"Things should be easier."

Such generalized statements carry no specific references that we can index. As forms of abstract knowledge, they carry no time-index (when), person-index (who), place-index (where), context index (under what circumstances), etc. Without such extensionalizing, the statement invites us to treat them as absolutes and universals. Yet if we fall for that, we thereby create insidious and dangerous maps. When we question and explore generalizations, we inquire into their form, usefulness, validity, practicality, etc. Are they well-formed or ill-formed?

- *"Who specifically?"*
- *"Specifically when, where, under what circumstances?"*

Figure 6.1: Linguistic Distinctions of Generalizations

6. *Universal Quantifiers:* Allness words.
7. *Modal Operators:* Words indicating style of operating.
8. *Lost Performatives:* Sentences stating general principles.

6) Universal Quantifiers

When we quantify our statements with *universals,* we generalize from one or a few items to a whole class. To do this we use *allness* words. That is, we code our statements in words that describe things in *all or nothing terms* (e.g., all, every, none, everybody, always, totally, absolutely, etc.) These universal terms enable us to over-generalize freely from our experiences. Even a one time event can become 'the way it is everywhere, for everybody, for all time.'

"*Nobody* pays any attention to me."

"*Everybody* hates me."

"Why do I *always* get the bum deal?"

Generalizing in this way means that we not only create a conceptual map, but that we quantify our statements globally using universal terms. This gives our talk a tone of absoluteness. Korzybski called such all-or-nothing language "one valued" or "two valued" abstractions. Talking in this way conveys the sense that the world is simple, having no complexity, no multiplicity in causation, no systemic factors or contributing factors, no indetermination of fuzzy boundaries so that we can summarize most things in either/or terms.

Of course this creates a polarization of thought-and-emotion, "It is this or that." More often than not, this mis-maps the system-filled world and completely overlooks the fact that most things occur in steps, stages, and along a continuum.

"Nobody pays any attention to what I say."

"I always avoid situations where I feel uncomfortable."

"The only way we can solve this problem is by..."

To gently question global maps full of universals, explore the 'allness' terms.

> *"Nobody has ever paid even the least bit of attention to you?"*

A response like this runs with the exaggeration expressed in the statement to highlight the exaggeration. Simultaneously, it calls for the person to consider exceptions to the generalization.

> "A single exception to the generalization starts the client on the process of assigning referential indices and insures the detail and richness in the client's model necessary to have a variety of options for coping." (p. 83)

Many statements occur which only *imply* universalization without actually stating such.

> "You just can't trust people."

> *"Nobody? A person can't trust another single human being? Have you ever trusted anyone? Suppose you allow yourself to imagine a circumstance in which you could trust someone."*

Empathetically asking such questions invites the speaker to re-examine his or her map of the situation and to reconnect it to a broader range of experiences, and to do so while actually looking for counter-examples. Such counter-examples call this way of thinking into question and so encourage a new re-mapping of the generalization.

There's another way to respond to this. We can offer a current experience as a counter-example. Do this by translating the generalization from an abstraction and connect it to *immediate* experience.

> *"Do you trust me right now in this situation?"*

> *"If this is true, then I should not trust you in this situation right now, should I?"*

Responding in these ways, and with these lines, describes conversational reframing. We will explore the magic of such lines in a later chapter. Early NLP called these 'Sleight of Mouth' patterns; because that sounds manipulative, we have renamed them as *Mind-Lines* (1997/2000).

Finding and eliciting counter-examples to an over-generalization begins the process of de-framing the old belief that the person had once upon a time generalized. It removes the old frame of meaning around the experience. Sometimes this leaves a person temporarily in a state of 'not knowing what to think or feel.' The person has no frame for understanding the experience. When we offer a new frame of meaning, we offer the person a new way to perceive, think, feel, and act.

We can now explore differences. Doing a contrastive analysis between two experiences enables us to identify specifically *the difference* that makes a difference.

> *"So what is different between the persons who you can trust and those that you cannot trust?"*
>
> *"What stops you from trusting someone?"*
>
> *"What would happen if you did trust someone?"*
>
> *"What would allow you to trust them?"*

You probably already have an intuitive wisdom about the *allness* words. You know to question immediately whether you should track over to your mental movie a frame that establishes a universal principle that is forever true.

"You never do anything right around here; I don't know why they let you work here."

> *Never? Never at any time? You really think that I'm that hopeless?*

7) Modal Operators

The phrase *Modal Operators* comes straight from the linguistics of Transformational Grammar. When you hear this term, think, *modus operandi,* or *MO*—a person's *style of acting*. A modal operator refers to those linguistic terms that indicate a person's *'mode'* of *operating* in the world.

Among the possible 'modes of operating' are the following: *necessity, desire, possibility, impossibility,* and *choice.* These terms also indicate a generalization, in this case, a generalization about how to operate in the world and the rules about behavioral operations.

As indicators of a person's *mode or state,* these terms identify the higher frame or conceptual state from which we operate at various times and in relationship to various activities, tasks, etc.

> Do you 'have to' go to work (necessity mode),
>
> Do you 'get to' go to work (desire mode),
>
> Or do you have the 'choice' of going to work (choice mode)?

Do you 'need' to exercise (necessity mode) or 'can' you exercise (ability mode)? 'Can' you stand criticism and use it positively (ability mode), or is it that you 'can't' stand criticism (inability mode)?

As modal operators, these terms indicate our *'mode'* of response. Some operational modes, our *modus operandi,* create limitations, prohibitions, pressures, and impoverishment for us. They generate a conceptual state (a meta-state) which limits our sense of choice and thereby transforms or textures the kind of 'reality' we experience. People who live in *necessity mode, impossibility mode, and inability mode* tend to experience lots of pressure, stress, constraints, negativity, etc.

Conversely, people who live in *possibility modes, desire modes,* and *ability modes* typically live more positively. They look for possibilities, take action, and follow their dreams.

When we respond effectively to such 'state words' we enable ourselves or another to break down these generalizations and/or to expand our boundaries and depotentiate limitations.

> "I have to think about offending others; what if I hurt their feelings?"

> "I can't stand criticism."

As we delete and leave characteristics out, we create rules, principles, beliefs, etc. (generalizations) for our *modus operandi* in the world. We generate these *operational styles* in our mental maps as we use these special linguistic distinctions called the Modal Operators. I 'have to,' 'must,' 'need to,' etc. These words describe or map out the operational mode of *necessity*. Other operational modes include: *possibility* ('can,' 'may,' 'want to,' 'get to,' 'can'), *impossibility* ('can't,' 'not possible,' 'may not,' etc.).

With the modal operators of necessity, the speaker has deleted the consequence. So we ask about that.

> "I have to (must, need to) consider the feelings of others."

> *"Or what? What will happen if you don't?"*

With the modal operators of impossibility, the speaker has deleted the inhibiting forces.

> "I can't stand to make a mistake."

> *"What stops you from standing mistakes?"*

> *"What prevents you, blocks you, inhibits you from making a mistake and learning from it and refining your skills?"*

> "I can't trust people."

When we hear a statement like this, we already intuitively know that there are human beings who do trust other human beings. It can happen, 'trusting people' is a human possibility. It's not in the same category that we put impossible things: "I can't fly with my arms." "I can't leap tall buildings in a single bound." We know that the world is rich enough to allow people to trust people. If it's possible, then what could stop or prevent a person from having this experience? The way they have mapped it as a possibility. Is it possible in the person's mapping? Or has that person mapped it as impossible? If so, then we can begin an inquiry:

So tell me, what stops you from trusting people?

What would happen if you did trust someone?

What resource would you need to trust someone?

As the person answers, or attempts to answer, he or she is forced to look more thoroughly at the mapping. Typically, at first, the person has no answer, no map. This invites the person to begin to elicit or create referent experiences to help with the mapping. It usually activates the person to restore deleted material about trust and to produce a clearer and richer map about the trusting process. Magic happens in this kind of questioning. Magic happens as the questions facilitate the person's re-connecting to unmapped experiences, stepping aside from inhibiting and sabotaging maps, and designing new possibilities.

The Meta-Modeling does not have to stop there. We can inquire in other ways that help coach the person in expanding and enriching his or her map about trusting, communicating, speaking honestly, etc. We do this by inquiring about needed resources. Such meta-stating questions enable the person to begin texturing his or her state with the needed resources:

Do you know anyone who can and does trust people?

Can you imagine someone trusting people from out of a sense of safety and confidence?

What would allow someone to do that?

What would it be like if trusting others enriched your relationships with them and made life more full?

Would you like to operate from the same frame of mind that empowers them?

8) Lost Performatives (Unspecified Speakers or Map-Makers)

Here's another term that John Grinder brought from TG. *Lost Performatives* refers to evaluative statements in the form of generalizations about the world, people, life, etc. which are *un-owned.* That is, the person who performed the evaluating and the map-making has deleted him or herself from the statement.

The result? We have a definitive map-statement about reality with no map-maker in sight. Since there's no indication of *who* performed the mapping operation, it's easy to forget that *someone* mapped the generalization and to treat it like a known and unquestioned *fact.*

Lost Performatives typically function as *rules, principles, and paradigms* for life made up by these ghost mappers. Yet, given that the performer has excluded him or herself from the statement, and so from our awareness, the map-maker takes no responsibility for the map. The statement appears out of the blue; it presents itself as self-evident, as universally applicable, as absolute 'truth,' and as unformed by a *human* map-maker. Because these Lost Performatives sound like mandates from heaven, they invite us to step into the 'deity mode' in our thinking and speaking.

"Boys shouldn't cry."

"Don't talk about yourself; it'll go to your head and people won't like you."

"It's too dangerous to take risks investing."

"Always watch your backside around here!"

When we consider the indexing question of *who performs* the action of mapping the construction of reality in a certain way, we ask about the speaker of the generalization. Generally, we intuitively know to ask, "Who says that?"

But when we delete the performer ('performative' in TG), we have a surface expression that's not connected to any speaker. Bandler and Grinder noted this:

> "There is no indication in the Surface Structure that the client is aware that the statement made is true for his particular model; that there is no indication that the client recognizes that there may be other possibilities." (p. 106)

This is where the *Lost Performative* often becomes tricky enough to trick even our usual intuitive awareness. The more the statement fits with a situation, the more self-evident and a matter of the 'common sense' of a given culture, the less likely we are to question it. Instead, it evokes the "Why, of course!" response. It then seems *unquestionable.*

> "Business is business; in business you just sometimes have to do what you have to do."
>
> "What do you expect of politicians? They're all alike: crooks at heart."
>
> "Culture is just too big for one person to change. That's for idealists."
>
> "We know that you can't really change 'personality.'"

There's an important principle at work. When we frame something as *unquestionable,* it cannot even come up for suspicion. We just assume it as real, valid, and 'the way it is.' And even more tricky about this is that it gets us all at the very place where we are most informed and intelligent. The more we know, the more we have studied, the more research we have under our belt—the more we have *made up our mind.* This sets the subject; it closes the subject. It ends all questioning, thinking, exploring.

You, like me, are most liable to being blind (paradigm blind) in the domains of knowledge that you know the most about. In those areas you are most seduced by your current knowledge. This is why, as Thomas Kuhn (1962) suggested in *The Structure of Scientific Revolutions,* it's the folks *outside* of a paradigm who are most likely to see the blind spots and the solutions that the experts *inside* cannot. So it's the *Lost Performatives* inside of our domain of expertise that can most deceive us.

What can we do about this?

We can set the frame, 'every statement is made by someone,' and then inquire about that someone. We can inquire about the context and time and place of the speaker of a generalization.

Who says that?

When did he or she say that?

In what time or circumstance?

To whom?

About what?

These questions enable us to recover the contextual information surrounding the generalization. When we do this in a dialogue, we invite the other to "see these generalizations as true for his belief system at a specific moment in time" (p.107).

"It's bad to be inconsistent."

Who said that?

Upon what criteria did the speaker base 'badness?'

How do you know that we should similarly evaluate it as bad?

What was the social, economic, political, racial, gender, interpersonal, etc. context of that statement?

In *Lost Performatives* we have a statement but no speaker. And when we have a voice echoing in the chambers of our mind, but no embodied source, it seems like the voice of a God, a Demon, an alien Entity, or another Personality. We have a linguistic observation encoded in a verbal map, but no map-maker. By deleting the *performer* of the mapping we are left with no contextual information about the time, place, identity of the map-maker, etc. All that remains involves only a generalized rule or principle. It's like the smile of the Cheshire cat ... suspended in air without the cat. And such statements typically leave the impression that it stands as an absolute truth for all times, places, people, etc. This can create a lot of unsanity, inappropriate rules, and even hurtful advice.

Conversely, we bring a touch of sanity to such unspecified statements when we index these concerns:

> "We all know that it's wrong to slow the group down."
> *Who says this?*
> *Wrong in what way or for whom?*
>
> "You just can't change personality."
> *Who said that? When?*
> *What change models and techniques did that person have available at that time?*

Summary

- To map is to generalize. When we draw conclusions about things, events, people, etc., how they work, what we should do, what they are, we create a map for navigating. Such mapping shows up as understandings, beliefs, principles, rules, etc. and so formulates our frames of reference and frames of mind.
- We now have linguistic markers for generalizations: Universal Quantifiers, Modal Operators, and Lost Performatives. More will show up in the next chapter.
- Using, enhancing, and training our linguistic intuitions to hear these linguistic markers so that we can question and inquire about them empower us to Quality Control them. This allows us to communicate with precision and elegance. It allows us to perform linguistic magic.

Chapter 7

The Magic Model Part III: Distortions (Part I)

The Meta-Model provides
"a great set of rules to guide your thinking."
Sid Jacobson (1986)

Distorting images, representations, structures, sequences, etc. is part of our power to think and to map reality. Our nervous system cannot deal with the form of the energy manifestations that exist in the electromagnetic field. So it *distorts* light waves as it literally transforms them into a *code* that we can use. Then the encoding of our rods and cones is *transduced* to yet another form, and then the nerve impulse is transduced to yet another form of chemical exchange, and so on it goes.

To map is to distort. From the first neurological maps to the higher sensory representations, to words, to concepts, etc., distortion explains how we make our internal models of the world. In modeling, we pick one code to *stand for,* and represent, something else. Distortion drives every mapping function.

We have no choice but to distort. After all, there is no flawless or totally accurate reproduction. Even a photograph distorts things. The picture you pull out of your wallet of your family has distorted their size—your loved ones are not *that* small! And they are not *flat two-dimensional* beings, are they?

As *distortion* drives the lower levels of mapping, it also organizes the higher levels of cognition as we 'make sense' of the see-hear-feel components. This isn't a bad thing. It's just the way abstracting happens at all levels of mapping. We are always making shifts in how we represent sensory data.

This can function as a really good thing as in fantasy when we distort information to plan, rehearse, create, and imagine a wide range of possibilities. Every time we fantasize a better or different design for the layout of the furniture in our living room, we are using the modeling function of distortion to create new possibilities. Architects fantasize, artists distort, so do movie-makers, inventors, etc. Distortion plays a central part in all creativity and invention and powerfully enriches our world and supports our highest skills.

Distortion can just as well limit the richness of our experiences. We can hallucinate terror, horror, trauma, misfortune, etc. and experience intense emotional pain. As usual, it all depends upon context and intent. We can use distortion to discount a loving affirmation, "She *just* says that because she wants something."

It can also create good feelings in response to 'negative' events, "I learned so many wonderful things through that job loss (accident, divorce, bankruptcy, down-sizing)." Under this category of *distortion,* we will find linguistic expressions that indicate various degrees of having altered or changed a representation.

In the *Communication Magic Model* there are five linguistic distinctions that encode significant distortions—distortions that may represent a radically ill-formed map and so create pain, limitations, and self-sabotaging signals. For the most part, unlike most of the previous language patterns, we do *not* have an intuitive sense about how to deal with them.

As a result, most people are unskilled and unprepared to deal with the linguistic fraud that can be perpetuated upon them by these linguistic forms. They make up so much of our mental framework for thinking and making sense of things that we typically do not even sense that there's something wrong with them.

This means several things.

1) *Lack of Intuition.* It means that you will *not* sense anything wrong with using the following linguistic distinctions for thinking and reasoning. You have been *trained* to think in these formats. They make up the very coding of the matrix of your mind. To now step

back with the eyes of a magician and question them will (at first) seem 'weird,' 'wrong,' 'strange,' 'funny,' and counter-intuitive.

I've encountered this many times over the years as I have taught the Meta-Model. For example, many have wanted immediately to argue that they can indeed 'read the minds' of others! That distortion is so much a part of their everyday thinking, emoting, relating, and experiencing, that they can't believe it's a linguistic and neurological distortion. Others will argue that 'Cause—Effect' *is* real. Uninformed by modern science and philosophy, they misperceive that the way we *punctuate our perception* of one event affecting another event is our *map* about such. It may truly provide us a true and useful map. But 'causation' is still a mental perception. The Newtonian 'laws' of physics are the mapped representations that we have come to understand, use, and believe in, within the domain that Newtonian physics are valid.

2) *Defenseless.* It means that you are pretty much *defenseless* against being tricked and duped by these linguistic forms *unless* you know them. If we all are trained to think and reason *using* these linguistic distinctions then we do *not* have a natural and intuitive sense of them as ill-formed formats.

This allows any and every spin-mister to use them for linguistic deception and fraud. It allows every manipulator of words to use them for tricking people. Of course, your best defense against them is your *awareness* of them. This is where your magician mind and eyes will give you the meta-knowledge and meta-awareness *not* to be seduced by the games.

3) *Already Seduced.* It means that our natural tendency will be to agree with these linguistic patterns of ill-formed maps. If our natural 'logic' does not work to give us an automatic signal that something is amiss here, we are not only left without a signaling system, we are predisposed to believe in these ill-logical forms. This is why we have to teach logic and critical thinking in schools. Our natural 'logic,' the psycho-logic of our nervous system and brain glories in these ill-formed structures. It's how we create our sense of reality.

Because of the length of the Linguistic Distinctions of Distortion, I have separated this presentation into two chapters. This chapter covers nominalization and mind-reading; the next chapter covers cause-effect, complex equivalences and presuppositions.

Figure 7.1: Linguistic Distinctions of Distortions

9. *Nominalization:* Verbs turned into nouns.
10. *Mind-Reading:* Reading the motives, intentions, and emotions of another person.
11. *Cause — Effect:* Inventing a causal structure about events.
12. *Complex Equivalences:* Equating events, ideas, emotions.
13. *Presuppositions:* Assumptions about life, existence, people, etc.

Turning Words (Grammar) into Movies

We 'make sense' of linguistic data by *representationally tracking* words onto the imagined screen of our mind and turning them into see, hear, feel, etc. referents. Nouns and verbs give us the basic actors for our movie. Nouns give us persons, places, and things. With nouns we clutter up the space of our movie with the objects.

We then get these objects moving, acting, and changing when we add verbs. Verbs describe what the nouns *do*. The objects run, jump, dance, hit, yell, embrace, love, reject, wonder, touch, etc. With verbs, we tell a story. If we only had nouns, we would have menu lists; we would only have a clutter of things like we have in any closet.

But with verbs, ah!, with verbs, the closet comes alive! Verbs make the toys of our mind come alive. It endows them with energy, movement, action, drama. Now the noun items that we have tracked to the screen have something to do, somewhere to go. So into the scenes that the nouns have suggested (a beach, blue skies, gentle breeze) we track the *action*.

> "Jim ran along on the white sand, almost in slow motion because the sand was so deep. With every step, he sank into the sand and it was only with effort that he slowly pulled loose to sink yet again."

With adjectives and adverbs, we add various qualities to our movie, texturing the description to make it rich and fuller. The italicized words in the following paragraph highlight this function of the modifiers.

> "Jim ran *lazily* along on the *white* sand, almost in *slow* motion because the *thick* sand was *so deep*. With *every* step, he sank into the sand and it was only with *strenuous* effort that he *slowly* pulled loose *only* to sink yet again. He always ran like this, he had to given the nature of the sand. That's why you shouldn't run on the beach, you should walk on a beach."

You can see that, can't you? And if you step into that movie and see it from within, you can feel it as well.

The three sections that I have underlined reflect the three generalization distinctions: Allness, Modal Operators, and Lost Performative. These are harder to see and track. "Always" makes the movie last forever. "Had to" reveals a hidden belief about the beach. And we probably code the words, "That's why you shouldn't run on the beach, you should walk on a beach" as a higher hidden frame or as the words of one of the people on the beach.

The Un-track-able Nature of the Linguistic Distortions Patterns

All of that is fairly straightforward and obvious. Well, it is compared to what follows. What follows is not. The following linguistic distinctions are very difficult, if not impossible, to *representationally track.* Why? Because they are much more conceptual. They involve higher level abstractions.

As an overview, *Nominalizations* (verbs turned into nouns) encourage us to *freeze frame* our movie so that the actual *actions* become static and suddenly we fill our mental world with conceptual entities.

> "My relationship with management here has become problematic and suggestive that we'll have to re-enter negotiations, or termination will be inevitable."

Picture that!

Mind-Reading (reading the motives, intentions, and emotions of another person) eliminates the 'how do you know process' and so encourages us to imagine an actor in the movie *just knowing* what others are thinking, intending, feeling, etc.

> "It's come to this because my supervisor dislikes me and has it in for me; he has since I got here. He's that kind of person. He has an agenda against everyone who questions him; his ego is out of control."

Now picture that!

Cause—Effect (inventing a causal structure about events) invites us to simplify our movie by putting one noun-item in such a relation with another that the first totally explains the second.

> "The employees around here make me so angry; you can't count on them. They're lazy to the core and will use anything to excuse them; that's why production has gone down and profits are at an all time low."

While we cannot really see these events *causing, making, and forcing* the effects, it seems like we can. We can write, draw, and diagram X leading to Y leading to Z and when we do, it seems so logical, so right, so true.

"She *makes* me angry." Okay, unspecified verb. "She *makes* me angry when she uses that better-than-thou tone and rolls her eyes upward dismissing my ideas." Ouuuu, that seems see-able! How could you question that? "You always make me late." Ah, the magic gets deeper.

Complex Equivalences (equating events, ideas, emotions) are impossible to see but, once again, they *seem* seeable. In the first example under Cause—Effect, we had an example of this:

> "They're lazy to the core ..."

Yet we cannot actually see 'lazy' or 'laziness.' Those nominalizations hide the underlying actions, use a generalized label, and assert that the actions on the primary level, perhaps 'lying on the couch watching TV,' *is* the same as, equal to, the internal state and concept of 'laziness.' Now we're into pure Trance Land where the language seduces us to hallucinate freely.

Presuppositions (assumptions about life, existence, people, etc.) offer us beginning assumptions that we just have to go with to make sense of things. Let's use the cause—effect example again:

> "The employees around here make me so angry; you can't count on them. They're lazy to the core and will use anything to excuse them; that's why production has gone done and profits are at a low."

What's just assumed and presupposed here? The idea that emotional states like anger can be created apart from our thinking and experiencing. The idea that all the employees, without exception, are lazy, that they are nothing but lazy, that laziness presupposes responsibility (being 'counted on'), that production and profit are solely and exclusively functions of what labor does, etc. How do you picture any of those assumptive frames?

I said it was tricky and deceptive.

With the mind and eyes of a magician, you will be able to see through these distortions. Knowing your verbal map is not the same thing as the territory, you'll more quickly train your intuitions about these mapping dangers.

9) Nominalization

This term, 'nominalization,' is part of the jargon which NLP inherited from Transformational Grammar. *Nominalization* refers to *naming* (as in 'nominate') or *giving names* to actions or ongoing events. When we name actions we turn processes (verbs) and evaluative qualities (predicates) into static entities (nouns). *Nominalizing* ongoing processes transforms actions and movements into 'things,' entities, and fixed products. As it deletes the processes, the movement, it eliminates awareness of the dynamics.

When we do this linguistically, we create a model of the world that's fixed, static, unmoving, permanent, and finished. It settles everything. It freezes our movies and turns them into snapshots. 'Relationship' (a nominalization) sounds like all of the *relating* and *interacting* has somehow come to an end. 'Motivation' sounds like an entity that we either have or don't have. It shoves *moving toward* and *moving away from* motives outside our awareness.

Nominalizations lead us to believe that we live in a fixed, static, and unchanging world. As we think that, we are then led to think that there's little to nothing we can do about it, that things don't change, and that we have no power to make things better. Freezing actions, processes, systems, etc. in this way most effectively creates a limiting, impoverishing, and victimizing model of the world.

The linguistic process of nominalization involves a complex transformational process in which a process word (or verb) appears as a finished and static thing. In TG, what occurs as movement at the Deep Structure gets distorted into a static noun-like label at the Surface Statement. Or, to use our representational tracking metaphor, what was once seen, heard and felt as an ongoing process gets transformed into a static object. The verb turns into a noun.

Suzette Elgin (1980) described these pseudo-nouns in a colloquial way. She said that nominalizations are "verby things turned into nouny things" I like that. It's memorable. Nominalizing creates nouny things out of verby things with the result that in a nominalization we have some *hidden verbs*.

This distortion can powerfully impoverish a cognitive map. How? It does so when we respond to these noun-like terms as if the referent is fixed and frozen in reality and beyond our influence. We forget about the verb hidden underneath the noun-like cloak.

"She has made a *decision* to not speak up to him since he's the boss." A 'decision' seems final, fixed, and unchangeable. Yet a 'decision' involves ongoing 'deciding'—a process of moment to moment decidings not to speak up.

Conversely, when we *de-nominalize,* we re-map the static-like thing so that we can see and sense the ongoing processes. Doing this enriches our map.

> "Reversing nominalizations assists the client in coming to see that what he had considered an event, finished and beyond his control, is an ongoing process which can be changed." (p. 74)

How do we test language to figure out which nouns are true nouns (persons, places, things) and which are pseudo-nouns (verbs and actions)? We can check out and differentiate a noun from a nominalization by seeing if it will fit into the linguistic phrase,

> *"an ongoing ... "*

True nouns indicating persons, places, or things will not fit into this scheme.

> "An ongoing chair" "An ongoing door" "An ongoing book"

Pseudo-nouns indicating processes, however, will fit into this format, and make sense.

> "An ongoing decision" "An ongoing marriage" "An ongoing failure" "An ongoing motivation"

These make sense. I can see them when I representationally track them to my mental screen.

Use this syntactic frame to test words that sound like, look like, and feel like concrete things, but actually hide a verb underneath the noun-like garb.

> "My divorce is painful" actually means —
>
> *"The experience of divorcing induces a lot of pain."*

"I experience a lot of pain in the process of going through the divorce of my spouse."

"Our terror blocks us" actually means—

"Thinking-and-feeling in fearful images, representations, terms, etc. blocks us."

"Your perception is seriously wrong" actually means—

"How you perceive the situation contains some important errors"

"My confusion about math just locks up my comprehension."

"When I fuse together several factors about math, I find it hard to get a hold of a clear picture of how the math works."

We have a second test for nominalizations—the *Wheelbarrow Test.* Can you put (or imagine putting) the referent of the nominalization in a wheelbarrow? (Or, in a chair, on a table, etc.) We can put the references of true nouns, the tangible things, in wheelbarrows, on tables, etc. We cannot, however, put the non-tangible referents of the pseudo-nouns on tangible things. This will not work with ongoing processes, especially the nominalizations that refer to *thinking,* imagining, having 'ideas,' etc.

Form a visual image from the sentence. Then see if you can imagine placing the referent of the non-process word (the nominalization) in it.

Given the complex ill-formed nature of nominalizations, how can we perform our magic and question ourselves or another to expose, explore, and challenge the supposed 'concreteness' of the action?

"I regret my decision."

"What if you decided to reconsider the values that you used in deciding, and then to alter what you first decided?"

"What is there about the deciding that you did which you now regret?"

"Is there anything stopping you from re-deciding and changing your thinking about that?"

In the statement "I can't stand her insensitivity," we cannot put *insensitivity* into a wheelbarrow. Yet it does make sense if we say, 'an ongoing insensitivity.' This tests the nominalization of the term, 'sensitivity.' Next, to de-nominalize that term, we begin to explore the verb hidden within it. We ask:

What is she not sensing or being responsive to?

What lets you know that she lacks in sensing or being responsive?

What would you want her to sense and respond to?

De-nominalizing involves identifying the hidden process within the so-called noun so that we can explicate the workings of that process. This is the magic that makes the static words come alive.

"Frustration"	*Who or what frustrates whom?*
"Happiness"	*Who feels happy about what?*
"Productivity"	*Who produces what?*
"Relationship"	*Who relates to whom, and how, and when, and under what conditions?*
"Skill level"	*Who demonstrates skills, toward what subject?*
"There's a lot of tension there."	*Who is tensing his or her muscles in response to what?*

Some nominalizations seem especially insidious. They seem disconnected from any verb. This confusing vagueness arises from having been derived from another language. When troublesome nominalizations like this strike our consciousness, we do not detect the representation processes at all. For instance:

Wind	*How does the air move?*
Mind	*How do you entertain thought?*
Religion (from Latin, "to bind back")	*What do you greatly value?* *To whom or to what does your belief bind you?* *How does this binding occur?*
Self-esteem	*In what way do you value yourself?* *According to what standard?*
Pain	*What hurts? Where?*

Would you like a more poetic approach that might provide a different frame about nominalization? Okay, here goes. In giving verbs names (nominalizing) we take a *frog-in-process* and knight it with a magic wand. Presto, frog becomes a prince. Suddenly the hopping, jumping, moving frog full of life and energy transforms into a *princely-noun*, who just stands still, posing, looking good, doing nothing.

Such nominalizing typically provides a significant challenge to clarity. Once the frog-like verbs put on royal robes, they lose all their movement and activity. They begin to just stand around and adopt a cold, superior lordly stare. Disdaining all of their previous leaping about (like true frogs), they put on airs by freezing all their movements.

In nominalization, it becomes difficult to tell *what* actions the terms actually *refer to*. They become more conceptual, abstract, and vague. Nounified words which are really verbs referring to processes look like and sound like '*things*.' The term reification describes this 'thing-ifying.' It comes from the verb 'to reify,' which derives from the Latin '*res*,' a thing, a real thing. To reify is 'to regard an abstraction (concept, idea) as if a material thing.'

In terms of clarity of communication and sanity of mind, when we use nominalizations, we send *false signals to our brains*. The messages we send and mental mapping that we engage in contains a very different structure from the territory. The linguistic coding cues us to think-feel and respond to the no-thing referent as if it were a solid, stable, static-like thing rather than a process of movement and fluidity. We cannot put the referent of these terms in a wheelbarrow or on a table. If we could, the no-thing process would not stay there, but move and leap and jump.

As mental abstractions of verbs, nominalizations lose all details and specificity about the hidden movements. They not only send poor signals to the brain about processes, but deceptive messages. Linguistically, nominalizations operate as impostures. Though dressed up as nouns, they mask underlying processes.

To use our mental screen for tracking from language to clear and precise de-coding, nominalizations need to be decoded. So we de-nominalize, unless, of course, we want to hypnotize. For hypnotizing, nominalization works like magic as it sends people inward on searches for meaning. But for clear, precise communication, we need to find the hidden verb and re-language it as a verb. When we do this, we wave the magic wand over the nominalization, ask some probing questions about suspended movements, and presto, a frog re-appears where there had been a stuffy noun. This transforms the static language allowing us once again to see the action. In this way we linguistically arrest the nominalization, disrobe it, strip-search it, and discover the process beneath the cover-up.

Some of our best nominalizations that really hypnotize occur when we give names to the processes of the mind, to the no-things that we *think*, to our conceptualizing, imagining, abstracting, philosophizing, etc. When we label higher mental abstractions, we name *activities* of a mind in action as if they were things. It is in this way that we create such 'things' (conceptual things) as good and bad, love and all emotional states, social phenomena (acceptance, peer pressure, society, government, law, etc.), theological phenomena, values, criteria, etc.

These words serve as symbols for *intangible referents* like our experiences of thought (ideas and concepts), our labels for experiences (trauma, forgiveness, insult, praise, etc.), and for conceptual hypothesis (gravity, electrons, etc.). When we reverse this and de-nominalize, we strip the nounified process words, recover the hidden verb, and then treat the verb as we would any other unspecific verb—we index its specifics.

"Let's improve our communication so that our relationship will give us more satisfaction."

> *How do we communicate with each other now?*
>
> *How would you like to communicate?*
>
> *What facet of our sending messages back and forth in an exchange needs improving?*

Denominalizing empowers us as we reconnect to the referent actions and processes. When we do not question or challenge the nominalizations, we experience the word and its referent as static and permanent. As our brain receives no messages of movement, we sense permanence, unchangeability, and even being stuck.

Endowing the process world and the world of mind with such static labels creates mental states of concreteness, or 'misplaced concreteness,' as Bertrand Russell said. We then feel and behave by that map. As the delusion continues, we begin to respond as if others equally see and share these attributes about things. Then together we live in the shared conceptual 'reality' of the frozen universe of 'things.'

10) Mind-Reading

As a linguistic distinction, *mind-reading* refers to the statement which declares, claims, or assumes knowledge of the internal state of another person (i.e., their thoughts, emotions, values, intentions, etc.). We speak *as if* we can *read the other person's mind.* Of course, we cannot. Yet we often talk as if we can. Reading our own mind is tough enough!

> *"You're feeling disgusted that I've pointed this out."*

Mind-reading statements are ill-formed to the extent that we do not explain *how* we know or suspect what another thinks, feels, wants, experiences, etc. They are ill-formed also to the extent that we deliver them as un-owned Lost Performatives. When we talk about another's *internal world,* without having received direct communication from that person, we engage in this ill-formed, distorted language pattern.

> *"Everybody at work thinks I'm stupid."*

The semantic ill-formedness in mind-reading involves the speaker's belief that he or she knows (or can know) the internal state, mind, emotions, intentions, etc. of the other *without asking*. Some people overtly believe that. Others act as if their 'intuitive' skills are so refined that they can accurately read others.

Mind-reading expressions presuppose too much. They presuppose that we can tell what's going on in another. People skilled at calibrating to non-verbal expressions sometimes fall into this trap, eventually developing an over-confidence in reading the general states of another.

In mind-reading, we have a combination of deletions, presuppositions, and referential index shifts. These often indicate feel-see, feel-hear synesthesia patterns or cross-sensory patterns. That is, we feel lonely, guilty, scared, paranoid, depressed, etc., and *feel* some intense emotion, and so we *project* our feelings onto others. We then state our feelings as if they belong to the other.

At the heart of the distortions in *mind-reading* we have the speaker deleting the processes (the how) whereby he or she knows the mind, heart, intuitions, etc. of another.

We would not have mind-reading if the speaker made his or her guesses about another tentative and allowed the other to correct the guess.

> "It seems to me that you're feeling frustrated and want to get out for a change of scenery, am I reading this right?"

Failing to do this prevents the speaker from *checking out* his or her guesses since there is no invitation for the other to provide a clarification.

As *cause—effect* expressions (the next distinction) limit choices by presupposing that some cause outside of oneself 'makes' or 'forces' one to have this or that emotion, experience, idea, etc., *mind-reading* limits choices by assuming one already knows what another thinks-and-feels. There are lots of problems with this, as I'm sure you can tell. Oops! I just did it. Subtle, right? And, suggestive. With that one I just indirectly suggested that *you can tell.* For one thing, when we make this assumption, we typically will not even bother to inquire about the other's thoughts, feelings, values, etc. There's no feedback loop. People who frequently mind-read tend not to express their own thoughts and feelings, but may expect others to 'just know' what they think-and-feel. In interpersonal relationships this creates a no-win, double-bind situation which undermines friendship and true intimacy (e.g., sharing, disclosing, etc.)

Whether there are people who can read the minds-and-emotions of others is not the question. Such phenomena may occur. Perhaps we will eventually learn processes, methods, and techniques that will enable us to do such.

Yet since most of us have a difficult enough time reading *our own* thoughts-and-emotions, intentions, and motives, etc., this ought to warn us against assuming too much about mind-reading others'. First we need to become skilled in reading our own minds and in running our own brains. Further, since "the source of vast amounts of inter-personal difficulties, miscommunication and its accompanying pain" (p. 105) arises from mind-reading, this should caution us to go slow in this area.

How do we question or inquire abut mind-reading so that we can challenge it? We primarily focus on indexing *how* the person knows what he or she claims to know about another.

How do you know that everybody thinks this about you?

How do you know that John feels disgusted with you?

How specifically does this process occur and how do you know this?

"Susan never considers my feelings!"

How do you know that Susan does not consider your feelings?

"You have lost respect for our president!"

I have? What about me gives you that impression? Is it something I've said or done?

We often mistake *intimate calibration* with mind-reading. Obviously, when you live with someone for a period of time, you get used to them. You pick up on the other's patterns of thinking, emoting, responding, etc. You become intimately acquainted with that person's beliefs, values, attitudes, opinions, etc. You get used to the cues and triggers in them and in the environment. You *become highly calibrated* to the other's style, states, and orientation. Eventually, you'll become fairly skilled at 'reading' that person.

The danger that then occurs is jumping to the conclusion that you can read that person's mind. State calibration is not the same as mind-reading.

For some people, the longer they relate, the more naturally they fall into the mind-reading trap. This is not necessarily a bad thing or dysfunctional. Again, it depends entirely upon the quality and nature of any given relationship. It can be playful, seductive, and a way to deepen intimacy. It is the kind of mind-reading which does not allow each person to have the last word about his or her own state that becomes toxic and harmful. "I know you! I know what you want."

It is when people become calibrated to each other but fail to 'pace' each other's values, principles, visions, understandings, beliefs, etc. that they fall into using hurtful mind-reading. This then adds to the conflict. Then each person will attempt to *tell* the other what the other *really* means and intends! At this point, mind-reading becomes toxic, morbid, and unsane. It leads to a communication pattern known as 'crazymaking.'

Mind-reading as a language pattern differs from *Lost Performatives* in that it identifies or describes internal states. Lost performatives typically pass judgments.

"You should be a man and not cry!"—a lost performative.

"You're trying to hurt my feelings"—mind-reading.

When people offer us *inaccurate mind-reading statements* we typically feel them to be insulting, intrusive, foreign, and 'controlling.' People who receive such statements will typically feel misunderstood, invisible, controlled, invaded, etc. On other occasions, inaccurate mind-reading statements will elicit an energized state wherein someone attempts to explain his or her true feelings and to assert his or her truths. Typically the person will do this in a defensive way.

With the knowledge and experience of being an adult we are able to 'read' very young children pretty accurately. It's simple. But, of course, they are so obvious. So as we simply describe some of their anticipations, it seems like we can read their minds. Magic! A few cues of behavior, facial expression, a typical pattern, and we seem to know just what they're up to, and what mischief they are about to get into. This occurs before the age of secrets when a child discovers that adults can't read their minds.

Yet danger lurks here. Too many inaccurate mind-reading statements by parents, teachers, or other adults often invite children to develop a distrust of their own mind. If we constantly tell them that they feel something, really believe something, really intend something, etc. and they accept that foreign attribution (whether by naive innocence, fear, intimidation, obedience to adults, etc.), this can invite them to disown their own judgment and come to distrust themselves. If the child retains consciousness of this, he or she may feel caught between two conflicting messages. This kind of 'crazymaking' may then cause a splitting off of the self in order to cope with the double messages (Bateson, 1972).

Accurate mind-reading statements, conversely, can sometimes enable a person to discover his or her thoughts, motives, etc. and so feel validated. Gentle, tentative mind-reading often occurs in therapy as an essential part of the healing. The therapist's 'reading' of the client's mind, motives, intentions, desires, etc. and articulation aims to communicate a validation and acceptance. Yet, depending upon how the client 'reads' this, this also can backfire. That's why a therapist has to do it with gentleness and tentatively. He or she must let the client ultimately accept, temper, or reject the mind-reading statements. In adult lives, the 'magic' of being truly seen by another, and appreciated can bring a special delight and pleasure.

Summary

- The linguistic markers that identify the distortion patterns introduce us to the higher levels of word magic and open our eyes to why communication becomes so difficult when we use them.
- We cannot easily track from the language of *Nominalizations* and *Mind-Reading* to our internal screen or movie. When we automatically engage in such, we are hallucinating, pure and simple.
- There are ways to train our linguistic intuitions so that we're not easily duped or deceived by these language patterns. If you have the mind and eyes of a magician who knows the map/territory distinction, you can easily learn to recognize such magic around you and create such.
- May the webs that you weave with your magic bless and honor and tie yourself and others up in patterns of respect, resourcefulness, and productivity.

Chapter 8

The Magic Model Part IV: Distortions (Part II)

"The Meta-Model is an explicit set of questions as well as a model for asking questions."
Dilts (1983, pp. 77–79).

Now for the conclusion of the distortions. We began exploring the deeper magic, the un-track-able magic involved in the language patterns under the category of distortions in the Meta-Model. In this chapter we will finish that description.

Figure 8.1: Linguistic Distinctions of Distortions

9. *Nominalization:* Verbs turned into nouns.
10. *Mind-Reading:* Reading the motives, intentions, and emotions of another person.
11. ***Cause—Effect:*** **Inventing a causal structure about events.**
12. ***Complex Equivalences:*** **Equating events, ideas, emotions.**
13. ***Presuppositions:*** **Assumptions about life, existence, people, etc.**

11) Cause—Effect

Cause—Effect statements assert causation. They assert that one thing necessarily leads to, makes, or *causes* another thing. To make such a statement indicates beliefs and presuppositions about the way things, emotions, thoughts, experiences, and events relate to each other. We typically encode our ideas about 'cause' with causal verbs (e.g. make, cause, force, etc.), although we can do it with almost any active verb (e.g., present, go, drive, etc.).

In causation language, we suggest or imply a linkage between stimuli and responses, a linkage or relationship, which may or may not have any actual direct or logical connection. Most of us develop our ideas of causation from events that demonstrate macro-level causation. Someone throws a rock at us; it hits us and we both see and feel a bruise welling up on our skin. So we say, "Tommy *caused* it."

In the world of macro-effects, such 'causation' as a conceptual category works pretty well. Newton saw an apple fall from a tree and theorized about the unseen force of gravity. In his model of physical forces and the field of Newtonian physics, gravity *causes* things to fall.

Of course, this *concept* of causation does not exist externally. It's a conceptual way of thinking about things, a way of symbolizing and encoding relationships between events. We create that concept using the modeling process of distortion. In the realm of Newtonian physics, it works sufficiently well. It allows us to build homes and bridges, cars and planes, to explain and model billiards, and to establish many facets of law regarding responsibilities.

This becomes less valid and useful when we apply these rough ideas of *cause and effect* to complex systems and to human mind-body systems. New and different features enter into the fray.

Bateson described the effect of kicking a stone or hitting a ball on a billiards table. The *effect* that we get in each case, while complex, can nevertheless be generally predicted and understood. Take into account all of the forces, the dynamics, and the energies inside of the various environmental contexts and contributing influences (temperature, wind, etc.), and we can pretty much figure out cause—effect relationships.

But kick a dog. The trajectory of that dog is much less dependable than the trajectory of a rock or a billiard ball. Why? Because there's latent energy within the dog. Kick your child or your neighbor, or the policeman on the corner, and again, the trajectory of where that person goes in *response* to the kick is dependent upon more factors than just the physics of your kick.

Yet all too often we attempt to use the same linear macro-level cause and effect thinking on neuro-linguistic systems that involve mind, emotion, value, meaning, history, memory, imagination, etc. Here linear *cause—effect statements* can become very inadequate and ill-formed.

This is especially true when we attempt to assign a single, linear *cause* in complex systems like relationships. We confuse and mix up the influencing factors that belong to us (e.g., the things we do or can do, the responses that we can make) with sources outside of ourselves that cannot affect things.

We say, "Jim *makes* me angry." But that statement follows the kind of format that, at best, only works with the strict Newtonian physics of inanimate objects. That's like saying, "George forced Mary to weigh 175 pounds."

Bandler and Grinder (1975) wrote,

> "*Some person causes some person to have some emotion.* When the first person, the one doing the causing, is different from the person experiencing the anger, the sentence is said to be semantically ill-formed and unaccepted. The semantic ill-formedness of sentences of this type arises because it, literally, is not possible for one human being to create an emotion in another human being. [Actually] the emotion is a response generated from a model in which the client takes no responsibility for experiences which he *could* control." (pp. 51–52)

Although the two events are here encoded, one 'the causing' and the other 'the result,' and do occur one after another, we do not necessarily have a closed-case of *causation*. This might involve a different kind of relationship, it might be a correlation, an accident, a sequence within a systemic network of responses, etc.

How do we question this model about cause—effect relationships? How can we inquire and explore it so that it empowers the speaker to look at the facts again, to take responsibility for his or her responses, to move beyond a single cause to recognize with multiple causation and contributing factors? The Meta-Model provides several questions:

Does Jim *always* make you feel angry when he does that?

Has there *ever* been a time when you didn't respond with anger to that?

Do you *have* to feel anger at that?

What *forces* you to feel anger at that?

What explains the difference between the times when you feel anger and those times when you don't?

Are there any other contributing influences to this feeling?

To gain a clear image of another person's model of the world, we need to see their behaviors, talk, and emotions in a way that *makes sense* given the way they have mapped things. Until then, we do not truly understand.

Cause—effect statements can create semantic ill-formed-ness and generate personal limitations when they map things so that we feel as if we have no choice in responding. This is implied in the statement "He makes me angry." There's magic in that statement. But it's not the good kind. If I map things so that my emotions are the results of the actions of others and that I have little to no ability to affect things—to resist the person's provocations, to stop giving those actions that much meaning or power—then my map limits my options. I feel controlled.

Implied causation typically shows up simply in direct active tense verbs. "She makes me feel depressed" linguistically is related to the more direct version, "She depresses me." Both have the same meaning. "You bore me" means, more fully, "You make me feel bored."

"She makes me angry" or "He scares me" represent vague images impossible to track *solely from those words* to our mental screen. Somehow the words invite us to represent one person performing some action that thereby leads to, causes, makes, or forces another person to experience some inner state of thought or emotion. If we blindly assume it is true and *run with the statement,* we then respond as if this map of the world accurately represents things.

"He scares me."

"Now, there, there; don't be upset. I'll talk to him about that."

How do we question and explore a cause—effect statement? How can we work our communication magic? Simply by inquiring into *how* the causation works.

How specifically does she 'make' you angry?

Does her action 'make' you feel angry? Does it always have this effect in you?

Has she said or done those things and you did not respond with anger?

Cause—effect statements frequently identify synesthesia patterns. These see-feel and hear-feel circuits describe the underlying neurological mapping (more about that in the last chapter).

"These ideas excite me." ("These are exciting ideas.")

How do these ideas evoke you to feel excitement?

What about these ideas excites you?

"Oh, John, you do everything just right to *make* me feel really loved!" Here is a cause—effect statement at work creating positive magic—the magic of romance and emotional bonding. Anything wrong with that? Not if we map it with mindfulness.

Mindful mapping that springs from the mind of a magician allows us to choose our magic spells and potions. Then we can map the world so that every sunrise, smile, sound of children playing, people going to work, etc. becomes a *cause* for more pleasure, appreciation, and motivation. It may be 'semantically ill-formed,' but it works. It works wonderfully to make our lives richer and fuller. If we mindfully set up the rules of the game in our own mind so that all kinds of everyday events will make us healthier and happier—then we have magic that works beautifully.

Statements that make predictions about the future contain cause—effect statements.

"You'll never be happy with him!" The predicted causation, 'will never be' puts the effect of being 'with him' into the future. Since cause—effect statements identify how things work, or what controls what, concepts of responsibility frequently get tied up with this pattern.

Implied causation can show up using various causation words (e.g., that, since, because). "I'm sad that you forgot our anniversary" (substitute 'since,' 'because,' 'inasmuchas,' etc.). Causation ideas can also hide beneath the word *but*. We can use 'but' to reference the reasons and conditions that we believe cause a situation.

> "I want to leave home, but my father is sick."

By implication, the father's being sick makes or causes the speaker here to experience an inability, he can't leave home.

> "I don't want to get angry, but she is always blaming me."
>
> "I don't enjoy being uptight, but my job demands it."

In response to these cause—effect statements, we can facilitate the enrichment of a person's model and sense of choice simply by questioning the universality of the statement.

> *Do you always get mad when she blames?*
>
> We can ask for more specificity.
>
> *How specifically does her blaming make you feel angry?*
>
> We can inquire more about the cause—effect relationship.
>
> *If she didn't blame you, you would not get angry at her?*

We have a 'special kind of deletion' occurring in statements that involve causation, when the causation involves a system of interactions, but the statement only details one side of the inter-relating. In addition to the *universals* ('always,' 'never') in the following lines, we have an incomplete model of an inter-action.

"My husband is always arguing with me."

"My wife never smiles at me."

Bandler and Grinder wrote,

> "The image of the processes or relationships of *arguing with* and *smiling at* are incomplete as only one person in the relationship is being described as having an active role. When faced with Surface Structures of this type, the therapist has the choice of asking for the way the person characterized as passive is involved in the process." (p. 85)

This *cause—effect deletion* surfaces another important linguistic distinction. It comes from Bateson's (1972) work with symmetry. Bateson noted that in relationships, we can have symmetrical and non-symmetrical relations.

Symmetrically, if "I am your peer," then of necessity, "you are my peer."

But non-symmetrically, if "I am your father," the converse is true. If, "I am your brother," you may or may not "be a brother" to me, you may be a sister.

The words 'argue with' indicate a symmetrical relationship. If I "argue with" you, this of necessity implies that you also "argue with" me. After all, it takes two to argue. With symmetrical predicates, the Meta-Model suggests the magic of *shifting referential indices*.

Then you also argue a lot with your husband?

This statement allows us to expand our mapping of cause—effect relationships as it helps us expand our vision to see the larger picture. It expands the context and introduces the sequences of actions which have effects which then become the next actions in the sequence.

A non-symmetrical predicate shows up in the example involving the words, 'smile at.' It does not take two to smile. Logically, while one person may never smile at another, the other may smile, may even typically smile at the first one. Yet psycho-logically while no logical necessity demands it,

> "... our experience has been that the converse is frequently psychologically accurate. Often the client states a generalization about another person ... the converse is true." (p. 87)

Simple cause—effect statements imply a linear world. To the extent that it does, it goes wrong. In a world of complex systems, most 'causation' involves multiple factors and systemic influences. Simple causation leads to another toxic response, blaming. Dr. Dennis Chong has written a small book on this, *Don't Ask Why?!* But he goes too far in absolutely rejecting and forbidding any causation. By contrast, systemic, non-linear causation that describes multiple contributing factors facilitates owning responsibility and staying solution-focused.

12) Complex Equivalences

From *cause—effect* statements, we jump to the next stage in mapping magic, *Complex Equivalences.* This refers to the creating of a complex generalization wherein we claim that one thing *means or equates to* another thing. We do not merely assert causation. We assert something more.

> "She *makes* me angry when she rolls her eyes like that. I know what that *is,* it *is* a challenge."

This linguistic mapping goes further, it equates two experiences and creates a piece of neuro-linguistic magic—magic that can either curse or bless, empower or dis-empower.

> "I hate his tone, it is not only insulting, but threatening."

This as much as says that my experience of hearing his tone of voice *is the same as* my experience of feeling threatened. His tone not only makes me feel threatened, it not only triggers and stimulates that, but I have to classify it and frame it as threatening. That's what it *is*. Now we have equivalence and identification.

> "He doesn't appreciate me; he never smiles at me."

Perhaps at one time his 'not smiling' *made* or *caused* her to feel unappreciated. She believed that his actions 'caused' her emotions rather than recognized that she participated in the process by giving the actions those meanings. But now, something more complex has emerged. Now his not smiling *means, is, or equals* 'being unappreciated,' 'not appreciating,' 'disapproval,' etc. 'Not smiling' has been elevated from a sensory-based referent that could be put into numerous categories to now being put in one and only one category: 'Disapproval.' That's what it *is*; that's what it *means*.

The complexity in these equivalences does not lie in their structure. Structurally, we have a very simple form, namely,

> *This* = *That* (X equals Y)

The complexity in this equivalence arises from the *thinking* that produces this neuro-linguistic equation. By paying attention to how we create equivalences, we can learn a great deal about how we construct beliefs out of generalizations in the first place.

When we equate two things that differ, and then treat them as synonyms of the same phenomenon, we create a *Complex Equivalence*. Typically, this involves two phenomena that do not even exist on the same logical level as when we equate an externally verifiable experience ('She doesn't smile at me') with a *meaning attribution* of an internal state ('she doesn't appreciate me,' 'she disapproves'). The first description gives us a see-hear-feel referent that we can empirically test. It exists in 'the world out there.' The second phrase does not. The second refers to a higher level of meaning and results from the way we construct the significance of the act, to the meaning we attached to the stimuli. Then we do our magic. Then we say the magic words that cast the spell, "They are the same." And so they become—to us, in our neurology.

Not smiling = Unappreciated
External Behavior = Internal State or Significance

If we map these equations into existence, then they *are* neuro-linguistic constructs. This also means that we can unglue them. If treating them as equal creates the equation, then treating them as different unglues them. This gives us the magic wand by which we can blast away these concrete-like assertions about what a thing 'is,' the very assertions that make up the cultural realities we live in.

Dissolving magic begins as we question these generalizations individually in terms of unspecified nouns, verbs, relations, etc. Or, we can go for the larger frame by questioning the construction itself. The Meta-Model describes the logic of a *complex equivalence* using the form or equation: *X = Y*. Here X stands for the external behavior (EB) and Y stands for the internal state or significance (IS). This provides some shorthand for quickly profiling the form and structure of these semantic equations.

> "When she doesn't smile at me (EB), I know she doesn't appreciate me (IS). ... See, there she goes with her disapproval." (Mind-Reading)
>
> *How do you know?*
>
> "She's frowning and raising her eyebrow."
>
> *And ...?*
>
> "Well, that shows her disrespect and rejection of me."

Here, when we flushed out the Mind-Reading, we found it embedded in a larger frame, a Complex Equivalence. And with that, the magic just got deeper.

> *So a frown and an eyebrow rise is disapproval? That's what it means? And it always means that? It can't mean anything else? It has to mean that, right? And so every time I see you frown or your eyebrow rise, I can count on that being a signal that you are disapproving of me, right?*

These provide some of the ways that we can question Complex Equivalences as we hear them in language. Use your listening and pacing skills to make the formula explicit and then begin to inquire about when, where, and how it works. You'll notice also the magical power of shifting referential indices (from the speaker receiving this equation to giving it). This can powerfully loosen up these kinds of mind frames.

So when you don't smile at him, that must also mean that you don't appreciate him, right? And I can count on any non-smiling from you to mean your disapproval. Is that how this works?

Inside such equations are allness frames (Universal Quantifiers), so check them out.

Does his not smiling at you always mean the lack of appreciation?

What experiences have lead you to draw this conclusion?

13) Presuppositions

Presuppositions refer to the ideas and beliefs that we *assume* from the beginning as 'true' and 'real.' A presupposition consists of those conceptual understandings that must *exist as true* in order for a statement to make sense. We take these higher frames, paradigms, and understandings for granted as we assume their reality, truth, and importance. We hold them without questioning. We presuppose them. By etymological definition, a presupposition refers to 'what comes before' (pre) 'that holds our statements, understandings, and/or beliefs' (position) 'up' (sup).

What do we presuppose? We presuppose Cause—Effect relationships. We presuppose Complex Equivalences. We presuppose Lost Performatives that we've heard all our lives. We presuppose words are real and objective.

In language, *presuppositions* contain the working and hidden assumptions that drive our model of the world.

> "Presuppositions are what is necessarily true for the statements that the client makes to make sense (not to be true, but just to be meaningful) at all. ... Presuppositions are particularly insidious as they are not presented openly for consideration." (p. 53)

This Meta-Model distinction allows us to identify and detect our basic assumptions, both those that enrich our world and those that impoverish. As we expose the limitations that this mapping magic creates we free ourselves from the outside-of-awareness frames that make up our mental world. We do this by asking,

- What has to be true for me, or this other person, to even utter this statement?
- What has to be true for it to make sense?

Assuming that the speaker is not crazy, but that his or her perception makes sense and has its own internal logic,

- What am I missing that supports this?

Frequently these hide as descriptions or clauses within statements.

> "I'm afraid that my son is turning out to be as lazy as my husband."

This description of the son's laziness reveals the mother's frame. She expresses it not overtly, but covertly as an assumption. This makes it all that more subtle and difficult to catch. She does not explicitly say it, she just assumes it.

A great many *syntactic environments* facilitate the presence of presuppositions. Any statement that follows main verbs like *realize, know, ignore,* etc. frames a presupposition. There is a list of 36 syntactic environments for presuppositions in *The Structure of Magic* (1975, Appendix B).

> "*Since* you understand this so quickly, we can go ahead with some illustrations"

In that sentence, the speaker presupposes everything after the word 'since.' Sneaky, huh? Yet as you learn this distinction, you too will be able to use it to perform your own magic with words. Ah, I did it again. Did you catch it? I just presupposed everything in that last sentence after the word 'as.' Yet once detected, we can simply question or challenge the presuppositional frames-of-reference which we hear.

> "How specifically do you know that your son or your husband acts lazily?"

To identify and flush out presuppositions, we can use several sentence completion forms. The following syntactic stems gives us a format:

- *There exists ...*
- *It stands as possible that ...*

We can examine the presuppositions in any sentence offered to us by utilizing these sentence stems. Because presuppositions indicate a speaker's basic reality-organizing principles, when we identify presuppositions, we identify the person's highest frames of reference. These governing frames are really unquestioned assumptions from family, culture, school, and even language. And inside of many of these are old spells that hold old post hypnotic suggestions about life, people, human nature, success and failure, purpose, etc.

Here we will find the most unconscious beliefs—mostly absorbed from family, culture, school, and religion, without much thought. Korzybski talked about *undefined terms,* and urged that we bring a mindful recognition to these undefined terms. In undefined terms we blindly assume all kinds of ideas and concepts, concepts that make up our epistemological and ontological beliefs and which can unknowingly create lots of limitations and problems. If we do not recognize and identify the *undefined presuppositional terms* by which we operate, we will not fully understand our own maps or distinguish the territory from such unconscious mapping. Conversely, when we detect, identify, and challenge our undefined terms, when we test them, we "lay on the table our metaphysics and our assumed structures" (1933: 155).

In *Frame Games* (2000), we flush out presuppositional frames by learning how to 'Name the Game.' Upon game detection we can then explore the rules of the game, game set-up, purpose and agenda, players, scoring, etc.

The Structure of Magic

There you have it, 13 distinctions in neuro-linguistic mapping that encode and govern the very structure of neuro-linguistic magic. These 13 distinctions highlight mapping processes which are neither good nor bad in themselves. In themselves, they are just the ways that we use linguistic symbols to send messages to our neurology. Yet in various contexts, and given contextual outcomes and criteria, we can use them to create limitations, inhibitions, dysfunctions, and problems. When so used, they harm and hinder, they create dragons and demons, they cast black magic spells, they prevent the development and use of our resources.

Numerous *linguistic markers* cue us about these mapping distinctions. We can use these to sound the alarm that a potential mapping problem of fluffiness, deletion, rigid rules, or corruption has occurred. Seeing and hearing these linguistic markers as warning signals empowers us to notice how we have mapped things, how they work productively for us or against us, and how we can enrich our impoverished maps.

In this lies the function and usefulness of the Meta-Model. This communication magic model enables us to take a meta-position to our cognitive maps and check them out for usefulness, accuracy, and desirability. If we discover a particular restrictiveness in one of our maps that causes pain or that prevents us from living more fully, we can use the Meta-Model distinctions and questions as a technology for expanding our model of the world.

The Meta-Model Strategy

There's an overall *strategy* regarding *how* to use language to touch human lives with magic. While I have already described it, here it is again. When you do this, you access the powers of a magician to *meta-model*:

- *Listen carefully* as a person expresses him or herself using everyday expressions.
- *Representationally track* the words to your mental movie screen.
- *Notice the missing and/or unclear parts.*
- *Explore, question, and challenge* those unclear parts to fill in the details of your mental movie.
- *Invite the person to map* more enhancing and supporting ideas for increased resourcefulness.

As you do this, you will recover the deleted, generalized, and distorted parts of the map. If these are unclear parts that impoverish one's thinking, then you coach the person with questions that enrich those parts. This activates the magic in the speaker's own mind and body. As your questioning invites the person to reconnect to the experience out of which the linguistic model came, it facilitates a new opportunity for re-mapping.

By design, we elicit greater clarity and precision in order to depotentate (de-power) the person's 'rules,' assumptions, and frames. This assists the other to build more empowering models of the world. When we speak about *meta-modeling* someone, we mean identifying language 'violations of well-formedness' (e.g. deletions, vagueness, imprecision, fuzziness, and distortions) and challenging the mapping in a way that generates a richer mental map and increased mindfulness.

Questioning lies at the heart of meta-modeling. This questioning involves using a set of questions which allows another to fill in the details, redraw the map, and create better generalizations. The questions gently call into question the way the current map has been formed, especially the ill-formed facets of structure, syntax, and meaning. Asking questions activates the person's neuro-linguistic mapping powers and puts the speaker back into the role of an active creator of his or her framing of life.

What we call *challenges* in the Meta-Model are simply the *questions* that we use to elicit higher-quality information. When we ask the basic indexing questions (i.e., *what, which, when, whom and how)* we rattle the cage of the old mapping. We invite the person inside the matrices of belief frames to wake up and recognize the made-up nature of this 'reality.'

Meta-Modeling and the 'Why?' Questions

Did you notice that the Meta-Model, for the most part, does *not* ask *why* questions? There's a reason for that. *Why* questions pose a special problem. *Why* questions tend to evoke explanations, reasons, history, rationalizations, excuses, and defensiveness. Rather than obtaining specific details, *why* questions get *'becauses.'*

Why did you do that?

Why are you that way?

Why do you like that?

Yet there are different kinds of *why* questions. There are some *why* questions that enable us to gather high-quality information. For example, we can ask the *why of intention or of teleology.*

Why do you want to do that?

Or, we can ask the *why of importance.* That provides marvelous information about another's world.

Why is that important to you?

Why does that mean so much to you?

These *why* questions allow us to explore the higher levels of the mind. They allow us to obtain the high quality information that's encoded in our governing frames of explanation and understanding. Conversely, it is the *why of source* or origin questions (asked within or under the old frames) which typically reinforce the generalizations and justify them.

The Meta-Model's questions provide a technology for asking the best kind of questions for drawing out and actively engaging a speaker. That's why it's great for information gathering. We begin by assuming that our language suffers from incomplete, fluffy, and unclear representations. The questions function as a kind of *de-fluffifying* process as they call for more and more clarity and precision. Jacobson (1986) described the Meta-Model as providing 'a great set of rules to guide your thinking.'

> "Remember that language is a reflection of what is in our minds. If our words come out like a tossed salad, well ... So listen to your language when you talk with people ..." (p. 106)

When you use the Meta-Model to guide your thinking, you will sequence, order, and structure the way you represent things in more productive ways. As these questions become habitual in your speech and then intuitive, you will think in many of the same ways that Perls, Satir, and Erickson thought when they performed their therapeutic magic. This will further develop your magician's mind and heart.

The Meta-Model questions enable us to explore the meaning structures, hence the neuro-semantics frameworks of our internal mapping.

> When and where does this behavior occur?
>
> What stimulus typically elicits this response?
>
> What does this response mean about your values?
>
> What are you seeking to accomplish?

There are also meta-questions in this communication magic model. These enable us to step back from the entire mapping process and to inquire about the *form and structure* of languaging itself and the frames that it sets. These enable us to look at the mapping processes as we check out the person's deleting of possibly critical information and his or her style and manner of generalizing and distorting.

Using these questions enables us, as listeners, to *stay in sensory awareness* as we gather information. It empowers us from going inside and generating our own experiential meanings rather than staying with, and eliciting, the speaker's. In the place where we might otherwise make reference to our own experiences (e.g., "I know what you mean, why back in 1983, I had a similar experience..."), we use the questions and explore *the person's* mapping.

As we facilitate communications between ourselves and others in an effort for more clarity and precision, we no longer will fill in pieces from our own model. Filling in the pieces with our own map defeats our purpose. Then we meet the other person at our model of the world rather than his or her model. If we have the heart of a magician, then these Meta-Model questions will enable us to meet the other person truly at his or her model of the world.

Summary

- Though we live in a real world, we do not operate directly or immediately upon that world. We operate indirectly through our maps to guide our behaviors and responses.
- These maps necessarily differ from the territory by the three processes of generalization, deletion, and distortion.
- The map is not the territory it represents. Much human suffering and limitation occurs because of impoverished maps. Even though the world is rich enough to support us, our problems often involve the maps we use in navigating the territory.
- The Meta-Model gives us a way to identify the structure, syntax, and meaning of human mapping, a way to transform impoverished linguistic maps, and a magic wand to touch human minds and hearts with magic.

Chart 8.1: The Meta-Model of Language

1. **Simple Deletions**
   "They don't listen to me."
   Who specifically doesn't listen to you?
   "People push me around."
   Who specifically pushes you?

2. **Comparative and Superlative Deletions** (Unspecified Relations)
   "She's a better person."
   Better than whom? Better at what? Compared to whom, what? Given what criteria?

3. **Unspecified Referential Indices: Unspecified Nouns and Verbs**
"I am uncomfortable."
Uncomfortable in what way? Uncomfortable when? Who specifically doesn't listen to you?
"He said that she was mean."
Whom did he call mean? What did he mean by 'mean'?
"She rejected me."
How specifically did she reject you?
"I felt really manipulated."
Manipulated in what way and how?

4. **Unspecified Processes—Adverbs Modifying Verbs**
"Surprisingly, my father lied about his drinking."
How did you feel surprised about that? What surprised you about that?
"She slowly started to cry."
What indicated to you that her starting to cry occurred in a slow manner?

5. **Unspecified Processes—Adjectives Modifying Nouns**
"I don't like unclear people."
Unclear about what and in what way?
"The unhappy letter surprised me."
How, and in what way, did you feel unhappy about the letter?

6. **Universal Quantifiers** (Allness, Generalizations that exclude exceptions)
"She never listens to me."
Never? She never so much as listens to you even a little bit?

7. **Modal Operators** (Operational Modes of Being—One's Modus Operandi)
"I have to take care of her."
What would happen if you didn't? You have to or else what?

8. **Lost Performatives** (Evaluative statement that deletes the speaker)
"It's bad to be inconsistent."
Who evaluates it as bad? According to what standard? How do you determine this label of 'badness?'

9. **Nominalizations** (Processes transformed into static 'things.')
"Let's improve our communication."
Whose communicating do you mean? How would you like to communicate?
"What state did you wake up in this morning?"
How specifically did you think and feel when you woke up?

10. **Mind-Reading** (Attributing knowledge of another's internal thoughts, feelings, motives)
'You don't like me.'
How do you know I don't like you? What leads you to think that?

11. **Cause—Effect** (Causational statements of relations between events, stimulus-response beliefs).
"You make me sad."
How does my behavior cause you to respond with sad feelings? Do you always feel sad when I do this? How specifically does this work?

12. **Complex Equivalences** (phenomena which someone equates as the same)
"She's always yelling at me; she doesn't like me."
How do you equate her yelling as meaning she doesn't like you? Can you recall a time when you yelled at someone that you liked?
"He's a loser when it comes to business, he just lacks business sense."
How do you know to equate his lack of success in business with his lack of business sense? Could other factors play a role in this?

13. **Presuppositions** (Silent Assumptions, Unspoken Paradigms)
"If my husband knew how much I suffered, he wouldn't do that."
How do you suffer? In what way? About what? How do you know that your husband knows or doesn't know this? Why do you assume that his intentions would shift if he knew. Does your husband always use your emotional state to determine his responses?

The Meta-Model

Patterns/ Distinctions	Responses/ Challenges	Predictions/ Results
1. Simple Deletions		
"They don't listen to me."	Who specifically doesn't listen to you?	Recover the Deletion
"People push me around."	Who specifically pushes you?	Recover the Ref. Index
2. Comparative & Superlative Deletions (Unspecified Relations)		
"She's a better person."	Better than whom? Better at what? Compared to whom, what? Given what criteria?	Recover the deleted standard, criteria, or belief
3. Unspecified Referential Indices (Unspecified Nouns and Verbs)		
"I am uncomfortable."	Uncomfortable in what way? Uncomfortable when?	Recover specific qualities of the verb
"They don't listen to me."	Who specifically doesn't listen to you?	Recover the nouns of the persons involved
"He said that she was mean."	Who specifically said that? Whom did he call mean? What did he mean by 'mean'?	Recover the individual meaning of the term
"People push me around." "I felt really manipulated."	Who specifically pushes you Manipulated in what way and how?	Add details to the map
4. Unspecified Processes—Adverbs Modifying Verbs		
"Surprisingly, my father lied about his drinking."	How did you feel surprised about that? What surprised you about that?	Recover the process of the person's emotional state
"She slowly started to cry."	What indicated to you that her starting to cry occurred in a slow manner?	Enriches with details of the person's referent
5. Unspecified Processes—Adjectives Modifying Nouns		
"I don't like unclear people."	Unclear about what and in what way?	Recover the projection of the speaker's sense of feeling 'unclear' or 'unhappy'
"The unhappy letter surprised me."	How, and in what way, did you feel unhappy?	
6. Universal Quantifiers		
"She never listens to me."	Never? She has never so much as listened to you even a little bit?	Recover details to the extent of a process and counter-examples
7. Modal Operators (Operational Modes of Being)		
"I have to take care of her." "I can't tell him the truth."	What would happen if you did? What wouldn't happen if you didn't? "You have to or else what?"	Recover details of the process, also causes, effects, and outcomes

Patterns/ Distinctions	Responses/ Challenges	Predictions/ Results
8. Lost Performatives (Evaluative statement/s with the speaker deleted or unowned)		
"It's bad to be inconsistent."	Who evaluates it as bad? According to what standard? How do you determine this label of "badness?"	Recovers the source of idea or belief—the map-maker, standards used
9. Nominalizations (Pseudo-Nouns that hide processes and actions)		
"Let's improve our communication."	Whose communicating do you mean? How would you like to communicate?	Recovers the process and the characteristics left out
"What state did you wake up in this morning?"	How specifically did you feel, think, etc.? What behaviors, physiology, and internal representations make up this "state?"	Specifies the verb and actions
10. Mind-Reading (Attributing knowledge of another's internal thoughts, feelings, motives)		
"You don't like me..."	How do you know I don't like you? What evidence leads you to that conclusion?	Recovers the source of the information—specifies how a person knows
11. Cause—Effect (Causational statements of relations between events, stimulus-response beliefs)		
"You make me sad."	How does my behavior cause you to respond with sad feelings? Counter Example: Do you always feel sad when I do this? How specifically does this work?	Recovers under standing of how a person views causation, sources, and origins—specifies beliefs about how world works
12. Complex Equivalences (Phenomena that differ which someone equates as the same)		
"She's always yelling at me, she doesn't like me."	How do you equate her yelling as meaning she doesn't like you? Can you recall a time when you yelled at someone that you liked?	Recovers how the person equates or associates one thing with another. Ask for counter-examples to the meaning equation. Could other factors play a role in this?
"He's a loser when it comes to business; he just lacks business sense."	How do you know to equate his lack of success in business with his lack of sense about it?	
13. Presuppositions (Silent Assumptions, Unspoken Paradigms).		
"If my husband knew how much I suffered, he would not do that."	How do you suffer? In what way? About what? How do you know that your husband doesn't know this? Why do you assume that his intentions would shift if he knew? Does your husband always use your emotional state to determine his responses?	Recovers the person's assumptions, beliefs, and values that he or she just doesn't question. Specifies processes, nouns, verbs, etc. left out.

Chapter 9

The Evolution of Magic Part I:

How New Developments in the Meta-Model Enriched it

"A word is worth a thousand pictures."
Robert Dilts, 1979

Over the years numerous changes have occurred in the Meta-Model. We'll explore some of these in this chapter and the next. Why review this history? Why explore the changes? In order to more fully develop and understand the Communication Magic Model. Doing this will give us yet another look at the model and deepen our appreciation of how it works. As we view the set of linguistic distinctions and questions from yet another perspective, we will be able to develop even more of the mind, heart, and eyes of a magician. It may also open up room for anticipating future changes in the model.

The Model Developed a Structure

In the beginning the Meta-Model was without form. The ideas were there, the terminology was there, but it was structureless. It appeared first in no sequential or orderly form. There were no diagrams, no charts, no lists, no menus. In the beginning, there were wonderful understandings about linguistic mapping and distinctions, but the ideas lacked a user-friendly form.

Look inside the first volume of *The Structure Of Magic,* and you will find no list or chart of the model. In fact, you have to engage in some extensive hunting and searching if you want to gather up the pieces of the paradigm and synthesize them. As others did this later, charts like the ones in the previous chapter began to appear. If you want to comb through the original book to collect the pieces of the Meta-Model, you will find some things about nominalizations in Chapter 2 and a few more in Chapter 3. This created a good bit of consternation for the early trainers.

It remained for others to formulate the model into an orderly form. Dilts (1975) seems to have been the first to have identified and numbered the Meta-Model distinctions. In a paper, "Application of the Meta-Model to the Socratic Method of Philosophical Inquiry" which he later published as *Applications of Neuro-Linguistic Programming* (1983), he identified 11 distinctions.

During the late 1970s, 80s, and 90s, charts contained as few as 8 to as many as 13 Meta-Model distinctions. The largest number that I have heard of came from NLP Trainer Charles Faulkner who said that he had found 17 patterns. By contrast, only 8 appeared in *Magic Demystified* (1982) by Byron Lewis and Frank Pucelik. In the end they listed 12 distinctions, putting 5 sub-patterns under "Referential Index" (pp. 76–83).

During the intervening years, numerous developers and authors suggested various structures for organizing, understanding, and working with the Meta-Model. I will explore some of these in this chapter as a reflection of how the Meta-Model grew and expanded over the years, moving out of the therapy field and into business, sports, management, writing, etc.

Formatting and Structuring the Meta-Model

The very first formatting of the Meta-Model occurred in 1976 with the second volume of *The Structure of Magic*. In that volume, Bandler and Grinder suggested the following as "useful in organizing our experience both in therapy" and in training seminars:

1) Gathering Information
2) Identifying the limits of the client's model
3) Specifying the techniques to be used for change (p. 165).

About the same time, Dilts (1975) suggested the following three categories as "the natural groupings of the Meta-Model violations."

1. Information Gathering
   a. Deletions (Del)
   b. Unspecified Referential Index (URI)
   c. Unspecified Verbs (UV)
   d. Nominalizations (Nom.)
2. Setting and Identifying Limits
   a. Universal Quantifiers (UQ)
   b. Modal Operators (MO)
3. Semantic Ill-Formedness
   a. Complex Equivalence (CEq.)
   b. Presuppositions (Ps.)
   c. Cause—Effect (C—E)
   d. Mind-Reading (MR)
   e. Lost Performative (LP)

In organizing the Meta-Model this way, Robert emphasized its value for (1) gathering high-quality information, (2) setting and identifying personal limits within one's model of the world, and (3) working with, identifying, and expanding the quality of one's meanings in life. Dilts (1983a) wrote:

> "For me, this is what the Meta Model is all about: being able to increase your efficiency in anything by finding out that kind of specific information. Knowing anchoring, knowing strategies, or any technique by itself isn't going to get you anywhere unless you know *how* and *when* to use them. ... The Meta Model is all about asking these kinds of questions. What do you need? What would happen if you did?" (p. 5)

It makes perfect sense to use the Meta-Model as an information-gathering technology. After all, it grew out of the questions that the therapeutic wizards Virginia Satir and Fritz Perls asked their clients. Such questioning explicates how a given *model of the world* works, what elements make up that mapping, its linguistic structure, and how a person 'knows' what he or she knows. It allows us to make explicit the magic spells that people live in. Of course, when we do that, our questioning can simultaneously have the effect of breaking the spells that are ill-formed.

From this we can identify the most basic and essential questions in the communication magic model:

What do you know?

How do you know that?

How do you know that you know?

Organizing Magic Via Representational Systems

Another attempt at structuring and ordering the Meta-Model occurred early in the history of NLP. Lewis and Pucelik (1982) attempted to correlate the Meta-Model distinctions to the representational systems (i.e., the visual, auditory, kinesthetic, and auditory-digital channels). They presented each distinction and offered generalizations in their attempt at a correlation.

> "This [Reversed Referential Index] is a common pattern used by individuals operating from the kinesthetic system." (p. 82)

> "Remember that 'visuals' organize experiences in such a way as to prevent 'contact' with those around them." (p. 83)

> "This Meta Model violation, unspecified verbs, is particularly common to individuals operating out of the kinesthetic category." (p. 91)

> "This pattern [The Modal Operator of Necessity] is typical of someone operating out of the visual model, especially under stress. In this way, a 'visual' can verbally externalize his frustration or anger at a person or situation and at the same time exclude himself from having any responsibility for the situation." (p. 95)

This way of looking at the Meta-Model certainly provides an interesting speculation between possible correlations in surface expressions and the underlying sensory system. Yet these correlations do not fit very well for most people. Undoubtedly that's why we do not find them carried over into other NLP books. This means that our preferred sensory system of encoding things (the VAK) does not control or govern our linguistic mapping. What we now know about the operating functions of systems and the governance of meta-levels suggests the very opposite. It is the linguistic mapping that recruits the sensory systems.

A Linguistic Anchoring System

Mention any word that you know and something comes to mind. Words work in eliciting or anchoring associations to sensory-based referents. They evoke memories of experiences. Words operate as anchors which trigger or activate us to use our representational screen.

Notice what comes to mind with these words: a juicy strawberry, the White House, a zebra, the Great Pyramid of Egypt, your childhood home, Donald Duck. *Something comes to mind* if you know how to 'make sense' of those words. But what? What comes to mind? If, on the inside, you see, hear, smell, feel, and taste something that corresponds to the sensory-based facets, then we say those words *work*. They work as they trigger associations which we have connected to them.

Words elicit associations. In this, the Meta-Model functions as an explanatory paradigm regarding *how* we organize our linguistic anchoring system so that we can 'make meaning' of things.

Yet words not only work via their associative and representative nature, they also work via the process of eliciting frameworks of meaning, categories, contexts, and contexts of contexts. This means that some words do *not* merely trigger direct Stimulus—Response associations. Instead, they trigger us to establish an entirely different and higher set of associations. They trigger categories or classes of evaluation—mental frames and frameworks. These non-sensory based or evaluative-based words take us up, up and away to the higher matrices of our mind.

'Book' specifies a category. While it points to no specific book, we can still make a picture of it. At least, we can picture a prototype book, one that stands for our idea of this category of things. This becomes much less possible when we use evaluative words: 'an insightful book,' 'a challenging book,' 'a book that initiates a paradigm shift.' Such words *work*, not to generate pictures, but to elicit (or even create) conceptual understandings. Each qualifying word invites us to go meta to yet another higher category. Each qualifying term invites us up a level to a new meta-state frame.

Transformational Grammar began the current understanding of linguists about our internal transforms from a 'deep structure' of representation to the surface structure expressions. That was the model current at the time when Bandler and Grinder first created the Meta-Model. But even then, the field of linguistics was in such a state of flux that all of this was about to change. At first those dedicated to TG pursued it even after Chomsky gave up D-structure. They persisted and developed Generative Semantics. But that went nowhere. Later, Space Grammar and Cognitive Grammar invented a different format for thinking about meaning—its structure and transformation. They showed that 'meaning' also arises from meta-level categories. These categories identify the *domains* or *contexts* that govern the meaning.

Today the Meta-Model provides insights into both of these domains: associative meaning and contextual meaning. It does so by showing *how* we first associate external sights, sounds, sensations, and experiences with internal structures (e.g., words, linguistic phrases, grammatical transforms, etc.).

It also does more. The Meta-Model also recognizes that we have, construct, and use many higher level constructs (e.g., generalizations and distortions). We create and use *class terms* of categories as we move up into higher levels of abstraction. This creates 'domains of knowledge' that we use as our mental *contexts* by which we understand words. This means that we 'make meaning' of some things, not so much by mere word association and anchoring, but also by the way we abstract to higher levels to create generalizations *about* our thoughts. This is where connotations, intensional definitions, categories, cognitive domains, and presuppositions give us a higher and different level of meaning. And sure enough, the Meta-Model provides us a way to explore and identify our meanings at these levels. It gives us a way to identify our neuro-semantics at these levels and to transform them so that they will work for us in more enhancing ways.

Dilts (1979), in explaining the Meta-Model, rephrased the old line about a picture evoking a thousand words. He wrote, *"A word is worth a thousand pictures."*

Why would this be so?

Because while the *meaning* of a word, to a given person, *begins with* the pictures, sounds, and sensations which that word evokes, it only begins there. It does not end there. Meaning involves a lot more than *representation,* it also involves *reference.* (This, by the way, describes one of the key ways that Neuro-Semantics differs from NLP as indicated in *Meta-States* and *Frame Games.*)

We think in categories. By categorizing, we put things and people into mental boxes and then those boxes into yet higher boxes. Eleanor Rosch describes our thinking using basic-level categories.

Charles Faulkner, having extensively studied Cognitive Linguistics has noted that many NLP practitioners have narrowly assumed that the Meta-Model only treats words in a rigid stimulus—response situation, "as conditioned responses." He asserts that we should also recognize how that language itself operates in a semantically laden way—"human language is necessarily semiotic."

> "You listen to somebody say they had an accident, or 'I am really troubled,' and you make sense of that for yourself without really knowing the other person's representations for it." (Dilts, 1979, p. 12)

This occurs because *context* itself drives and governs representation. So we must explore the context domain—the person's encyclopedic knowledge of a domain, the context of contexts, and the categories used.

Present State to Desired State Algorithm

The Meta-Model puts several magic wands into our hands, wands which allow us to perform varieties of magic. One *magic wand* of this model involves using the 'present state to desired state' algorithm. This algorithm moves a person from his or her current state of mind and emotion and transports a person into some desired state. Wisely using this algorithm enables us to recognize *what* to meta-model. Obviously, we do not need to meta-model everything in someone's communications. Rene Pfalzgraf (1989) noted this in an article on Meta-Model III.

> "Ineffective challenging usually occurs when the person challenging has no idea what they are going for i.e., the NLP practitioner does not have a well-formed outcome. There are too many meta-model patterns present in each sentence to effectively challenge all of them."

So, as an information gathering tool, if we meta-model every linguistic violation that is ill-formed, we would overwhelm ourselves with too much information and fail to recognize the crucial from the trivial and the leverage points in the neuro-semantic system. An effective map does not have to detail *everything* in the territory. We can leave out trees, bushes, alleys, and all kinds of things on a city map and still get around just fine. We can generalize the direction of a freeway without worry about putting in every turn and twist in the road. We can even distort the size of the freeway—coloring it red and making it very thick without deluding anybody that when they drive onto the freeway, it will be a mile wide.

How do we make our decisions about *what* to meta-model? Dilts (1979) suggested an algorithm. This algorithm is a simple formula and serves as a larger framework for moving ourselves or another from a *present state* to a *desired state*. When we use this structure in our mind—it governs our questioning about three things: the two locations and the needed resources. After we tease out the information on present and desired states, we then focus on coaching someone to access and develop the needed resources. We go after the resources as transitional mechanisms to create a bridge for the person from one state to the other. Eventually Dilts turned this algorithm into the *S.C.O.R.E. model*. He explained,

> "One of the difficulties experienced by early meta modelers was gathering too much information. ... *Present state desired state* is the overlay ... to put on your information when you use the meta model. Essentially, everything else is going to be irrelevant other

> than present state and especially desired state information." (Dilts, 1979, p. 33)

The letters S.C.O.R.E. stand for:

> **S**ymptoms: present state symptoms we want to change.
>
> **C**auses: factors that contribute to the symptoms.
>
> **O**utcome: the desired state.
>
> **R**esources: the mechanisms that move one from present state to desired state.
>
> **E**ffects: the results and consequences of the desired state.

In Brief Psychotherapy, de Shazer (1988) and associates refer to the same process in different terms. They use the metaphor of the *miracle question.*

> "Suppose that one night there is a miracle while you are sleeping and the problem that brought you into therapy is solved. How would you know? What would be different? How would your husband know without your saying a word to him about it?" (p. 5)

We have a similar question in NLP. After we obtain a clear description of a present state, we ask about the desired state. This is the miracle or magic question:

> "If you had a magic wand, what would you do differently? What would you see, hear, or feel?" (Dilts, 1979, p. 33)

Robert tells a story about John Grinder using this question. When he was once at a liquor store, he noticed a lady there who had all the external signs of alcoholism. When it became evident that she needed a ride home, John gave her a lift.

In the car, she asked him a question, "Why do you drink?"

He answered saying that he liked the taste of wine, but he also said that he didn't drink very much. Then, "being the magician that he is," he asked her a series of questions that eventually coached her to mapping a new reality for herself.

"But that isn't the real question you wanted to ask me, is it?"

She burst into tears. "Yes, the real question is, 'Why do I drink?'"

And so they began to talk. Eventually, John shifted her from that present state of distress to a more desirable state. He did so with a question that teased her. "But the question *why* do you drink is not really the question that you want to find the answer to either."

She said nothing.

Then, after setting up more interest and tease, he said, "The real question is, 'What would you be doing if you weren't drinking?'"

This magical question shifted her from thinking about the problem state of drinking and why she drank (a causation focus of the contributing factors). It invited her to go somewhere else, namely, to attending to the nature of the *solution state*. What would that be like? What would you be doing, feeling, etc.?

Personally I like the miracle or magic question so much that I have built an entire Meta-States Pattern around it (*The Secrets of Personal Mastery*). It all began by considering what any question like this evokes.

> "What would life be like the day after the miracle?"
>
> "What would you be thinking, feeling, doing, etc. if you were not engaged in this current distressful state?"

These questions invite a respondent to begin to access specific sensory-based information about life *apart from* the problem. These questions invite one to *outframe* the problem and to associate into the new description, to step into it, and to personalize it. This begins to build, for that person, a new reality. No wonder *desired state questions* are some of the most important and life-changing questions that we can design or ask.

What would it be like if you fully experienced X?

What would you see, hear, or feel?

How would you know that you are experiencing X?

The Model was Organized in Logical Levels

As noted earlier, by the mid 1980s, most charts organized the Meta-Model in terms of the three modeling categories (i.e., deletions, generalizations, and distortions). At first, they organized these lists from simplest to more complex (deletions to distortions). By 1987, many had turned this around to present the higher levels first. This is reflected in Figure 9.1.

Ordering the distinctions as a logical level system draws attention to the fact that we have *deletions* in every linguistic distinction. In Cause—Effect statements, we have deleted the connection. In Mind-Reading, we have deleted the process of how we know or how we have made our guess about another person's mind, intentions, and motives. In Complex Equivalence, we have deleted how we created the equation between the items existing on different logical levels. *Deletion,* as a modeling process, occurs in the processes of generalization and distortion. It represents a smaller unit or *lower* level.

Figure 9.1: The Order of the Meta-Model

Distortions
- Mind Reading (MR)
- Lost Performative (LP)
- Cause—Effect (C—E)
- Complex Equivalence (CEq)
- Presuppositions (Ps)

Generalizations
- Universal Quantifiers (UQ)
- Modal Operators (MO)

Deletions
- Nominalizations (Nom)
- Unspecified Verbs (UV)
- Simple Deletions (Del)

Similarly, we have *generalizations* in most of the Meta-Model distinctions. We generalize how things work in causing or leading from one thing to another (C—E). We generalize the basic pattern of meaning (CEq) as we specify that a External Behavior (EB) equals an Internal State (IS). We generalize about the basic thoughts, emotions, and intentions in others (MR). But, conversely, we may have no generalization when we simply delete the specifics of who, how, when, where, etc.

By the time I wrote the notes for Richard Bandler's Master Practitioner Training (1989), which is now the book *The Spirit of NLP* (1996/2000), Richard had made some other changes in his structuring of the Meta-Model.

Figure 9.2: The Logical Levels of the Meta-Model

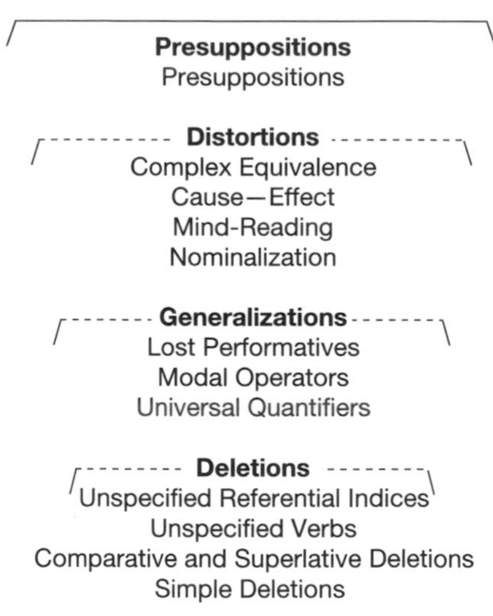

For instance, he *inverted* the Meta-Model so that it began at the top with the largest level distinctions. He had moved 'nominalizations' from the category of deletions to the larger grouping of distortions. Among the other changes, he separated *presuppositions* from the category of distortions and was beginning to use it to describe another modeling process. This also appears briefly in Lankton's (1980) work, *Practical Magic* (p. 54). There, in the space of two paragraphs, he noted the idea of the operational logical levels within the Meta-Model, but did not go on to develop that idea.

In presenting this schematic, Bandler said that the Meta-Model was a system of logical levels. The higher modeling process (presuppositions) *drives* (or organizes) the levels below it, and the next highest process (distortion) drives generalizations and deletions below it (Figure 9.2), etc. I have noted the logical levels of the Meta-Model in a chapter about 'logical levels' in *NLP: Advanced Modeling Using Meta-States and Logical Levels* (1997).

The Magic of the Higher Levels

What significance does this re-structuring of the logical level system inherent in the Meta-Model have? There are several.

First, it highlights the fact that *higher levels organize and modulate the lower levels.* This partly explains the power of Meta-Model questions and how they challenge and shift things at a higher level of mind. Changing things at a higher level generates a pervasive effect, an effect that governs, controls, and organizes the transformations at lower levels. This means that at the lowest level in the system (the linguistic distinctions of *deletions),* we will get the smallest 'chunk' of information. At this level, indexing and asking for specifics provide details of great precision. While these many details fill in the missing pieces, they may only address trivial concerns rather than crucial ones.

As we move up to the distinctions under the category of *generalizations,* we begin to get larger chunks of information—'beliefs'. This gives us information about how a person has structured his or her world in terms of action style (*modus operandi)* and 'rules' for living (LP).

When we get to the distortions category of linguistic distinctions, we have access to a person's internal world that deals with causation (C—E), meanings and associations (CEq), values and states (Nom), and beliefs about the states of others and what causes those states (MR). Yet the largest level of all flows from a person's presuppositions—those unspoken assumptions in beliefs about knowledge, meaning, self, destiny, etc. (Ps).

What does this mean in terms of learning to use the Meta-Model effectively? By recognizing the logical levels in this model, we can ask logical level questions:

> What 'chunk' size of information do I need?
>
> At what level does the person's difficulty exist?
>
> At what level will I get the most useful and valuable information?
>
> At what level can I intervene to get the most pervasive impact?

System Magic

Another valuable understanding arises when we recognize the logical levels of the Meta-Model. As a *system* of interactions, what we do in one part of the system will reverberate in other parts of the system. This systemic awareness, in turn, leads us to think in terms of *leverage points,* and places where the smallest alteration can have the largest effect. It alerts us to how moving up to higher levels will sometimes generate emergent *meta-level phenomena* that we can't explain as merely 'the sum of the parts.'

From out of the mind-body system of representing data (non-verbally and linguistically), of working with symbols and systems of symbols *emerge* new qualities and properties. This explains the power of beliefs (and beliefs about beliefs) in governing perception, body functions, autonomic nervous system operations, health, and experience. Of course, the Meta-States model more fully explicates this domain as it describes how each higher *state* operates as a frame and a self-organizing attractor in the system.

Even though our representations at any level may not accord with, or fit, the territory at all (and may even represent *nothing at all* in the territory!), *as* we represent *and* then develop other thoughts-and-feelings (beliefs) *about* those representations, so we construct a system of thoughts-and-feelings about those. These higher level cause—effect relationships, complex equivalences, presuppositions, etc. will indeed become *actualized* (literally, real-ized) in the body. The representations will become somatized and then govern our neurology. It is in this way that our *mind* becomes *muscle,* that ideas and concepts become *embodied* in us.

When that happens, we truly have *neuro-semantic reality.* When this happens in an unthinking way, it operates as a 'semantic reaction' and when conscious and mindful, a 'semantic response.' We are that kind of a class of life. So from our linguistic encoding of ideas, we develop our neuro-linguistic and neuro-semantic states. We then respond to the world via our neuro-linguistic and neuro-semantic mappings. As an attractor in a self-organizing system, this mapping molds, governs, determines, and controls our felt sense of 'reality.'

Prior to the cognitive behavioral model of NLP and the Meta-Model as an explanatory system, we might have very well called all of this 'magic.' We might have put it in a mental box of 'self-fulfilling prophecies.' Now, however, we recognize the structure of this magic. This opens our eyes to *how the 'magic' works.* Yet we also know more.

What else does it allow us to know and do?

It gives us access to all kinds of *incantations of growth, potential, sanity, and resourcefulness.* How? By giving us a way to use the same languaging processes in our nervous system-and-brain. The same processes by which we create 'black' magic which curses, defeats, sickens, toxifies, and destroys us—*the same languaging processes* give us the power to create 'white' magic by which we can bless, strength, and empower, make life whole and sound.

Misunderstanding 'Ill-formedness'

The Meta-Model speaks about, and focuses on, 'semantic ill-formedness.' This refers to the magic of mind that encodes ill-formed maps via our words. This brings me to the interesting, but strange, version of the Meta-Model that Dennis Chong (1993) has created. While his expertise as a medical doctor shows up in his 1994 book, *The Knife Without Pain,* on using hypnotic communication for surgery, his attempt at updating the NLP communication model leaves much to be desired. Mostly he seemed to take the phrase, 'semantically ill-formed' to mean something really 'bad.' And his bugaboo is the cause—effect distinction. His reading led him to think that Bandler and Grinder "denounced" cause—effect (p. 105).

This misunderstanding of what an ill-formed representation meant in TG and how NLP has used it as a way of testing for more enhancing structures, led him to write off *causation* as a totally useless concept. 'Causal modeling' he wrote 'is a complete mismatch of the territory' (p. 168). He goes further when he asserts in his own denunciations against causation:

> "... it has been clearly shown that a system based on the structure of Y → X is the condition for a mad world." (p. 231)

Well, don't tell that to architects, engineers, designers, etc. Scientists everywhere use the concept of 'causation' to great effects even though *philosophically* we recognize that it's not real, but only a concept. Newtonian physics, which mostly uses linear causation, has enabled us to experience the scientific revolution of the nineteenth and twentieth centuries. It has empowered us to build bridges, skyscrapers, engines, tools, cars, trains, planes, etc. It has allowed us to model billiard playing, sports, and many other fields involving movement, change, speed, etc.

This misunderstanding led Chong to conclude that every 'why' question must also be bad and inevitably lead to 'blame.' Now certainly asking existential *why* questions that invite a negative framing, can create semantic distress.

> "Why am I this way?" "Why can't I get my act together?" "Why is she such a snot?" "Why can't things go better for me?" etc.

'Why' questions do frequently lead to blaming and accusing. And true enough, many people ask *why* questions in order to escape responsibility.

"Why did you do that to me?" "Why can't you learn to think before you speak?"

In this, I agree with Chong on his general emphasis about not asking 'why.' Yet there are other kinds of why questions, *why questions* that increase our resourcefulness and enable us to create very empowering maps.

Intentional Why: Why do you want that? What will that do for you?

Value Why: Why do you feel that's so important? Why do you care about it as you do and invest so much of yourself into it?

Explanation Why: Why do things fall to the ground when I release them? Why does it seem that the sun moves through the sky?

Causation or Source Why: Why do you repeatedly undermine your success in that way? Why do you frame things as you do today?

Summary

- As the Meta-Model has grown and evolved over the years it has dropped its Transformational Grammar and therapeutic beginnings and has become a more general model of how language works its magic in our minds and bodies.
- The changes in the model have made it more streamlined and user-friendly. It has given us charts and diagrams and a set of distinctions and questions.

Chapter 10

The Evolution of Magic Part II:

The Model Dresses Up for Business

The usefulness of any model depends on how it is actually used, what people do with it, and how it changes or becomes refined over the years. The Meta-Model began as a communication tool, modeled from therapists and for therapists. It was intended for therapeutic communications. It soon outgrew that.

It began as a TG tool for distinguishing the transformational levels and using the transformational rules for modeling how meaning is transformed from level to level. But it soon outgrew *that.*

In this chapter, I will conclude the evolution of magic with a look at how it fits business, how it moves up and down the levels of thought, enables us to create new generalizations and set new meta-state frames.

The Business Precision Model

Sometime after Bandler and Grinder went their separate ways (1981), John Grinder teamed up with Michael McMaster and created a fascinating version that both reduced and expanded the Meta-Model. They designated it the *Precision Model* (1983/1993).

They designed this particular adaptation of the Meta-Model for the context of business and to be used by management. They offered it as both a model and a set of procedures for managers when seeking to obtain the highest quality of information possible. They sought to provide a "systematic way of controlling the quality of the language information" (p. 11) and to provide "information engineering skills" (p. 179). If all of this sounds dry and technical, that's the tone of their book. It's strictly business.

In re-designing the Meta-Model, they engineered the *Precision Model* to allow managers to accomplish several purposes:

1) Gather the highest quality of information.
2) Ask explicit questions by which they could obtain the precise information needed by directly responding to language cues. They called these 'Pointers.'
3) Determine the level of quality needed in a given context by using 'Frames' and 'Frame Procedures.'
4) Use various frames for managing the process of moving from present state to desired state.
5) Learn numerous procedures that maintain the frames to guarantee efficiency.

From these objectives, they engineered the *Precision Model* and equipped it with three sets of tools: Frames, Procedures, and Pointers. The *Pointers* reduce the Meta-Model to five linguistic distinctions: unspecified nouns, unspecified verbs, modal operators, universal quantifiers, and comparative deletions. They described this model as a set of "tools to engineer information flow channels" (p. 30) and the Meta-Model distinctions as "precision tools" or "technology" for converting low grade information into "high quality information necessary for precise planning and execution in business" (p. 45).

In *translating* the therapy-dominated language of the Meta-Model for business contexts, Grinder and McMaster created a lot of new terminology. For instance, they labeled the Meta-Model distinctions *'pointers'* and the effect of tracking from low grade quality to high grade quality as *'blockbusting'* (busting a block of over-generalized information). This enabled them to present the Meta-Model in the greatly reduced format of:

- 1st pointer: Noun Blockbuster (Unspecified Noun, Referential Index)
- 2nd pointer: Verb Blockbuster (Unspecified Verb)
- 3rd pointer: Universal Blockbuster (Universal Quantifiers)
- 4th pointer: The Comparator (Comparative Deletions)
- 5th pointer: Boundary Crossing (Modal Operators)

In this re-doing of the Meta-Model, Grinder and McMaster called the linguistic markers "the special language markers." For a Comparator, they suggest the *Difference Procedure* by asking, "What is the difference between...?"

While this facet of the precision model *reduced* the Meta-Model and limited the distinctions, the next set of tools expanded the Meta-Model. In doing so, it introduces meta-level phenomena for governing language and experience, namely, *Frames or Contexts* (anticipating the current developments in Cognitive Linguistics and Neuro-Semantics). In this way, the Precision Model delivers two kinds of tools:

> "... a set of Frames which identify and establish the context or boundary conditions within which information is being elicited, and a set of Precision Model questions which develops the high quality information within that context." (ibid., p. 25)

Grinder and McMaster presented three basic Frames with six Procedures for maintaining the frames:

1) *Outcome Frame*
   The outcome frame identifies and establishes the desired target state. It is a verbal mapping of the outcome which the participants want to achieve. The outcome provides a context for focusing resources. It also provides an explicit standard of relevance and efficiency within which to organize information.

2) *Backtrack Frame*
   The backtrack frame refers to the mechanism by which we can review or trace the development of information maps relevant to the outcome. We can use it to verify a shared map of understandings and to establish a context for the next step. In backtracking we rephrase things in order to precisely summarize a development of understanding.

3) *As If Frame*
   The 'as if' frame establishes a contrary-to-fact "context or frame in which the desired information or behavior then becomes available" (p. 134). Here we ask questions as if we do not know the meaning of a term or phrase.

"Let me pretend to be naive about this margins-inventory situation. Specifically, see how many ways you can describe to me that this problem might be solved."

Then, within these Frames, they offered six Procedures—processes for touching our business lives with the magic of efficiency:

1) *Evidence Question*
"How will you know? What will serve as evidence to you?" These evidence questions provide a powerful organizing device to a skilled manager to enable him or her to "get in a principled way contextualized to the point information" (p. 69). Present State/Desired State Frame is the most pervasive organizing principle in the model. "What will you accept as evidence?"

2) *Difference Question*
"What is the difference between the present state and the desired state?" This specifies the steps and stages needed to move from one place to another. These stages involve: *defining the difference, pathfinding, surveying,* and *evaluating.* Re-processing the Difference Procedure over and over focuses precisely the 'problem' as the 'difference' between present state and desired state.

Pathfinding describes the creative and brainstorming process of coming up with alternatives choices. The manager seeks primarily to tap into all of the available information in the individual maps and to co-create with the group a richer and fuller shared map. In pathfinding we move continually to more fully specified verbs until we achieve adequate precision.

Surveying refers to filling in the details of a path selected for reaching a certain outcome.

Evaluating makes a choice among the paths (alternatives) surveyed that will lead one to the desired outcome state. Here one makes a choice about a specific pathway.

3) *Efficiency Challenge*
"What factors do you know which will eliminate this potential course of action?" "Will this work?" This prevents wasting time on non-feasible alternatives.

4) *Relevancy Frame*
"Is this relevant?" "How is it relevant to what we're seeking to do?" This frame is designed to directionalize a discussion toward an outcome in a principled way. It does so by keeping the conversation on track and preventing 'a veritable avalanche of free associations.' A manager should challenge relevancy immediately and courteously.

 "Would you please connect that question with the outcome we're presently working on?"
 "I don't understand the relevance of that remark with respect to what we're doing here right now—please explain ..."
 "... your last statement throws me—how is that pertinent to what this part of the meeting is about?"

5) *Recycle Frame*
"How else might we increase funds for investment?" "How else might we improve the quality of our product?" This frame enables us to loop back through a word or phrase that we find 'so rich with potential hidden material' that we find it profitable to keep returning to enrich our map (p. 130). "How else might we ... [supply the verb]?"

6) *Missing Link Procedure*
"How will that achieve what we want?" This adapts the relevancy challenge in order to develop new branches of pathfinding.

By incorporating frames and procedures into the *Precision Model,* Grinder and McMaster transcended a logical level to expand the Meta-Model with some higher level linguistic phenomena. Cognitive semantics and grammar speak about this in terms of *domains, contexts,* and *categories.* This allows us to move up from the *content* of a conversation between persons where imprecision and vagueness occurs and to set some magical frames (see

Figure 10.1: Precision Model Frames

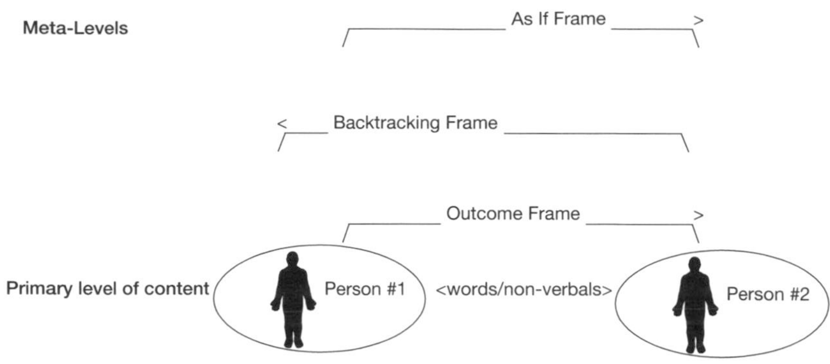

Figure 10.1). This allows us to set and invoke larger *frames-of-reference*. We meta-state the content with thoughts-and-feelings about *outcome* (where we want to go and what we want to achieve). We meta-state the situation further by bringing the other frames to perform other feats of magic, namely, *Backtracking* (refreshing our representations of where we have been), and *As If* (pretending and imagining future possibilities).

With the Outcome Frame, we are able to set a larger domain which allows us to *think strategically* as we use the communication questions. These enable us to step continually out of the content frame to check where we stand with the person (or persons) with whom we're communicating. Not knowing where we stand in such a process (whether in business, parenting, negotiating, etc.) makes it almost impossible to know how to maintain appropriate context. "Information is precise only if it is in context." (p. 145).

> "The Precision Model demands that you know where you are in the process and provides the tools enabling you to know. Failure to clearly differentiate where you are, that is, to be constantly aware of the context, often results in inappropriate responses to comments or information." (p. 143)
>
> "The Precision Model not only enables a manager to know where he is at any time in the process of problem solving, it insists that he knows where he is. Maintaining context and specificity will be accomplished only if a manager knows where he is in the process." (p. 163)

Magic Flexibility

We have seen how we generalize to create our maps and the linguistic magic that we can perform by indexing the specifics of our generalizations. Typically, in Meta-Modeling we 'chunk down' to details. We move *down* the scale of specificity-to-abstraction as we elicit more and more specifics using the questions that explore and challenge a mental formatting of the world. Early on Bandler and Grinder noted that the overall effect of this leads to *de-hypnotizing* because it reconnects a person to the experiences out of which the map arose.

Zink and Munshaw (1995) noted this reductionistic power of the Meta Model and described it in a paper, "Collapsing Generalizations and the Other Half of NLP." Their overall critique urged that we should not only engage in reduction, but should also move up the scale in generalizing. Doing so is very important for creating new generalizations in the form of beliefs. Yet in offering this critique, they seemed to have drawn several conclusions about the Meta-Model that I think are unfounded.

> "That the Meta-Model is a deductive tool should be extremely obvious, as its primary function is to reason from the general to the specific. It deconstructs generalizations; it roots out distortions and recovers deletions." (p. 20)

Because it reduces, Zink and Munshaw argued that NLP has developed too much of a reductionistic attitude and has developed too little use of induction in building up generalizations. This complaint certainly has some validity. One of the ways they sought to demonstrate it was by suggesting that reductionism has contributed to fewer and fewer new developments in NLP during the 1990s.

> "We think we know why there has not been more truly generative change in the field of NLP in recent years ... the major problem is: an over-reliance on *reductionistic thinking and paradigms."* (p. 17)

> "Many NLP procedures—the V-A-K Strategies Model, the Sensory Submodalities Model, and Meta Model of Language in particular—are intended to reduce Map scale." (p. 24)

Without question, the Meta-Model certainly focuses, at least primarily, in chunking down, yet it also contains processes by which we chunk up as well, chunk up and create new generalizations. The magic goes *up* as well as *down*. Bandler and Grinder illustrate this in the transcriptions entitled, "In the Vortex" (Ch. 5). By just meta-modeling a client, they have the therapist saying the following:

> "Let me get this straight: you're saying that your mother's not noticing what you did for her means that she wasn't interested in you?" (p. 127)

They commented, "The client again verifies the generalization involved." This *verifying generalizations* describes an important purpose and process of the Meta-Model. This takes a person *up the scale of abstraction* as the person thinks *about* the generalization and then sets a frame of validation over it. Doing this involves a meta-stating process.

> T: "Ralph, have you ever had the experience of someone's doing something for you and you didn't notice until after they pointed it out to you?"

> T: "The therapist decides to challenge the client's generalization—here he chooses to begin the challenge by shifting the referential indices ... and therefore, the generalizations are transformed." (pp. 127–8)

Here we have two additional meta-modeling processes—we have *shifting referential indices* and *transforming generalizations.* When we shift references and apply a statement back to the speaker, it not only challenges the statement, but frequently invites the speaker to construct the generalization in such a way that it *applies* the statement to him or herself. They may have used a map which they simply had never applied to themselves. This invites the speaker to create a new generalization. Sometimes this creates great insights as the person accesses counter-examples to their other generalization. The result? The magic of a new, more balanced generalization.

> T: "Did you not notice what they had done because you weren't interested in them?"

> R: "No, I just didn't notice ..." (p. 128)

Here the client *drew a new conclusion*. He moved up a level of thinking, and in doing so this accomplished two things. It began to deframe the old generalization and it transformed the old one into a new one. The magic tore out the old ideas that had been mapped about relationships and the new magic stimulated the creation of more effective mapping.

In the Meta-Modeling that followed in the original text (*The Structure of Magic*), we have an example of a therapist shifting referential index time and again. Each time it had the effect of eliciting a new and more empowering generalization.

The same occurred when the therapist challenged the Modal Operator. The client said that he didn't communicate his love directly. The therapist asked a Meta-Modeling question,

> "What prevents you from telling her?"

The person eventually answered that "nothing stopped him," and that he guessed he could. In saying this, he thereby built a new generalization—a new map that allowed him to answer in this way. This offers another means of evoking a person to 'chunk' up to a new understanding using one of the communication magic questions.

> "What stops you? ... The therapist uses the technique of asking for the generalization, the outcome of the client's actions which he finds scary." (p. 134)

Here Bandler and Grinder demonstrated Meta-Modeling as *asking for the generalization.* Interestingly enough, it evoked the following response, a response that indicates a logical level shift.

> "Nothing, that's what's so scary. (laughing)" (p. 134)

Note the meta-stating response. In the first statement ("Nothing") the speaker acknowledges that he could not find or create a generalization that would now fit his model of the world. This indicates a new generalization. For this 'nothing' signifies the existence of a 'no-thing,' or as we might say, 'a blank.' As he moves up to a higher level to consider 'what stops him,' he has become aware that 'no-thing' stops him.

Then, *to* that awareness, he immediately experiences another thought/emotion. "That's what's so scary." This indicates another upward move as his consciousness now *reflects back* onto its previous product (the no-thing of 'nothing') and entertains a lighthearted scariness *about* it. This is the magic of meta-stating. What is the quality of this higher level *fear*, this fear of realizing that nothing was stopping him from just expressing his love? Well that depends upon how he has framed that idea.

All of these are *meta-jumps within the Meta-Model,* and I have drawn them out here because some trainers and writers have apparently overlooked these *chunking up* facets in the Meta-Model. Overlooking these has led them to think about the Meta-Model as only involving reductionistic processes. Yet the Meta-Model itself does not *only* reduce and deframe. Certainly the challenging questions of the Meta-Model ask for more specifics, index time, place, person, context, etc. Yet the model itself also chunks up to create new frames. It shows how we abstract from the experiences and ideas to create higher level beliefs.

Meta-modeling involves summarizing and articulating the unarticulated generalization that the person uses as his or her presupposition. We see this demonstrated in "Transcript 2" (*The Structure of Magic,* pp. 134–153). When the client said that she "kinda hinted" to her roommates to let them know what she wanted, the therapist asked, "How do you kinda hint?"

She said, "I do things for them."

> "Then, since you do things for them, they're suppose to know that you want them to do something in return?"
>
> Comment: "The therapist decides to check to see whether the client will verify this generalization ... by repeating the entire generalization to the client." (p. 142)

Here, *articulating a presupposition,* by fully expressing a person's generalization and then inviting him or her to verify it, moves a person up to the generalization, and then above the generalization to run an ecology check on it. In this case, it worked. First the client said "It sounds sorta funny when you say it like that." This indicates a meta-level awareness of an evaluation *about* the generalization. Specifically, the person continued to comment *about* the statement.

> "Like I'm not being honest or something, but you just can't go around demanding things all the time or people will not want to give them to you." (p. 143)

Moving to a meta-level, via this meta-modeling type of questioning, evoked *an even larger level generalization,* the person's operating presupposition for relating and communicating. It meta-stated the client in an open-ended way. In fact, shortly thereafter, the therapist discovered that this statement brought them to *the very edge of her map,* and of course, that's one of the best places to touch people with magic—right at the edge of their maps. They are so receptive there!

> T: "What prevents you?
>
> B: "I just can't, ... I JUST CAN'T."
>
> T: "Beth, what would happen if you asked for something when you want it?"
>
> B: "I can't because people will feel pushed around if I ask for things from them." (pp. 146–7)

Then *shifting referential index* again, the therapist asked:

> "Are you aware that ... you came to me and asked if I would work with you?" (pp. 148–9)

In commenting on this, Bandler and Grinder wrote, "the therapist relativized the client's generalization." As soon as she recognized that, he then applied it back to her situation. As he did, it enabled Beth to create a new and more enhancing generalization about herself and about speaking more assertively about her requests. All of this illustrates the inductive power and usage of the Meta-Model.

Meta-Model Generalizing

In my opinion, Zink and Munshaw (1995) have generated another misunderstanding of the Meta-Model. Defining a 'generalization' as "the act or process of deriving or inducing a general conception, principle, or inference from particulars" (Oxford English Dictionary), they concluded that the definition of generalization was wrong as given in *The Structure of Magic* (p. 216).

> "A generalization is NOT 'the process by which a specific experience comes to represent the entire category of which it is a member'." (p. 21)

By way of contrast, they explained their analysis as follows:

> "That's an entirely different breed of cat and is more properly called *categorization*—reasoning by category. A generaliz-ation describes or defines the essence of a class, while categorization merely stands in for any member of a class. Categories remain concrete and literal while generalizations are figurative and symbolic because they are abstractions."

Lakoff (1987), an earlier proponent of Transformational Grammar who later developed Generative Semantics and then went on to work in the field of Cognitive Linguistics, wrote a book on category distinctions. In it he enumerated *several kinds of categories,* although he primarily made the distinction between the classical theory of categories (Aristotelian) and prototype theory (developed by Eleanor Rosch). He analyzed the prototype theory of categories as involving several features including family resemblances, extendable boundaries, central and non-central members, goodness-of-fit, radical structures, idealized cognitive model, etc. In other words, we have many different kinds of 'reasoning by category,' and not just one monolithic kind of 'categorization,'especially the Aristotelian form of category alluded to.

The same holds true also for 'generalization.' We can distinguish different kinds and qualities of generalizing—generalizing at different levels of concreteness and abstraction. Synthesizing and distilling a number of instances of something (e.g. work situations) will lead to a 'generalization.' Using the Aristotelian classic definition of category, Zink and Munshaw conclude:

> "If the work Map contains the essence of multiple and varied work conditions then it is a generalization; should it be reducible to a single instance, it is a categorization." (1995, p. 22)

However, to use Rosch's prototype theory of categories, the first instance simply articulates the heart of the generalization, while the second offers an example of the generalization that has such "goodness-of-example" that it operates as a prototype. The multi ordinality of the term 'generalization' allows for this much flexibility in meaning. For me, this completely calls into question the following judgment:

> "One of these principles, Surface/Deep Structure, holds that our Maps can be reduced to single concrete examples. If this is true, then the Surface/Deep Structure concept precludes abstract thought." (p. 22)

I do not buy this as the original intention in *The Structure of Magic* regarding the Meta-Model nor in the original Chomskian model of Transformational Grammar. Asking "specifically what, when, who, where, etc." does not *necessarily* imply that "our Maps can be reduced to single concrete examples." It only implies that asking such sends a map-maker back to his or her internal references. It is asking for behavioral equivalences of the abstractions. Doing this sometimes deframes the maps because the person will not be able to find specific concrete cases. At other times, it confirms the maps inasmuch as the person does find some prototypical instances. This enables the person to explore the degree their reference supports the generalization, the degree it does not, to look for characteristics left out, distortions, etc.

Meta-Stating Power inside the Meta-Model

If the Meta-Model and the meta-modeling challenging questions not only 'chunk' down, but also 'chunk' up, then such questions can evoke and facilitate *meta-states.* I've mentioned this earlier, now I'll explain what that means.

Suppose someone inquires:

> Is there actual *meta-stating* in the original Meta-Model of Bandler and Grinder?
>
> Do we have any examples of *meta-stating* in the book *The Structure of Magic?*

Yes, definitely. Actually, we have already seen this in *The Structure of Magic* text. We saw it in the previous exchange. That dialogue illustrates how the meta-modeling questions actually encourages a person to 'go meta' in order to access a meta-level state of awareness. For example,

> "What stops you?"
>
> "Nothing, that's what's so scary. (laughing)." (p. 134)

If *meta-stating* is going to a higher level of thoughts and emotions than our current state, then when this speaker accesses a mental state of awareness that 'nothing stops me,' this state of *possibility* evokes yet a higher state, *fear of that potential.*

In addition, consider this next quotation which models the meta-level shifting that Richard and John found in Satir's work.

> "When you ask questions like, 'How do you feel about that?' (whatever *that* might be) you are, in fact, asking your client for a fuller representation (than even the Deep Structure) of your client's experience of the world. And what you are doing by asking this particular question is asking for what you know is a necessary component of the client's reference structure. ..."

Here, at the very beginning of the development of the NLP model, Bandler and Grinder address the two directions that consciousness can take.

1) First, at the primary level, it moves outward to the world.
2) Then, it moves back and onto the experience and products of consciousness (i.e. the thoughts, emotions, etc. that we produce). This creates a meta-state.

In the first case we experience our thoughts-and-emotions *going out* to the world beyond us—to the events, experiences, and words that we encounter there. When that happens, our consciousness engages the world, it wraps itself around the information that we find there, it then represents that data, processes it, and so responds to it.

In the second case, we experience our thoughts-and-emotions as *reflecting back onto themselves.* This accesses our self-reflexive consciousness. As we experience this back-tracking of mind, we move up a logical level. Now our thoughts-and-feelings no longer take notice of things 'out there,' instead they take cognizance of the things 'inside.' In the first, we experience thoughts-and-emotions *about* something external. In the second, we experience thoughts-and-emotions *about* something internal.

"How do you feel *about* your feelings *about* this experience?"

In the *Meta-States Model* (Hall, 1995/2000), a meta-state is simply *a state about another state,* hence a mind-body state that has reference to a previous mind-body state. A meta-state jumps logical levels. We move upward to think *about* our thinking, emoting, experiencing, etc. This moves us to a meta-level of awareness. We simultaneously transcend our own thoughts and include them inside of a new frame. This brings us to a new level. We experience meta-level phenomena: thoughts about thoughts, feelings about feelings, 'second-order abstractions' (Korzybski), our reactions to our reactions, or what Bandler and Grinder (following Satir) called 'self-esteem.' They wrote,

> "This new question, which is characteristic of Satir's work, is: 'How do you feel about your feelings about what is happening?'

> This is essentially a request on the part of the therapist for the client to say how he feels about his reference structure—his model of the world ..." (p. 160–1)

To illustrate, Bandler and Grinder provided an illustration of a client upset and angry because Paul "just doesn't care about cleaning up the house." Upon discovering that Paul directly and clearly stated this (so it is not mind-reading), the dialogue continues:

> "How do you feel about his telling you he doesn't care?
>
> I feel angry.
>
> How do you feel about feeling angry?
>
> How do I feel about feeling angry?
>
> Yes, how do you feel about feeling angry at Paul?
>
> Well, I don't feel so good about it." (1975, 162–3)

Bandler and Grinder recognized the strangeness of this question. So to explain, "How do you feel *about* that?", they wrote:

> "The therapist ... chooses to shift levels, asking the client about her feelings about her image of herself in her model of the world ... The client appears to be initially confused by the therapist's question requiring her to shift levels. This is a common reaction to such level shifts in our experience ..."

There are several things to note about this. First, this Meta-Modeling questioning obviously *chunks up* and moves a person to a higher level. It shifts logical levels as the questions facilitate the listener to move up the scale of abstraction and to create new generalizations at a higher level. So as this meta-function creates ever higher levels of meta-states, we see the meta-magic in the model. So yes, there is meta-stating language in the Meta-Model, even though Bandler and Grinder knew nothing about the Meta-States model at the time.

Second, something seemed to have prevented Bandler and Grinder, at that point in their formulations, from recognizing all of this as a *meta-stating process.* What? It was what Virginia Satir told them. Satir had said that any answer to the question, "How do you feel *about* feeling X?" results in articulating the person's 'self-esteem.' Notice in the following quotations that Bandler and Grinder quoted Satir on this in both volumes of *The Structure of Magic.*

> "Changes at this level—the level of self-esteem—are extremely important, since a person's self-image affects the way a person organizes his entire experience or reference structure. Therefore, changes at this level of structure permeate the client's entire model of the world." (1975, 162–3)

> "This question is extensively used by Virginia Satir in her dynamic therapy—she describes this question as an excellent way to tap the client's self-esteem (the client's feelings about his feelings)—a part of the client closely connected with his ability to cope ..." (1976, 57)

This understanding blinded them from seeing the meta-question ("How do you feel *about* that?") as moving a person into all of the phenomena that emerge in the meta-levels of the mind. So as they unquestioningly accepted the assumption that this *reference structure* of a person's reality, a meta-level structure, which *"permeates the client's entire model of the world"* as a definition of 'self-esteem'—they failed to see these levels.

The Meta-States Model recognizes the structure of 'self-esteem' as one of the many meta-level phenomena that we construct as we move *above and beyond* our first experience to create ever-higher frames. Multiple other meta-level phenomena and structures similarly come into being when consciousness reflects back onto itself.

What does this mean?

It means that we can use the meta-modeling challenging questions not only for reducing and deframing impoverishing maps, we can also use them to chunk up to create new enriching generalizations. This occurs regularly whenever we ask:

"And what stops or prevents you?"

"How do you feel about experiencing those thoughts or feelings?"

"How would you like to think-and-feel about that?"

"What does it mean to you when you think or feel about X?"

Such meta-modeling elicits a person to reflect back on the products or experience of previous states, thereby evoking or creating a *meta-state experience*. It leads to shifting upward to higher logical levels, to transcend and include the previous states.

Summary

- Numerous insights, additions, re-organizations, usages, and extensions have occurred to the Meta-Model over the years. The extensions of the model mentioned here have obviously enriched it, expanded it, and given us more ways to do *magic* in our minds-and-emotions-and-bodies.
- But what about additional language distinctions to the original ones? What additional extensions to the Meta-Model distinctions themselves have arisen? We now turn to this subject.

Chapter 11

Magic from the Wizard Korzybski

Because we are a class of life that uses symbols, language enables us to perform magic-like effects. In previous chapters we have seen how the communication magic model of the Meta-Model (Chapters 5–8) provides us with specific understandings about *how* we can do 'magical' things with our words. After all, by languaging we create models of the world and these models govern our perceptions, feelings, thinking, acting, skills, expertise, etc.

The linguistic distinctions enable us to recognize and examine not only the content of our maps, but also their *form and structure.* They allow us to examine the effect of structure on our everyday lives. Also, as our constructed realities (or maps) affect our bodies, neurology, emotions, behaviors, and skills (the 'magic' we experience), alteration of the map inevitably transforms our experiences. There is much practical everyday value and usefulness of the Meta-Model:

- It gives us a way to listen to, and respond to, *everyday linguistic expressions*.
- It gives us a way to use everyday statements as a pathway to the mapping processes of the persons who generated them.
- The *linguistic distinctions* give us a path of language for hearing and recognizing in anyone his or her model of the world. Tuning our hearing to various *linguistic markers* we can actually detect, identify, and recognize semantic ill-formedness as well as well-formedness.

What's so important about that?

Our ability to detect the *structure* in a mental map (whether ill-formed or well-formed) equips us with some *especially empowering understandings*.

What?

First, we get an immediate awareness of, and *feel for*, the Map/Territory distinction. Then, almost simultaneously, we recognize that human 'problems' arise partly, or even solely, from poorly constructed maps. When we know that, we shift our focus in how we engage in problem-solving and responding. This leads to the marvelously useful consequence of *not* needing to get mad at our map or at someone else's map. After all, "It's just a map."

And, if it is 'just a map,' then we are not up against unchangeable genetic pathology. The problems that we experience and address, are expressions of poor mapping. *They are mapping problems.* This means that the problem with people lies not in them, but in their maps. People are not 'the problem.' 'The map' is the problem.

Imagine the difference this will make when asked, "What's the problem?" The problem is always some map—a mental or emotional map. So why get mad at people, fear people, feel disgusted with people, etc., when ultimately 'the problem' lies in *how* a person has mapped things? This changes a lot of things. It means that we can truly take a compassionate approach to people (and toward ourselves) when driven by stupid or toxic ideas. After all, *they* are not the problem. The problem lies in, and arises from, their ideas. This now allows us to *align with them* against the non-enhancing, non-empowering, non-productive ideas, and so enables us powerfully to influence them.

This understanding of the Map/Territory distinction has allowed NLP to adopt a very positive and person affirming approach. From the beginning Bandler and Grinder announced that "People are not broken; they work perfectly well." If certain persons produce schizophrenic speech and behavior, they do so regularly, systematically, and methodically. There's nothing wrong with them. As long as they run the schizophrenic program or map, they will continue skillfully to produce schizophrenia. The question is *not*, "How are you broken?" or "What's wrong with you?" The question is, "How do you do that?" "Teach me systematically to create those effects."

This alerts us to a navigational fact. Our maps can be inadequate, harmful, and even toxic. We often leave out important data. We often adopt or create inaccurate and unuseful generalizations about things. They may not correspond with the territory at all, or so poorly that they are nearly worthless. We often alter or transform structures, relationships, meanings (semantics), associations, etc. in our mapping so that they undermine and sabotage us. We often start from assumptions that make our experience more painful and unproductive. Whatever the 'problem,' more typically it is a mapping problem. Somehow we have simply not mapped something in a way that promotes our well-being.

But now we can!

How? By openly examining our maps to make sure they are *semantically well-formed*. We can examine them in terms of their construction, their form, their usefulness, etc. We can quality control our maps to make sure that they really will help us navigate various facets of life. If 'the menu is not the meal,' and we have an abbreviated menu, we can expand the menu choices. If we have a really old menu, we can update it. If the menu has become folded, smeared, or dirtied so we cannot even read it—we can replace it.

The Meta-Model entirely avoids the epistemological questions about the 'truth conditions' of the map. Rather than evaluating whether we have 'true' or 'false' maps, it focuses more pragmatically on other concerns:

- *Will our maps guide us to the places we want to go?* (i.e. healthy relationships, success at work, ability to achieve important goals, personal health and vitality, bonding, conflict resolution, etc.)
- *Do our maps have a structure that basically accords with the territory?* (Korzybski said that "structure and structure only" comprises the essence of 'knowledge.')
- *Do we have enough flexibility and openness in our maps to keep updating them as circumstances and events change?* (Rigid maps carved in stone will eventually become dated and un-useful.

In a process universe, we need flexible maps that allow us to keep adding to knowledge and to take feedback into account.)
- *Will our maps allow us to navigate effectively in the territory that we want to move in?* (We need to run an 'ecology check' on the effectiveness of our map. This quality controls the map for ecological balance. As we do this, we add 'effectiveness' as a criteria to 'accuracy of structure.')
- *Do our maps allow us to reflexively look at the maps themselves?* (Do we even recognize our thoughts, emotions, values, beliefs, etc. as maps so that we can evaluate our maps, de-construct maps, and re-map as needed? To do so keeps our mapping processes as an open system rather than a closed one.)

Extending the Meta-Model

The 13 distinctions that we have detailed in the Meta-Model offer linguistic distinctions about modeling, map-making, and well-formed structures. Yet they do not express the last work about such. Bandler and Grinder noted this at the beginning of their work in *The Structure of Magic,*

> "... our Meta-Model covers only a portion of the verbal communication which is possible ..." (1975, p. 107)

> "... we suspect that some of the research currently being conducted in Generative Semantics ... will be particularly useful in expanding the Meta-Model further." (p. 109)

Given this, what *additional distinctions* can we find, identify, and develop to *expand* the Meta-Model? What other typical linguistic distinctions occur in our everyday expressions of thought and ideas that can also cue us to ill-formed structures of deletions, generalizations, distortions, and presuppositions?

I began my own search for *missing Meta-Model distinctions* in 1990 as I engaged in an in-depth exploration of the foundational work of neuro-linguistics in the classic work of Alfred Korzybski, *Science and Sanity: An Introduction to Non-Aristotelian Systems and General Semantics* (1933/ 1994). After having presented the Meta-Model as part of the NLP training, and researched into Korzybski, I published a series of articles in *Anchor Point* (an International NLP popular magazine) on the missing Meta-Model distinctions (1992). These were later published in German (*Multimind—NLP aktuell* magazine) and were also translated into other languages, Russian, Spanish, etc. That work ultimately culminated in my doctoral studies and dissertation and a book, *Languaging* (1996). I have replicated some of that work here, as I have updated and expanded the Meta-Model.

Nine Additional Distinctions

While it is true that Bandler and Grinder built their neuro-linguistic model utilizing many of the ideas cultivated from Korzybski, they did not bring over many of his linguistic distinctions into NLP. They actually did not even refer to his *extensional devices* that he considered critical for both science and sanity.

Why not? I think primarily because of Grinder's Transformational Grammar background from which they took the majority of their distinctions. After all, TG was the linguistic model of the day. They may have very well passed over the crucial distinctions of Korzybski by not having actually read *Science and Sanity*. There's some indication of that. And yet General Semantics fits more with the current developments in Cognitive Linguistics.

As founder of General Semantics, Korzybski focused primarily on *neuro-linguistic distinctions* that empower us to avoid *confusing* map and territory. As an engineer, his genius went toward building a new language system that would offer a structure in accordance with both the territory and the human nervous system. As he studied mathematical systems, physics, biology, neurology, etc., he developed a vision of promoting the human sciences which he called 'human engineering,' that he would base on a *new Non-Aristotelian system of language.* He called this General Semantics. The 'General' here refers to a larger or meta-level frame about semantic structures. It was his pre-Bateson term for 'meta.' Thinking about General Semantics as *Meta Semantics* will give you an understanding of his focus.

The non-Aristotelian system of Korzybski counters the 'laws of thoughts' which Aristotle made explicit and upon which classical 'reasoning,' 'logic' and 'categorizing' depended. Korzybski vigorously disagreed with these so-called Aristotelian 'laws of thought' (as do most theorists today). Of Aristotle's three 'Laws' that he proposed govern reality, thought, and linguistics, we have the following:

1) *The Law of Identity:*
   In Reality:
      "Whatever is, is."
      "A thing is what it is."
   In Linguistics:
      "A word means what it means."
      "A term's meaning must remain constant in any discourse."
2) *The Law of Contradiction:*
   In Reality:
      "A thing is not what it is not."
      "Whatever does not exist is non-existent."
   In Linguistics:
      "A word does not mean what it does not mean."
      "Two negatives make an affirmative."
3) *The Law of Excluded Middle:*
   In Reality:
      "A thing either exists or it does not exist."
      "A thing cannot have contradictory properties."
   In Linguistics:
      "A proposition is either true or false."
      "Two contradictory propositions cannot both be true."
      "A class is either included in another class, or it is not."

Korzybski developed General Semantics to offer a non-Aristotelian system of languaging and theorizing about external reality and our linguistic mapping of it. This led him to posit the following as contrasts with the old Aristotelian system and the foundation of accurate mapping and languaging.

1) *The Principle of Non-Identity*
   We live in a process world comprised *not* of 'things' or substance, but of energy manifestations, patterns, structure, and

communication. So ultimately, nothing is the 'same.' No two things are the same, there are always differences. Even the same thing doesn't stay the same over time. This makes 'sameness' a pseudo-concept. External reality consists of 'a dance of electrons' while internal reality of communication, messages, patterns, and differences. We can only say, "For the sake of discussion, let's assume A will remain constant."

2) *The Principle of Contradiction*
To be more accurate we rephrase the Aristotelian principle, "A thing can simultaneously be classified as A and not-A depending upon the observer and the observer's purpose." An apple 'is' an apple *and* one bite out of it makes it a non-apple *to some degree.* Ten bites makes it even more of a non-apple. The point (or bite) at which the 'apple' became a non-apple is a *matter of degree.* If twenty bites makes it 100% a non-apple, then one bite makes it *less* of an apple as it moves it toward more of the non-apple class. 'Contradiction' is a function of our classifying, especially our either/or classifying that doesn't take degrees, grays, and fuzziness into account.

3) *The Principle of the Middles*
We eliminate the law of the excluded middles altogether and recognize the realms of grays, the fuzzy borders between things. "We can classify a thing as existing or not existing at a given time regarding a given context." We can evaluate a proposition as true and false given different levels of abstraction, contexts, times, observers, etc. Sometimes "both—and" more accurately describes things rather than "either/or."

As a *non-Aristotelian system,* NLP developed from Gregory Bateson and others using General Systems Theory, cybernetics, communication theory, and other disciplines. The Cognitive Revolution has similarly built its models on non-Aristotelian bases. Rosch (1975, 1977), Lakoff (1987), Lakoff and Johnson (1999), many current cognitive psychologists, and those in cognitive linguistics have similarly moved away from the old Aristotelian model and 'logics.' The Fuzzy Logic movement with its development of electronic equipment has introduced a whole realm of practical applications to fuzzy logic. The old classic theory portrayed logic as disembodied (hence not *neuro*-linguistic), transcendental (and therefore unaffected by an observer and not involving a performer), and absolute (hence not relative or context-dependent). Today we recognize 'logic' as psychological, embodied, observer-dependent, and therefore relative—relative to the body of knowledge, context, etc.

Extending the Meta-Model

The first 7 distinctions that follow come from Korzybski's General Semantics. As linguistic markers, they cue us about different ways that our language can be ill-formed and hinder us in mapping and engineering our neuro-linguistics and in communicating effectively.

> [As a point of historical note, Korzybski coined the phrase, 'neuro-linguistics' in his 1936 "Neuro-semantic and Neuro-linguistic Mechanisms of Extensionalization" published in the *American Journal of Psychiatry.* He also coined 'human engineering' in his 1921 book, *The Manhood of Humanity.* During the 1940s, he conducted general-semantic workshops that he called Neuro-Linguistic Trainings.]

Due to the length of this presentation, I have included the first 2 of these distinctions in this chapter, the next 5 in the next chapter, and then the last 2 in the following chapter. These additions to the Meta-Model enable us to work more magic as we work with language itself. These extend our tool box of neuro-linguistic markers.

Chapter 11:

1. Over/Under Defined Terms (O/U)
2. Delusional Verbal Splits (DVS)

Chapter 12:

3. Either/Or Phrases (E/O)
4. Multiordinality (M)
5. Static or Signal Words (SW)
6. Pseudo-Words (PW)
7. Identification (Id.)

Chapter 13:

8. Personalizing (Per.)
9. Metaphors (Mp)

Expanding the Meta-Model with these distinctions for more productive map-making, I have reformulated 7 Korzybskian distinctions using the Meta-Model format. I have packaged them in terms of neuro-linguistic *distinctions* and *questions*. First come the distinctions for detecting the structure of the mapping. Then come the questions to explore the poor map construction or ill-formed structures. This makes these distinctions explicit in a way that Korzybski did not. In this way, we can combine and synthesize these new and additional patterns to update the Meta-Model and identify more secrets for performing neuro-semantic magic.

The *distinctions* refer to the *language patterns* which indicate structures of mapping. These appear as the surface expressions or statements that we use as we communicate. Yet these forms often create conceptual limitations that impoverish our world.

To address this impoverishment, we question or challenge the linguistic structure. As we *meta-model,* we invite a person to re-connect to his or her *experiences* out of which the map arose and to re-map it more fully, appropriately, and usefully. We do this specifically by offering a question, response, or challenge that elicits from the person more specificity in indexing the referents or the construction of a more enhancing map. As meta-modeling engages a person's mapping processes, it activates unconscious processes. The early TG model called that the 'deep structure,' Cognitive Linguistics describe this as the over-arching hierarchies of 'cognitive domains' and 'matrixes of domains.' The meta-modeling process thereby initiates the magic of change.

[The following page numbers refer to *Science and Sanity* (1933/1994) unless otherwise indicated.]

1. Over/Under Defined Terms

Bandler and Grinder mentioned Korzybski and the role of 'extensional' and 'intensional' definitions in *The Structure of Magic, Vol. I*

(p. 56), although they (or a proof-reader) misspelled 'intensional,' confusing it with 'intentional.' When Korzybski described these two orientations, he labeled them *over/under defined terms.*

He said that we mainly over-define terms when we operate out of an *intensional orientation.* This means moving into the world assuming that our dictionary definition of terms offers a complete and satisfactory form of mapping.

> "We live, happy or unhappy, *by what actually amounts to a definition,* and not by the empirical, individual facts less coloured by semantic factors. When Smith$_1$ marries Smith$_2$, they most do so *by a kind of definition.* They have certain notions as to what 'man', 'woman', and 'marriage' 'are' *by definition.* They actually go through the performances and find that the Smith$_1$ and his wife, Smith$_2$, have unexpected likes, dislikes, and particularities—in general, characteristics and semantic reactions *not included* in their definition of the terms ... " (p. 415)

We have over/under defined most of our terms. We over-define (or over-limit) words *by intension* when we over-trust our formal verbal or dictionary definition. As we over-believe in our definition of the word as 'real,' we give it (in our mind) too much substance and concreteness. We under-define words by using too little *extension* (that is, failing to use sufficient specific facts and details that *extend* on out to actual referents which we can point to). This results in our generalizations becoming merely hypothetical (p. lii).

How does this relate to making a sane adjustment in the world of physical and psychological health, being effective in business, career, relationships, parenting, etc.? Korzybski noted that when we primarily orient ourselves in the world by intension, we create maladjustment. We then perceive, think, and evaluate reality by over-definitions, confusing our maps or 'verbalisms' with the territory. This invites us into the magical thinking that treats words as real as mac trucks and bagels.

Effective evaluating occurs when we *extensionalize.* We do this by pointing to the extensional facts. This operationalizes our terms. We create a better adjustment to things as we do so. This explains why the *deletion questions* in the Meta-Model work so magically to enrich our lives. As we become more specific, we index our concepts to specific people, times, places, and contexts. This interrupts the habit of over-generalizing which often shows up as the cognitive distortions of 'terriblizing,' 'awfulizing,' 'negative predictions of the future,' 'personalizing,' etc. (Albert Ellis, Rational-Emotive Therapy (1976).)

Consider what happens when a woman finds and marries 'a good husband.' What does this phrase regarding the conceptual linguistic reality ('a good husband') point to? It exists, totally and absolutely, *not* as something in the world, but as a *verbal definition* in the woman's mind. To the extent that she fails to recognize this, she sets herself up for disappointment and neurological shock. Ultimately, she will suffer some semantic reactions as she encounters the *extensional facts* (he snores, he leaves his dirty clothes around, etc.) of the particular man. Then, she will find the meal very different from what she thought the menu offered.

This also occurs with all other generalized terms that we build up and over-define in the mind while simultaneously under-defining extensionally. We over-trust our evaluative terms (in contradistinction to sensory-based words) like 'beauty,' 'ugly,' 'good,' 'bad,' 'productive,' 'useful,' 'wonderful,' 'exciting,' 'traumatic,' etc. This intensional orientation can do us significant harm in the way we live, and the expectations we map.

How? By primarily orienting ourselves in the world by means of intensional definitions of words, we over-develop a *hallucinatory adaptive style*. Talk about black magic! Fantasy becomes our main way of mapping what we hope for and expect. This doesn't condemn fantasy, it only reminds us that as we move *up* the levels of the mind to create a rich mental map about future desires, we *also* need to move *down* the levels and out into the external world to reality-test their usefulness. Feed forward *and* feed back.

The intensional style treats *words* as if 'real' and their formal dictionary definitions as 'real' without an external check. That's the problem. *Only* intensionalizing does not promote sanity or adjustment. We also need extensionalizing. If we want to engage in some valid reality testing or to effectively adjust ourselves to reality, we have to bring the intensional ideas back down.

S.I. Hayakawa (1980) described the difference between extensional and intensional meanings.

> "The extensional meaning of an utterance is that which it *points to* or denotes in the extensional world ... the extensional meaning is something that *cannot be expressed in words*, because it is that which words stand for. An easy way to remember this is to put your hand over your mouth and point whenever you are asked to give an extensional meaning. ... The *intensional meaning* of a word or expression, on the other hand, is that which is *suggested* (connoted) inside one's head. Roughly speaking, whenever we express the meaning of words by uttering more words, we are giving intensional meaning, or connotations. To remember this, put your hand over your eyes and let the words spin around in your head." (pp. 61–62)

The utterances we communicate ought to have *both* extensional and intensional meanings. "Angels watch over my bed at night" certainly has several intensional meanings, but no extensional meanings.

> "When we say that the statement has no extensional meaning, we are merely saying that we cannot see, touch, photograph, or in any scientific manner detect the presence of angels.' (ibid., p. 62)

This Intensional/Extensional distinction provides a valuable discrimination in our language use. Because extensional statements partake of an empirical and sensory-based nature, we can use them to bring an argument to a close.

> "This room measures fifteen feet long."
>
> "She received 100 more votes in the election."
>
> "We have increased production by 20% since the last report."

No matter how many guesses we make about the room from our intensional definitions, all discussion ceases when someone produces a tape measure. This is the power of *extending* our definitions down and out into the external world.

Not so with intensional meanings. Here discussions and arguments can go on forever.

> "This is a *beautifully* decorated room."
>
> "She is undoubtedly the *best* candidate for the job."

Statements not based on 'sense' can provoke all kinds of disagreements. When we say something that we cannot extensionalize on out, we cannot 'make' sense out of it, and it has the distinct possibility of being 'non-sense.' Then an utterance does not refer to sense data at all; so one cannot collect sense data to settle the discussion. The speaker's statement does not refer primarily to the external world, but to the person's *internal world of evaluations.*

Meta-Modeling Over/Under Defined Terms

As linguistic forms that lead to inadequate communications, we need to question over/under defined terms in the following ways:

(a) *Extensionalize the over-defined words of intensional statements* to evoke richer descriptions of the person's meanings.

What is the extensional evidence for this intensional term? Please *operationalize* what you mean in see-hear-feel language (e.g. behavioral terms). What can you point to?

(b) *Explore presuppositions in the undefined terms.*

This gets the speaker to put his or her epistemology, so to speak, out on the table.

What does this assume?

What have you presupposed in stating this?

(c) *Train yourself for the extensional orientation.*

The natural order of evaluation involves facts first, then evaluations.

What are the facts upon which you've based this term or this idea?

2. *Delusional Verbal Splits*

Don't you love that phrase, *Delusional Verbal Splits?* It's one of my favorites. Imagine what you can do with it:

> "Well, you've got a good point there and it would make sense, but not with the *Delusional Verbal Split* inside your statement."

Of course, before you use it to perform some magic with words, I suppose we ought to know what in the world it means!

This phrase highlights the General Semantics emphasis on the danger and problem of *'Elementalism.'* What does that means? Elementalism refers to how we can take language and use it to compartmentalize and dichotomize elements of a whole.

We do this, for example, when we speak about 'mind' and 'body' *as if* we can have one of these elements without the other. Try it if you like. Imagine a 'mind' apart from a 'body.' Or, imagine a 'body' apart from a 'mind.' They go together as part of the same interconnected reality, do they not? When we speak about them as separate, distinct, and unrelated, we create a false-to-fact map. Actually, it is always 'mind-body.'

We do the same with 'space' and 'time.' Korzybski noted that in the revolution in physics Einstein healed the delusional verbal split between 'space' and 'time.' He said that there was no *'and.'* He quoted Einstein and the way Einstein re-languaged it as the 'space-time' continuum. By hyphenating 'time-space,' Einstein presented a holistic understanding that more accurately expressed the newer understandings in quantum mechanics.

Taking his cue from this, Korzybski suggested a similar healing for other forms of delusional splitting of the world: 'mind-body,' 'thoughts-emotions,' 'neuro-linguistics,' 'neuro-semantics,' 'psycho-logics,' etc.

Elementalism occurs when we take reality-as-a-whole and split it up into parts or elements. If we remember that we do this only conceptually and linguistically, all will go well. But the moment we forget or confuse the map-territory distinction and begin thinking that the *elements* (which we can think about and talk about) *actually exist apart from the system,* we then treat these 'elements' of the map as if real, as if they have a separate and unrelated existence. Then things begin to go amiss.

In a way, this describes one of the magical uses of words. We can use words to sort, separate, divide, and categorize the ever-connected flow of processes of the world. By words, we can split up, sort out, organize, and punctuate the flux of reality. What magic emerges from this?

Lots.

Doing this allows us to create theories, understandings, hypotheses, etc. It enables us to create fields, disciplines, and areas of intellectual study. Verbally also (but not actually), we can split up the world by the way we language our conceptualization. By languaging we inevitably dichotomize the rich interconnectedness of the actual world. This creates *elements,* parts, pieces, etc. Later, if we forget that we have so slaughtered the territory in our mapping, if we forget to reconnect the systems, if we get so used to the parts, we may begin to believe that the *elements* exist as separate entities and heal them as separate entities. This is what Korzybski called *elementalism.*

In languaging, we can talk about 'body' *and* 'mind,' 'emotion' *and* 'intellect,' 'space' *and* 'time,' etc. The referents of these words do *not* exist as separate elements. They *cannot* so exist as separate elements. Their existence involves an interconnected process—systems of interactions embedded inside of other systems. We can only split them at the *verbal level* so that we can think about and talk about these parts. Breaking a system into parts and working with an individual facet often gives us the power to take control over that system.

Linguistically, we form and interact with these parts or elements as separate words. We do the same conceptually. This is where the unsanity begins. As we tear the inner-connected world apart, our terms become 'elementalistic,' and to that extent, false-to-fact because they do not accurately represent the territory.

Since we cannot actually or literally separate 'emotions' and 'intellect,' this division structurally violates the organism-as-a-whole generalization (Korzybski, p. 65). So with 'body' and 'soul,' and other verbal splittings. In these ways, we confuse our own understanding, hamper development and creativity, and create false-to-fact ideas. Using language *elementalistically* prevents us from thinking, speaking, and acting with our knowledge of systems. It prevents *systemic thinking, feeling, and responding.*

When we use elementalistic language, we construct poor and inadequate maps, maps which misdirect and impoverish our understandings of the world. As an elementalistic terminology assumes a sharp division between 'mind' and 'senses,' 'percept' and 'concept,' etc., it prevents us from thinking systemically.

Speaking half a century before Systems Theory, Korzybski (1933/1994) wrote,

> "Einstein realized that the empirical structure of 'space' and 'time' with which the physicist and the average man deal is such that it cannot be empirically divided, and that we actually deal with a blend which we have split only elementalistically and verbally into these fictitious entities." (p. 106)

> "The elementalistic 'absolute' division of the 'observer' and the 'observed' was false to facts, because every observation in this field disturbs the observed." (p. 107)

If we create or use *verbal splits* without remaining conscious that our words exist *only as words,* only as verbal representations, and that they only deal with verbal representations, we train ourselves in *delusional semantic reactions*. That is, we train ourselves to think in terms of one-valued or two-valued semantics rather than recognizing the infinite valued world (pp. 194–195).

> "In life, as well as in science, we deal with different happenings, objects, and larger or smaller bits of materials. We have a habit of

speaking about them in terms of 'matter'. Through a semantic disturbance, called identification, we fancy that such a thing as 'matter' has separate physical existence. It would probably be a shock to be invited seriously *to give* a piece of 'matter' (give and not burst into speech). ... I have had the most amusing experiences in this field. Most people, scientists included, hand over a pencil or something of this sort. But did they actually give 'matter'? What they gave is *not* to be *symbolized* simply 'matter'. The object, 'pencil', which they *handed*, requires linguistically 'space'; otherwise, there would be no pencil but a mathematical point, a fiction. It also requires verbally 'time'; otherwise, there would be no pencil but a 'flash'." (pp. 224–5)

Meta-Modeling Delusional Verbal Splits

To question and challenge a *delusional verbal split,* and the elementalisms lurking within, you can do any of the following:

(a) **Hyphenate** the delusional verbal split.

When you catch elementalizing and dichotomizing in language, stick in *hyphens*. Korzybski said this functional process of hyphenating enables us to reconnect holistic processes that we can only separate verbally.

> "A little dash here and there may be of serious semantic importance when we deal with symbolism." (p. 289)

This gives us, 'time-space,' 'mind-body,' 'neuro-semantic,' etc. Organism-as-a-whole words provide representations that remind us of the systemic nature of the world. They remind us of the holistic and inseparable processes with which we deal.

The device of hyphenating elementalistic terms enables us to stop dichotomizing and splitting up reality into parts. Since that results in inaccurate maps, we need a linguistic tool for describing a holistic world that works systemically, hence, organism-as-a-whole in a space-time world. Using hyphens enables us to create richer and more accurate maps, maps which cue us to the interactive *systems* around us.

(b) **Question the elementalism.**

Does X (the DVS) truly stand alone?
What context does X occur within?
Can we deal with X without also considering Y or Z?

(c) **Create holistic terms.**

Many terms are much more holistic. For instance, we can use psychosomatic, semantic reactions, neurophysiology, psychobiology, attitude (a mental-emotional state), etc.

(d) **Look for the systemic processes—the interconnected domains.**

Develop an 'eye' and awareness for systems of interactions. This will help to overcome the Aristotelian elementalistic perspective and equip us with *systemic thinking*.

Summary

- As *a semantic class of life,* we map our internal reality and model of the world by using language. We can do none other. To keep sane and productive in using language, we need to increase our *consciousness* that whatever we say about anything does *not* exist as 'the same thing as' that thing.
- We live simultaneously in two worlds. We live in the world of what we call 'objective reality,' *Plethora* (Bateson, 1979) and we live in the world of symbols, meaning, or 'mind,' *Creatura* (the world of communication, organization, semantic structures, etc.).
- In languaging, we operate at the verbal level of reality (the map level). Setting this awareness can save us from semantic reactions which arise when we confuse map with territory.
- We now have the first two linguistic distinctions which spring from the genius of Alfred Korzybski. You will find five more in the next chapter.

Chapter 12

Enriching the Magic from Korzybski

In this chapter we will finish exploring the other linguistic distinctions in Korzybski's *Science and Sanity*. These linguistic markers enable us to make new distinctions in listening to the mapping structures that we and others use as we communicate. Hearing them from an understanding awareness about their structures increases our options in how to respond effectively. It also increases our ability to quality control our communications. It gives us the mind and eyes of a magician.

In this, I have only briefly summarized a few of the central features in the massive work of *Science and Sanity*. In doing so, I have used the terms, ideas, and *extensional devices* of General Semantics to extend and expand the Meta-Model. These linguistic distinctions empower us to question, explore, challenge, and expand the structure of a linguistic map so that we can perform our magic more elegantly.

3. Either/Or Terms and Phrases

> Are you satisfied with your job?
>
> How do you best like to relax? Do you totally relax when you do that? Could you relax even 0.5% more?
>
> Do you prefer to study by listening or by reading?

Another Aristotelian way of thinking involves viewing and languaging things in *either/or terms*. Doing this creates two-valued terms. What's the problem with this? For the most part, this maps another false-to-fact distinction. It leaves out excluded middles, continua, both-and perspectives, degrees, gray areas, fuzzy or indeterminant areas, etc. It also creates over-simplifications and two-valued dichotomies.

When we make statements phrased in Either/Or formats, we then represent the territory and so orient ourselves to that representation *as if* we only have two choices in viewing, valuing, and responding. Typically, we polarize back and forth between the two choices, a map and choice that inaccurately represents reality.

Historically, we have struggled (even suffer) under the Either/Or orientation in psychology with the classic issues such as heredity/environment, nature/nurture, genetics/learning, etc. These false-to-fact concepts assume that we have to think about a person's characteristics in a bi-polar two-class category, and that these classes are mutually exclusive. It is *either* heredity *or* it is environment. So, which is it?

The excluded middle of Aristotelian logic drives us to this kind of thinking. "A thing either exists or it does not exist." This formulation excludes structures that make other possibilities available. Yet our experiences more typically involve an *interaction* between our genes and our environment, between the inherent hard-wire nature that our DNA prescribes and the nurture that we receive along the way. Both enter into the picture.

There is value in *Either/Or thinking.* It does sketch out broad outlines regarding things at the gross level: day or night, cold or hot, water or land, etc. It is when we totally exclude all middles that we create these very limiting maps for ourselves. Then we have no twilight or dusk. Non-Aristotelian thinking enables us to recognize that we may evaluate something as something other than 'true' or 'false.' It may also be 'ambiguous,' 'meaningless,' 'doesn't apply,' or the indeterminate, 'I don't know' category.

Structurally, either/or statements assume a two-valued cause—effect thinking (Korzybski, pp. 216–7). Frequently this offers an over-generalization resulting from the failure to take into account levels of abstraction and the nature of multiordinal and infinite-valued terms. When that happens, then we preclude seeing and recognizing more complex interactions, meanings that involve multiple layers, and things that are ambiguous in meaning until the context is specified.

More recently, scientists Lotfi Zadeh and Bart Kosko have popularized the idea of *fuzzy logic and reasoning.* The formal name for fuzziness is multivalence. The opposite is bivalence or two-valuedness, two ways to answer a question, true or false. Fuzziness means *multi*valence, three or more options, perhaps even an infinite spectrum of options. Kosko (1993) describes the fuzzy principle saying, "Everything is a matter of degree."

> "We can put black-and-white labels on these things. But the labels will pass from accurate to inaccurate as things change. Language ties a string between a word and the thing it stands for. When the thing changes to a non-thing, the string stretches or breaks or tangles with other strings." (p. 5)

> "Scientists had rounded off gray things to white and black things and then forgot about the rounding off and saw only a world of whites and blacks." (p. 14)

Meta-Modeling Either/Or Terms and Phrases

To question Either/Or language structures, and to get to the referent that may be outside the either/or box, use the following challenges:

(a) **Reality-test the Either/Or structure.**
Does this truly reflect an either/or situation?
Can I discover any choices in-between, any grays, or other considerations which may enter into consideration and influence my representation of this reality?
If I think about the two poles presented by these terms, what lies on the continuum between them?
If there was a scale from 0 to 10 what lies at 3, 5, 7, etc.?

(b) **Explore the possibility of Both-And.**
Could we have overlooked that in some way, at a larger frame, or in different contexts, both of these seemingly opposite responses stand as true?

In what way could we consider both of these choices as accurate and useful?

(c) **Add "etc."**
The use of the term 'etc.' not only signifies 'and so on,' but also, 'let the reader recognize that there are many other things that we could say about this, and that we have not uttered the last word about this.' In fact, Korzybski used *etc.* so often in *Science and Sanity* that he developed a very extensive system of dots and commas for conveying 'etc.' He believed that the liberal use of 'etc.' would help to establish an *extensional attitude and orientation*. He believed it would promote a healthy tentativeness. One of the key journals in the field of General Semantics today is called, "ETC."

Kinds of Nominalizations

In the classic NLP list of linguistic distinctions, *nominalizations* played a big role. These are the actions, processes, and verbs that have been *named* or *nominalized* so frozen in time and space and turned into a Thing-like-Entity. Relating becomes 'relationship.' Moving and having a motive becomes 'motivation.' With nominalizations, all of the life has been sucked out of the verb.

When we let the life and energy leak out of such terms, the terms become marvelous terms to use when we want to hypnotize. After all, to make sense out of these words a person has to go inside (a trance phenomenon) and begin to invent, create, and generate references that fit the term. That's why nominalizations make up so much of trance language.

> "And as the *realization* of your *ability* to experience an *expansive self-esteem* dawns on your *wondering mind*, you can begin to feel a deeper *relaxation* than you have ever before..."

In the field of linguistics, scholars specify many different *kinds* of nominalizations. This makes a lot of sense. After all, we can make many distinctions in the kinds, qualities, and properties of *processes and actions*. For instance, we can distinguish actions that involve completed and incompleted processes, those that involve primarily one person, two persons, or more. We can distinguish processes of external actions and internal 'mental' states, those of the past, the present, the future. Langacker (1991) distinguishes bounded and unbounded regions of actions.

In the following Korzybski distinctions, we have nominalizations that have taken on additional usages and qualities. These nominalizations involve more than the typical run-of-the-mill nominalizations. In them you will find new distinctions for casting and breaking spells.

4. *Multiordinality*

Nominalizations, as higher level abstractions, as *named* verbs, generally lose specific meanings and increasingly become broad and general enough for us to use them at many different levels of abstraction. This leads to multiordinality.

When a term gets to this stage of development, it actually stands for no specific referent. At this point, the words only have an over-generalized meaning, and the meaning changes according to *the level of abstraction* or context. Korzybski termed these infinite-valued terms *'multi-ordinal.'* What does that mean? It means that these terms have a *reflexivity* which allows us to use them on themselves. Linguists describe such terms as *polysemy or polysemous* (marked by multiplicity of meanings).

What's deleted in multiordinal terms is the *level* or dimension of abstraction of the generalization. When we turn 'thinking' (verb) into a noun-like word (nominalization), we have 'thought.' It sounds like a thing. "I have a thought about where we could go for dinner." Yet we can use this nominalization on itself, and at multiple levels. "I have a thought about that thought." This enables us to use these terms on many different levels of abstraction.

Now what might be surprising is that these multiordinal, infinite-valued terms include many of the most common terms we use everyday. We also argue about these highly *ambiguous* terms a lot without taking the time to identify the level of abstraction.

What are some examples?

> "Mankind, science, mathematics, man, education, ethics, politics, religion, sanity, insanity, iron, wood, apple, object, etc." We use them not as one-valued terms for constants of some sort, but as terms with inherently infinite-valued or variable referents (pp. 138–9, 433)

A majority of our everyday terms consist of names for *infinite-valued stages of processes with a changing content.* This is what makes them multiordinal in nature. As infinite-valued variables they are not true or false, but *ambiguous* in meaning.

Consider 'love' as a multiordinal term. We use this term to describe our thoughts and feelings about people and things (objects on the primary level). "I love Jane." "I love ice-cream." "I love my dog Nero." Though very different, yet our 'love' at this level has an actual referent, something you can see, hear, smell, touch, and taste. Our thoughts and feelings all involve an attraction, desire, want, etc. for the object.

Yet we also use this term in reference to concepts. "I love democracy." We can use it in reference to imagined experiences. "I would love being in love." These concepts are non-objects (no-things) that we have constructed and which exist only in the mind. They exist at a higher or meta level. When we say the following, we go further,

> "I love my love of democracy."
>
> "I love being in love" which creates infatuation.
>
> "I love the feeling of infatuation" which could be romanticism.

In the development of fuzzy logic and reasoning, Kosko (1993) describes the fuzziness of words. I here include his description because it provides another perceptive on multiordinality. In Kosko's model, multiordinal words stand for *sets.*

> "The word *house* stands for many houses. It stands for different houses for each of us because we each have seen and lived in and

> read about and dreamed about different houses. We all speak and write the same words but we do not think the same words. Words are public but the sets we learn are private. And we think in sets." (p. 122)

The *set* that the term 'house' refers to is also a fuzzy set or a multiordinal term. Though most of us will have a prototypical house in mind, 'house' also may include castles, trailers, mobile homes, duplexes, tine-shared condos, teepees, etc. Could the set of *houses* even extend to tents, caves, and lean-tos? It's all a matter of degree. Some structures seem to fit into the category better than others. They seem to be more like a *house* than do others.

If words operate like a fuzzy set, and we *think* in such terms or categories, can this happen to verbs, adjectives, and process works? Yes. *Old* house may specify a smaller *set*, but still a set of houses. *Foreclosed* house takes a verb (to foreclose), nominalizes it and then uses it as an adverb.

Consider the nominalization *marriage* and even the identity 'being married.' Suppose you ask an audience, "How many here are married?" At first this may seem like a clear, either/or, black-and-white digital *set*. But how does the person *in the midst of a divorce* answer? Or the person who has lived with another for a decade, without ever formally 'getting married?' Or the person who has a second wife? Or the person whose husband is an MIA (Missing In Action)? Fuzziness begins to arise as we explore the set.

Fuzziness really increases in our terms when we ask the audience to raise their hands in response to such questions as:

> Are you satisfied with your job?
>
> Are you tall, short, thin, fat, smart, honest?
>
> Are you resourceful, happy, focused?

Fuzzy sets, like multiordinal terms, are matters of degree, and depend upon the context, time, etc.

Meta-Modeling Multiordinal Terms

To question and explore multiordinal nominalizations, do any of the following:

(a) **Use co-ordinates.**
Use co-ordinates to assign single values to the variable to locate it in time and space (p. 139). When we identify time co-ordinates or space co-ordinates we contextualize specific referents. If a word or phrase expresses ambiguity, to understand its meaning we have to contextualize the level or dimension of our use. This makes the multiordinal word specific and precise.

(b) **Supply a context.**
Since these words essentially operate as terms without a context, supply a context for them. This enables us to then determine their usage and meaning. As we supply a context, we fix its meaning to a single referent (p. 436).

(c) **Chunk down.**
Chunk down to the specific referents at each level of abstraction. Develop 'a behavioristic and functional set of words' to map with specific descriptions. Using descriptive language orders the happenings on the objective level in sensory-based terms (p. 264). In science, we talk about operationalizing our terms; that's what this does. Functional words enable us to translate dynamic processes into static forms and static processes into dynamic forms. Korzybski wrote:

> "In science, we have to use an actional, 'behaviouristic', 'functional' 'operational' language, in which we do not say that this and this 'is' so and so, but where we describe extensionally what happens in a certain order. We describe how something *behaves,* what something *does,* what we *do* in our research work ..." (p. 639)

(d) **Check for reflexivity.**
This is the test for multiordinality. Check to see if you can reflexively turn the word back onto itself. Distinguishing multiordinal words as those that can operate on many levels

of abstraction enables us to recognize their nature and how they function in our languaging. Can you move to another level and still use the term?

"Do you love someone? Do you love loving them? Do you love loving love?"

"Do you have a prejudice? What about a prejudice against prejudice?"

"What science relates to this?" "Do you also have a science of this science?"

This reflexivity test will not work with non-multiordinal words. "What a beautiful tree!" "Suppose you had a tree of that tree?"

(e) **Put quotes around words.**
Since words are not the territory to which they refer, cuing ourselves by putting quotes around slippery words ('mind,' 'love,' etc.) provides a way to alert ourselves to the danger of forgetting their map-like quality.

5. *Static or Signal Words*

When we set or fix the context of a polysemous *multiordinal* term, we specify its meaning. As a result, we get a specific and definite meaning to the term. Yet if we do this in such a way that we construct a fixed and rigid meaning, then we construct a poorly built map—a *Static Word.*

Here we take a process, nominalize it into a polysemous, vague, ambiguous word and then inappropriately lock it down by giving it a fixed, rigid, 'true for all time,' and absolute definition. When a multiordinal term becomes static, we freeze it using Aristotelian logic (i.e., 'Whatever is, is.'). Later when we use such terms, we forget what we have done and confuse our verbal map with the territory. This enables us to lock in a multiordinal word at one level and freeze it so that it becomes 'static' in meaning for all time.

This gives it a one-valued significance, and so creates what Korzybski called a static or signal word.

Our tendency to *nominalize* verbs (by reifying processes) in the first place contributes to creating these static, definite, and absolutistic one-valued statements (p. 140). Then, as we create these static expressions, we are induced into absolutist and dogmatic state. We begin making statements that sound like pronouncements from heaven. Korzybski said that this creates a 'legislative semantic mood,' absolutisms, and 'the deity mode.'

> "We humans ... have a tendency to make static, definite, and absolutistic one-valued statements." (p. 140)

Of course, this fits with the absolutism of the Aristotelian laws of logic. 'Whatever is, is.' 'Nothing can both be and not be.' 'Everything must either be or not be.'

Yet when we ascribe to nominalizations a quality of certitude that they do not (and cannot) have, we emotionally load them with the result that they become 'heavy terms.' This powerfully affects our neurology. We then experience the words as the *things*. 'The thing-hood of words' results from the delusions we create by these static words. When we do this, we use our nervous systems as animals use theirs. These terms become a mere signal for reactions, rather than symbols that stand for something else. We come to believe without question that the words *'are'* the things they stand for. This shows up in the 'is' of identity verbs.

Meta-Modeling Static Terms

Use the following as processes for questioning and challenging these linguistic maps.

(a) **Loosen up the multiordinal term.**
Loosen the multiordinal term made so rigid and absolute by indexing who used it at a certain level on a certain date in a certain way. Flush out the hidden processes and verbs.

(b) **Extensionalize.**
Enumerate the collection of items out of which we create the generalization. Extensionalize by dating and timing the referents. *"Point out to me specifically what you mean."*

(c) **De-infinitize the state.**
Doing this makes it semantically harmless. Identify the stages and variables within the static over-generalized word. Index time, place, and person. As you do that, you will be communicating the message, "Not true for all time, all space, all people, etc."

(d) **Ask meaning questions.**
What do you mean by ...?

Understanding that we use words to construct or evoke meanings enables us to recognize words as creatures of our definitions. They are entirely arbitrary. At the verbal level, all words and sentences exist only as *forms of representations* that evoke semantic reactions in our nervous system.

The events outside of our skin are un-speakable, absolute, and individual. Our *words 'are' not* those things. Words and things occur on different logical levels. Our words merely express a verbalization *about* things.

Static words convey a false-to-fact understanding which leads us to over-evaluate words and to treat them as 'things.' This falsely ascribes an objectivity to words that they do not, and cannot, bear. We avoid objectifying words when we ask, *What do you mean by that word?* This also provides us with psychological 'distance' from language so that we begin to *feel* it at the kinesthetic level as truly *not* the territory, but just our *map of the territory.*

As we make a move to a higher level, and ask the meaning question at that level, it prevents the semantic blockage that arises when we treat words statically. *What do you mean by that word? How does your use of this word contrast with X?*

6. Pseudo-Words or Non-Referencing Words

Suppose we push a multiordinal polysemous nominalization so far up the levels of abstracting and detach it from the extensionalizing feedback to reality. What happens then? We create a non-referencing *Pseudo-Word.* This means that we can create mental and verbal maps that *mean* nothing in the sense that they *refer* to nothing in the external world. They do not *stand for* or *point to* anything.

So, just because we can make verbal *noises* or *spell out marks* on paper which look like and sound like words, this does not necessarily make them true words. Korzybski designated such pseudo-words as *'noises'* (in the auditory channel) and as *'spell-marks'* (in the visual channel).

This gives us linguistic maps that reference nothing. Nothing exists in the actual world or in the world of logic (logical existence) for which such words can stand as true symbols. These airy nothings, these verbal fictions have no reality in any dimension. Yet if we use them to navigate through the territory and take action based on such, disasters occur.

We can keep on generating 'words,' even when the symbols that we construct have no referent! Yet when we use words that refer to nothing outside ourselves, we are merely making noises. What shall we say of maps that allude to no actual territory? We might find them interesting, even entertaining. Science fiction glories in such. But are they useful when we want to convey accurate information or to orient ourselves to reality?

When we create and use such 'words,' words that only exist in the world of 'mind,' these *pseudo-words* become very tricky. This is because though they look like words, and sound like words, they do not reference anything. The lack of mindfulness about this can lead to lots of delusions, illusions, and deceptions.

Now a word that references nothing in the world of physics may reference an imagined thing in the world of mind and communication. We can talk about Alice in Wonderland. We can read about her, imagine her adventures. We can use the stories, events, and dialogues as illustrations. Yet *Alice* and *Wonderland* are only referencing the world of imagination. In the external world, they are non-referencing words.

Non-referencing words have no referent in either imagination or in physics. These *noises* made with the mouth or *marks* spelled on paper only give the impression of being real words.

How do we tell the difference between *true and pseudo words*?

What criteria can we use?

By definition, for a sound or image to function as a true word it must operate as a *symbol* which means that it *stands for* something. That is, it has an extensional connection with the world. To the extent that it stands for, or refers to, something, it serves as a true symbol, elicits internal representations, and mentally 'anchors' the referent. If it does not, it *merely stands as a noise*. It refers to nothing. Before a noise or image can function as a symbol, something must 'exist' (actually or logically). If it does not, then it simply functions as a *semantic noise*, hence a meaningless sign (p. 79).

Before a noise or a spell-mark can exist as a symbol, something must exist. When it does, the symbol can symbolize that existing thing, process, or concept. In language and 'knowledge' we have two kinds of existences: *physical existence and logical existence*.

Unicorns do not exist in the external world of unaided nature. They do *not* belong to zoology. When we apply the word unicorn to the field of zoology, we employ a pseudo-word. However, if we employ the word with reference to mythology or human fancy, the word there has a referent and so functions meaningfully as a symbol (pp. 81–82).

The ability to distinguish between words which operate as *true* symbols by symbolizing something that exists and those which function merely as *noises* represents a vital skill for clear communication, thinking, reasoning, and even sanity. If we *use noises* as if they were words, we create problems.

> "One of the obvious origins of human disagreement lies in the use of noises for words." (p. 82)

Because this literally involves 'the use of *false representations,*' Korzybski called this a form of fraud. He illustrated this with the word *'heat'* (p. 107) noting that grammatically we classify 'heat' as a substantive (noun, actually, a nominalization). Yet physicists labored for centuries looking for some 'substance' which would correspond to the substantive 'heat.' They never found it. It does not exist. Today we know that no such *thing* as 'heat' exists.

What does exist? Manifestations of 'energy' (processes) and interactions between processes that create or release thermo-dynamic energy. So we use a verb or adverb (thermo-dynamic) to represent the referent. Today we recognize that no such 'substance' as 'heat' exists, so we talk about the process of 'thermo-dynamics' as two objects or processes interacting.

Sometimes we use 'heat' to refer to our *sense of temperature,* the result of thermo-dynamic energy. 'Heat' speaks about a relationship between phenomena in motion. To use this non-referencing term as a word engages in a *linguistic fiction* false-to-facts.

No wonder the scientists looking for 'heat' found themselves ill-adjusted to reality. Here, the verbal symbolism of language did not point to anything. It had no reference. Linguistically, the word deceptively mapped a road that took people down a blind alley. The word had cast a spell that sent them on a fruitless journey.

Korzybski also illustrated this point using the word *'space'* (p. 228). 'Space,' in the sense of absolute emptiness, does not exist. As a word it stands as neither true nor false, but non-sense (a delusional verbal split). It makes a noise, yet it says nothing about the external world. Korzybski said that it stands as a label for a semantic disturbance, for verbal objectification, for a pathological state inside our skin, for a fancy, not a symbol.

He illustrated non-referencing words also with the word *'infinity'* (p. 205). The term 'infinite' refers to any process which does not end or stop. We use it legitimately as an adjective describing the characteristics of a process. We misuse it when we use it as a noun. So with the verbal fiction of 'owning' or 'ownership.'

> "We see the utter folly of racing to accumulate symbols, worthless in themselves, while destroying the 'mental' and 'moral' values which are behind the symbols. For it is useless to 'own' a semantically unbalanced world ..." (p. 549)

We label these verbal forms which have no actual referents as *pseudo-words*. These noises and spell-marks arise as mere mechanisms of our symbolism. They have the appearance of words, but we should not consider them words since they say nothing in a given context (pp. 137–8). In practical life, we often do not even suspect collections of noises or spell-marks in books to exist as non-referencing (p. 142).

In the field of Rational-Emotive Behavior Therapy (REBT), psychologists have highlighted common pseudo-words of unsanity that torment lots of people and send them to a pit of emotional hell. These include: 'awful,' 'horrible,' 'terrible,' etc.

These words refer to nothing. They function only as *emotional amplification words* that exaggerate a situation which a person does not desire. In REBT, a person learns to challenge this philosophical nonsense by inviting a speaker to explain *what* these evaluative words mean. What is 'awful' or 'terrible' about this? What does this mean other than just undesirable? What is meant other than 'intense dislike and aversion?'

> "Why is this experience 'awful,' 'terrible,' or a 'catastrophe?' I know that you don't like it and that you wish you didn't have to deal with it. I can see how unpleasant and distressful it feels, but why is it 'awful?'"

As we realize that many words have no referent, this enables us to *not* immediately buy into the reality of words. If you have lived your life under the delusion that 'words are real,' that 'if you can name it, it exists,' or 'a map is the territory it represents,' then you will probably find this shocking and disconcerting. Yet once you make this distinction, with your mind of a magician, you will develop a new automatic response to words. You will intuitively feel the symbolic nature of words. You will have the heart of a magician. This will give you a certain *distance* from words and a feeling, 'They are just words.' This neuro-semantic response will then empower you to respond to words as symbols.

Ultimately, our thinking-emoting arises from our linguistics. We can think no better than we use language. If we use an antiquated, primitive, and false-to-facts language, we will think in primitive and inaccurate ways. If we language unsanely, using words without true referents, we will begin to think-feel unsane and respond to the ghosts of our words.

In the early seventeenth century, Francis Bacon criticized "the idols of the market-place" and so addressed the issue of pseudo-words.

> "The idols imposed by words on the understanding are of two kinds. They are either names of things which do not exist (... names which result from fantastic suppositions and to which nothing in reality corresponds), or they are names of things which exist, but yet confused and ill-defined, and hastily and irregularly derived from realities. Of the former kind are Fortune, the Prime Mover, Planetary Orbits, Elements of Fire, and like fictions which owe their origin to false and idle theories." (Bacon, 1620, p. 68)

Meta-Modeling Pseudo-Words

To question non-referencing words in a way that challenges the appropriateness of the symbol, use the following processes:

(a) **Reality test the reference.**
Challenge pseudo-words by referencing them. Date and time index the referents. *Suppose I could see-hear-feel this, what would I see or hear or feel? To what kind or dimension of reality does this word refer? In what domain?* Find out to what field the term applies.

(b) **Explore the reference.**
What is the referent of this or that word? Does it exist in either the world of physics or in the world of mind? Could this term be a non-referencing word? Does this word truly have an actual referent? Or is it a fictional and constructed understanding of the imagination? Does this linguistic symbol reference anything that has actual or logical existence?

7. Identity/Identification

When we come to *identification,* we come to the factor which Korzybski considered primary to the sanity and/or unsanity in human functioning (p. lxxviii). In fact, he declared that *identification* itself represents the heart of Aristotelian logic (reasoning and thinking) and *the* basic false-to-fact structure. Read *Science and Sanity* and you will find that Korzybski as much as declared war on this process of *identification.* For him, it is the main thing which prevents people from thinking, evaluating, and operating as Non-Aristotelian.

By *identity* and *identification* Korzybski meant *identifying* phenomenon on different levels, or identifying a thing in an absolute way, even with itself. When this happens, we do not recognize differences. For him, identity meant *'absolute sameness* in all respects.'

Obviously, *'all'* in this definition makes identity impossible. If we eliminate the 'all' from the definition, then the word *'absolute'* also loses its meaning. Then we simply have 'sameness in *some* respects,' an acceptable concept. 'Same' in this way then has the significance of 'similar.' The concept of *similarity* enables us to create, work with, and use generalizations, labels, categories, etc. appropriately. If we alter the ideas of 'absolute' and 'all,' we no longer have 'identity' at all, only *similarity.*

This provides a much more accurate way of mapping the world. In the world of differences, nothing is ever the 'same.' Even the 'same' rock is not actually 'the same' from moment to moment when we recognize the sub-molecular world where the 'dance of electrons' continually causes change and process. The rock may be similar from moment to moment, even century to century, but it is not 'the same.'

Identification leads to many false evaluations and to the majority of evaluations that in human life create unsanity. Identity as 'absolute sameness in all respects' *simply never occurs in the world or even in our heads* (p. 194). Nor can it. Identification results when we fail to make distinctions. It reflects our confusing of differences between things, events, and orders of abstractions.

In the world we only deal with unique individual persons, events, and things. There only exists *non-identity* in the world of processes. Every event is unique, individual, absolute, and unrepeatable. No individual or event can be 'the same' from one moment to the next.

Identification begins early in life. Infants develop semantic reactions as they identify things that exist on different levels. When the infant discovers that his *cry* brings food, then neuro-semantically, his cry *'is'* the food (p. 201). He links his pre-word noises (crying) to the referent. Or, we may say that he *confuses* the two. They become *anchored* so that the one not only inescapably *leads to* the other (Cause—Effect), but *is* the other (Complex Equivalence).

In this way, we all learn to equate words with referents so that we develop an innate feeling that 'the map *is* the territory!' That we *feel this inside our bodies* speaks about how we have neurologically linked the experiences. Then our thinking and mapping about something *seems to be* that thing. Identification.

The infant does not distinguish map and territory. Indeed an infant child *cannot* make such a distinction, not at that stage. That comes later. Yet if we do not later correct that initial mapping, we develop all kinds of *semantic reactions* to words and ideas. Then, at the neuro-semantic level, words *are* real. At least, they feel real. Neuro-semantically, we fail to distinguish word and referent. This, of course, prevents us from being a magician with our words.

If someone calls us 'stupid,' we feel bad. We feel attacked and that we have to fight to fend off that attribution. The word itself *hurts.* Why? Because *in* our body, *the word is the reality.* This describes what we mean by identifying. When we identify, we program our neurology to *experience* our mapping as real. We then salivate in a stimulus—response way.

We can see in this that identification erroneously evaluates the products of our thinking-and-feeling as having objective existence. By ascribing external objectivity to words, we map untrue and very unuseful representations. Evaluation only occurs in mind, it is a meta-stating process. Also, the 'products' of our evaluation exist and operate only as a mental phenomenon at the level of thoughts [Wilber following Immanuel Kant calls this *intellibilia* (the 'eye' of intelligence) and not *sensibilia* (the 'eye' of the flesh or senses, 1983, p. 67).

Now the amazing thing is that we do not stop *identifying* at these lower levels. We engage in higher level *identifications* as well. We identify with multiordinal nominalizations! We take one of our neuro-linguistic states (e.g., love, joy, fear, anger, disgust, confidence, trustworthiness, manic-depression, etc.) and *identify* with them. Of course, when we do, we create some high level forms of unsanity as we make the identification static and either/or.

The Korzybskian language distinction of identification grows out of the tiniest nominalization ('is'). It can start as innocently as two things occurring about the same time, we jump to a Cause—Effect relationship, then we equate the two (Complex Equivalence), we then make that static, and we jump yet another level and meta-state our sense of identity with that.

An *Identification* statement makes an equation between things on different levels of abstraction. We create it via an equation which involves a confusion of the multiordinal nominalization, 'self' (the concept of self).

> "I am ... X"
>
> "He is an X."
>
> "She's nothing more than an X!"

These involve the two most dangerous forms of mapping false-to-fact (i.e., it doesn't fit the territory at all), namely, 'the "is" of identification,' and 'the "is" of predication.'

The 'is' of identification involves equating or identifying one's self with words, labels, definitions, understandings, etc. Humans in all cultures do this. We take our powers of functioning (thinking, feeling, speaking, behaving, relating, achieving, etc.) and identify with such. We identify with our beliefs, values, skills, roles, experiences, etc. We identify with our cultural practices, our religion, our race, family, etc. There's no end to the things, ideas, experiences, emotions, roles, etc., that we can identify with.

The "is" of predication involves predicating or asserting qualities. Neurologically, we even do this at the perceptual level. Hence, 'The rose is red.' Yet this actually fails to map the *interaction* of what we receive from the world and the contributions of our sense receptors (rods and cones). Predicating judgments (i.e., our evaluations, meanings) takes this to a higher level ('He is a jerk') as we *project* out onto the world our idiosyncratic evaluations.

These 'ises' show how one of the central linguistic makers of identification shows up in the *'to be'* verbs (is, am, are, was, were, be, being, been, etc.). David Bourland, Jr. (1991) has called the 'to be' verbs, "the deity mode" of thinking and speaking. 'This is that!' 'That's how it is!'

The damaging 'ises' thus take two primary forms: (1) *the 'is' of identity* ('I am ...' 'You are ...' 'That is ...') and (2) *the 'is' of predication* ('The apple is red'). Bourland created **E-Prime** (English primed of the 'to be' verbs) to eliminate this (see Appendix B).

Not all 'ises' create unsanity. When we use *'is' as an auxiliary verb* ('Jim is coming over,' 'Sally was going shopping') this 'is' simply contributes and supports another verb. So it creates no semantic difficulties. Nor does the *'is' of existence* do any harm. It simply points to events and things that 'stand out' in our perception ('She is over there by the tree.').

Korzybski noted that the identification process inherently arises from the very form of our subject-predicate language form (pp. 57, 188–191, 198, 250). Our language patterns assume the existence of identification inasmuch as when we form our basic statements we speak of predicating things. This presupposes an underlying level of existence comprised of substances.

When we engage in identifying, we experience a comparatively inflexible, rigid form of adaptation, low degree conditionality, and neurological necessity. This represents an animal type of adaptation, and one most "inadequate for modern man" (p. 195).

Korzybski also noted that identification occurs in all known forms of 'mental' illness. Yet in the world of process and non-identity (since every event exists as unique, individual, absolute, unrepeatable) no individual, 'object', event, etc., can exist as 'the same' from one moment to the next. So when we identify, we create a mental illusion. We create an illusion of a fixed and rigid map about reality. By identifying, we begin to live in a delusional world of our own making.

> "In heavy cases of dementia praecox we find the most highly developed 'identification'. [This] suggests that any identification, no matter how slight, represents a dementia praecox factor in our semantic reactions. The rest is only a question of degrees of this maladjustment." (p. 568)

In identifying, we erroneously conclude that what occurs inside our skin (e.g., ideas, understandings, concepts) has objective existence. Psychologically, we call this 'projection.' This means that we are identifying and then ascribing external objectivity to our internal experiences of feelings, words, ideas, meanings, etc. This generates a number of mental mapping mistakes: delusions, illusions, hallucinations (pp. 456–7).

Meta-Modeling Identification

To question and challenge identifications, and then to de-identify by recognizing the unique distinctions of reality, we can do the following:

(a) **Extensionalize.**
Extend your meanings out to the external world to make your referents clear. By specifying your referents, you prevent the identification. "What specifically are you a failure at?" "How does his experience make him a drunk?"

Korzybski said that the extensional method deals structurally with the many definite individuals that distinguish and separate (p. 135). We can extensionalize by indexing specifics (who, when, where, how, which, etc.), by making distinctions, by hyphenating, and by riding our language of the 'to be' verbs (E-Priming).

(b) **Differentiate realities.**
Because 'identity' does not occur in the world, as we reject the very concept of the 'is' of identity, we learn to orient ourselves more to differences and differentiation as fundamental (p. 93–4). This enables us to begin to look for, and specify, the absolute individuality of events.

How do these things that seem similar, and which you have identified, actually differ?

(c) **Sub-scripting words with time-dates or space-locations.**
To index a word to a particular time, place, person, event, etc. by using a subscript gives the term much more specificity. As we so extensionalize, we create more clarity of thought and expression. Hence, $\text{Science}_{\text{Aristotle, 300 BC}}$ differs radically from $\text{Science}_{\text{Einstein, 1903}}$. In modern science we speak about this as operationalizing our terms. What specific behaviors, actions, responses, etc. would we see, hear, and feel?

We index by sub-scripting. When we subscript we are forced to deal with the absolute individuality of every event at every time. Since the world and ourselves consist of processes, every Smith_{1950} exists as quite a different person from Smith_{1995}.

This individualizing assists us in making distinctions. Depression_{1991} differs from depression_{1994}; $\text{depression}_{\text{Bob}}$ differs from $\text{depression}_{\text{Susan}}$. By time-indexing, we specify the date of our verbal statements. We can do the same with person-indexing, place-indexing, and even process-indexing.

(d) **Practice silence at the unspeakable levels.**
If our map only seeks to represent the territory and never *'is'* the territory, then as we learn to 'stop the world' in terms of the chatty internal dialogue that runs in our heads or even the rush of our neurological VAK language (our sights, sounds, and sensations) we give ourselves a chance to sense and feel the gulf between the territory and our maps. In his neuro-linguistic trainings, Korzybski had people point at an object and maintain silence to anchor this awareness. 'Silence on the objective levels' installs a strategy of psycho-physical delay so that we don't react without thinking.

Train yourself to recognize 'the unspeakable level of experience.' This process describes a central technique for eliminating the 'is' of identify. In the place of repressing or suppressing,

> "... we teach silence on the objective level in general ... Any bursting into speech is not repressed; a gesture of the hand to ... the objects, or action, or happenings, or feelings. Such a procedure has a most potent semantic effect. It gives a semantic jar; but this jar is not repression, but the realization of a most fundamental, natural, structural fact of evaluation." (p. 481)

Notice how closely this technique corresponds to the early NLP technique of accessing the 'stopping the world' state (McClendon, 1991, Grinder, 1987). Stopping the world means stopping one's racing and disquiet internal dialogue. Doing this moves us from the meta-level of language representations and brings us back down to the wondrous sensory rich world prior to our languaging. This intense sensory awareness state gives us the chance and space to create a new mapping as we language our experiences in new and different ways.

Summary

- As a semantic class of life, we use language to map our way around. Yet because our Mapping *is* not the same as the Territory, we need the ability to hear and question the maps that we and others use. This is the heart of all meta-modeling—the skill of a magician.
- We now have seven additional linguistic distinctions that add to the magic that we can perform with words. This expands our repertoire.
- In the next chapter, we shall add two additional pieces of magic.

Part III

Using Magic in Communicating and Living

Chapter 13

Cognitive Magic

Letting there be more Magic

Our exploration has taken us into the *structure* of the magical way that language works in our communications with each other in the neuro-linguistic states we induce. It began with the original Bandler and Grinder Meta-Model (1975). In the past three chapters we have stepped back in time to the origin of neuro-linguistics itself, and to the magic that Alfred Korzybski offered in General Semantics.

In this chapter we shall step forward in time and explore the linguistic distinctions offered in the Cognitive Psychotherapies and add one of those to our repertoire of magic—Personalization. Then I'll suggest a final one—Metaphor.

In addition to the seven linguistic distinctions from Korzybski, I have added two more that will cue us about ill-formed maps and give us the ability to touch them with the magic of precision. These linguistic distinctions enable us to set powerful mental and emotional frames in communicating.

Rational Emotive Therapy and NLP

In the field of Cognitive Therapy and REBT, Beck (1976) and Ellis (1979) have created lists of cognitive distortions that specify how we filter information and perceive the world. These distinctions closely correspond to the Meta-Model distinctions. Some years ago I sent this to Dr. Albert Ellis when I was writing my dissertation and asked for his comments. He said he was surprised. When I later went to New York City to meet with him, he described his dislike of NLP but admitted that it was mostly because of his dislike of Milton Erickson.

Some of the following exactly replicate linguistic patterns that we have covered while others offer yet additional perspectives.

1) *Over-Generalizing* closely corresponds to Universal Quantifiers and Lost Performatives. In over-generalizing, we jump to conclusions too quickly and draw too broad a map about something.

2) *All-or-Nothing thinking* corresponds to Universal Quantifiers and the Either/Or distinctions. This kind of thinking cuts the world into over-simplistic categories.

3) *Labeling* refers to putting labels on events, people, situations and then responding blindly to the label as if it was the thing. This fits with Nominalizations, Lost Performatives, Complex Equivalences, and Identifications.

4) *Blaming,* as a cognitive distortion, operates from the all-or-nothing frame that assumes linear causation. We blame to relieve ourselves of responsibility. Many Lost Performatives involve this kind of judgment from some unidentified map-maker. Many Cause—Effect statements imply blame.

5) *Mind-Reading* in the REBT model replicates the Mind-Reading pattern in the Meta-Model.

6) *Prophesying the future* takes the mind-reading distortion further as it applies the same mental pattern to read the future. This relates to what Bandler and Grinder called "crystal-ball mind-reading" (1975, pp. 144, 147).

7) *Awfulizing,* as a cognitive distortion, pronounces the judgment that something is 'awful.' Yet what does this nominalization mean? What is the criteria for calling something 'awful?' Is it just labeling and name-calling? Or is it just a Lost Performative statement that floats around as a cultural meme for feeling really bad and helpless, a meme that isn't indexed at all? When we attempt to index 'awful,' and extensionalize the term, we find that *awful* and *awfulizing* are Pseudo-Words. They have no real or logical referent anyway.

8) *Should-ing* refers to using the word 'should' (a modal operator) and imposing one's 'shoulds' on self or others inappropriately. 'You shouldn't hurt other people's feelings.' When used in that way, Should-ing becomes a Lost Performative. A modal operator of necessity becomes a moralizing cognitive and linguistic pattern that attempts to set an obligation frame.

9) *Filtering,* as in 'filtering out the positive,' fits with the deletion patterns of the Meta-Model (Unspecified Referential Indices and Simple Deletions). Yet when we filter *out,* we also filter *in*. That is, we *selectively filter* for what we want to see, hope for, wish for, etc. Filtering indicates that we have set a frame that is now operating as a self-organizing attractor. Linguistically, *filtering* can show up as a Nominalization, Cause—Effect, Complex Equivalence, etc.

10) *Can't-ing* is another modal operator that a person can take and make their mental filter and frame of reference for abilities. "I can't stand criticism." This modal operator of impossibility (in the Meta-Model) becomes a cognitive distortion in REBT, one used to relieve responsibility, excuse from action, etc.

8. Personalizing

There are two distinctions from the list of the REBT Cognitive Distortions which do not seem to correspond to any of the Meta Model distinctions. These make up the categories of 'personalizing' and 'emotionalizing.'

11) *Emotionalizing* refers to using our *emotions* for gathering and processing information. In emotionalizing, we over-value 'emotions,' we take counsel of them and we treat them as information-gathering mechanisms rather than a reflection of how our values compare with how we perceive things.

Emotions actually describe a relationship—a relationship in our minds-bodies. Emotions emerge from, and reflect, the relationship between our *Model* of the world and our *Experience* of the world. The difference between these two subjective awarenesses is what we experience as an 'emotion.' Think of the difference as a movement and position of a scale that weighs and compares *Model* and *Experience*.

When the scale tips evenly, our *experience* fits with what our *model* forecasts, predicts, describes, etc. When the scale tips down on the *experience* side, the world is not living up to our *model* of it. This sets off *negative* emotions. We don't like what's going on. We feel endangered, threatened, or violated. When the scale tips up on the *experience* side, then we are getting more than our *model* expected. This creates *positive* emotions. We really like this.

In emotionalizing, a person reacts to things subjectively and so forgets that our 'emotions' are but the relative weight that emerges from two phenomena: our sense of Map and Territory.

12) Personalizing (as used in REBT) refers to perceiving things, especially the actions of others, as specifically targeted toward us and/or as an attack on us. When we 'take things personally,' we personalize. This leads us to perceive people, events, situations, etc. through egocentric filters. It sets the frame over whatever happens so that we take it in and use it as a reflection on ourselves. We even do this when things and events have nothing to do with us. This style for thinking and sorting obviously leads to an over-sensitivity, giving everything that happens in our environment an effect on our self-image, ego, self-esteem, etc.

These ways of viewing things arise originally, as does *Identification*, from the way a child's mind works early in life. A child views the world egocentrically, in terms of itself, and by assuming that the world revolves around itself. Young children don't know better. They can easily assume that events and talk by others says something personal about them. The cognitive distortion at work involves associating into all mental processing and interpreting it to mean something about oneself.

A person using these cognitive distortions sees, hears, and responds to information, events, words, etc. as if whatever occurs out there does so in a 'personal' way—as a statement or reflection on the self.

In *personalization*, a person believes that he or she stands responsible for external situations for which they could not possibly stand responsible. "It's my fault that the picnic got rained out!" From that way of sorting things, the person then jumps to the conclusion that if they so perceive things, they should *feel* such (emotionalize it). In 'emotional reasoning,' a person believes that *because* he or she feels a negative emotion, *there must exist* a corresponding negative external situation.

Such personalizing and emotionalizing show up in language in the personal pronouns (I, me, mine), words indicating oneself, and in implied formats.

"Tom's making a lot of noise because he's angry *at me*."

This expression involves a cause—effect ('because'), a complex equivalence (lots of noise equals (=) a state of anger), and personalization (the presupposition that Tom engages in the angry behavior and directs it at the person. Personalizing involves a higher structuring that attaches *personal significance* to events and communication that could just as easily be understood impersonally. It frequently lies behind (or above) other semantically ill-formed expressions.

Suppose someone says, "Linda is ignoring me." The way this person selectively focuses on things (also discounting and negatively filtering) encourages personalizing. If we then can ask what that *means* to the person, he or she might say, "I will never have any friends." In this cause—effect statement, involving some universal quantifiers ('never,' 'any'), we also have another personalization, along with crystal-ball mind-read of the universe!

What does that mean?

"It means I am all alone."

Personalizing feeds self-pity and 'the entitlement syndrome.' When habitually over-used, it can lead to the antisocial personality orientation.

Joe typically ended work by catching a drink with the guys before going home. When he got home, he would notice that the children would continue to play outside or watch TV. He would automatically think, "They don't care that I've been working hard all day." Similarly, if he arrived home late without calling and his wife Becky had already cleaned up after supper, he would automatically judge it. "That bitch never fixes a decent meal for me." He would then confront her with that (!). If she didn't respond immediately with an apology, he would think, "She's ignoring me! How dare she!" This obviously set the stage for more unhealthy interactions.

Meta-Modeling Personalization

To question and explore the meanings within a statement that involves personalizing, use the following orientations:

(a) **Inquire about how the process works.**
How do you know to treat it as personal rather than impersonal?

"How do you know that Linda is intentionally ignoring you and purposefully doing it to send you a message?"

(b) **Explore other possibilities.**
"If Linda was just preoccupied, how would you tell? What would indicate that?"

(c) **Go meta to explore the personalization as a possible habitual meta-frame.**
"Do you typically read the behavior or words of others as saying something about yourself? Do you tend to be sensitive about yourself regarding such things?"

"Could this represent a perceptual filter that you have learned to use?"

9. Metaphors/Metaphor-ing

When we look at language at both the level of individual words and statements, metaphors are everywhere. They *lurk in the corners*. They often *visit us* like *angels unawares*. At yet other times, we have to *smoke them out*.

Why are there so many metaphors in our language? Because language itself is metaphorical; it *operates* via the *structure* of metaphors. Ultimately, how we create language and use language is by presenting various symbols that *stand for* something else. This explains the metaphorical or symbolic nature of language itself.

If all language *boils down* to metaphor, then this also describes one of the essential ways that we conceptualize. We compare what we know with what we seek to know and understand. We use references common in our experience as a template, format, or structure for what we are learning. We relate one domain of experience to another. We bring one referent to bear upon another. You can see these ideas in the root meaning of the word metaphor itself: 'to bear'(phorein) + 'above, over, about' (meta). In metaphor-ing, we take one thing and use it as a model for how to think about, perceive, and understand another thing. Throughout this work, as you well know, I have *played* with the metaphor of *magic*.

Lakoff and Johnson (1980a) have pioneered works showing how metaphor operates as a basic process for structuring knowledge. They theorize that concrete conceptual structures form the basis for abstract thinking and talking.

> "We understand experience metaphorically when we use a gestalt from one domain of experience to structure experience in another domain." (p. 230)

Consequently, in thinking, perceiving, understanding, and talking we constantly find, create, and use metaphors from one experience to 'make sense' of another. The fundamental nature of metaphor 'is understanding and experiencing one kind of thing in terms of another.' As language grows and habituates, we lose sense of the metaphorical nature of words. The metaphors die, lose their luster, and become lost in the history of the term.

Gordon (1978) was the first to devote an entire book to the subject of metaphors. He presented an NLP approach to building isomorphic metaphors that would therapeutically address problems.

> "Metaphors are a way of talking about experience ..."(p. 9), "all communication is metaphorical" (p. 11), "What makes it possible for a metaphor to be influential is that it is isomorphic with the client's actual situation." (p. 50)

For Lakoff and Johnson, we live by our metaphors. Our metaphors govern our thinking and feeling, they structure our actions and performances, they order our culture and meanings. In *Metaphors We Live By,* they illustrated numerous common cultural metaphors that govern how we live.

Time is Money (e.g., Time is a Limited Resource; Time is a Valuable Commodity).
    You're *wasting* my time.
    This gadget will *save* you hours.
    I've *invested* a lot of time in her.
Ideas (meanings) *are objects.*
Linguistic expressions are containers.
Communication is sending.
    It's hard to *get* that idea *across to* him.
    I *gave* you that idea.
    It's difficult to *put* my ideas *into* words.
Happiness is up; sadness is down.
More is up; less is down.
Ideas are entities (the basis of nominalizations).
    Inflation is lowering our standard of living.
    The *theory* explains to me why language works.
    These *facts* argue against that theory.
Mind is a machine.
    My mind is just not *operating* today.
    I'm a *little rusty* on that subject.
    I've *run out of steam* about that problem.

These examples show how metaphors not only set our presuppositional frames, but also structure our attitudes about things. When we frame by metaphor that 'Theories are buildings,' then we want to set a good *foundation,* so that our theory has good *support* and won't *fall apart* or *collapse*. We'll need to *buttress* our ideas. When 'Love is a physical force,' then we can feel the *electricity* as we're *attracted* to another. Then the *atmosphere* feels *charged* with *energy*.

In this way we *live* our metaphors. As they structure our thinking and action, they come alive in our bodies and feel 'real.' That's why it sometimes feels counter-intuitive to even question them. As we embody them, we feel grounded in them as an epistemological structure of meaning. When we use metaphors in our thinking and speaking, we think and speak of one thing *'in terms of'* another. To do this we have to move to a meta-position (a meta-state) and set the second thing as a metaphorical structure over the first.

In so using metaphors, we engage in a top-down kind of processing (deductive reasoning). "How *strong* is your hope for success?" The metaphor of *strength* here sets the frame for one's hope. Intensity of strength ('strong') is related to the legitimacy and validity of one's sense of hope. The metaphor sets the frame (or meta-states) the primary experience.

Analogical communication includes metaphors, analogies, similes, stories, and a great many other kinds of figurative language forms. Such language connotates, it indirectly implies rather than directly denotes a referent. Such language endows communication with less directness, more complexity and vagueness, and more emotional evocativeness. It describes the language of the poet more than the scientist. I say 'more,' because scientists also use metaphor constantly, although they typically use it more as an explanatory device whereas the poet glories in it as an end within itself—for its beauty and charm.

To become sensitive to the metaphorical level and use of language, we need to think in terms of analogies and analogous relations.

> What term, terms, sentences, and even paragraphs imply or suggest some metaphorical relation?

> What metaphors does the speaker use to structure his or her thinking and framing?

Lisnek (1996) has noted the 'story' nature of communication and the Meta-Model as a technology for addressing such.

> "There is a term that applies to the story-telling model of communication—it's the 'meta' model. In simple terms, the meta model is based on the idea that people relate information in story form. As listeners of the story, we add to the information we hear or delete facts or impressions based on past experience and our interpretation of events. So, your version will assuredly be different from mine, even if we've both experienced the same event. (pp. 33–34)

> "When Arnie tells his best friend Mary about his rotten salary, he tells a story. ... The meta model of communication includes a set of patterns that allows us to examine how we generalize, distort, specify, or delete data as we relate information in our stories. We do this so that we can better position ourselves in negotiation by testing the stories of the other negotiator." (p. 34)

Notice the metaphors in the following:

> "What you claim is indefensible."

> "She attacked the weakest point in his line of arguments."

> "His criticisms were right on target."

> "They shot down all my arguments."

Since the overall frame-of-reference involves conflict, battle, war, we can identify the 'war' metaphor as the driving frame in these statements. The speakers analogously compare the communication exchange to soldiers battling to win a war. How does this differ from another possible metaphor.

> "Arguing with him is like a dance."

> "We danced around the core issue for a long time."

"The movements of our meanings whirled around with no pattern at first."

Typically, we think of metaphors as operating not so much as 'real' language, but as flowery language. Because of this, we don't take them as serious descriptions. Paradoxically, this has the effect of empowering metaphors in our neuro-linguistics so that they have more influence and power in our lives and emotions. Because metaphors operate at a meta-level rather than at the primary level, when we are focused on *content* we hardly even hear or notice the metaphors. This allows them to operate as meta-level presuppositions, which invites people to remain mostly unconscious to their presence and workings. So when someone says, "Now I feel like I'm getting somewhere," we may not even notice the 'travel' metaphor of journeying, adventuring, etc. "That was over my head" suggests a 'space' metaphor to ideas and understandings.

More recently, Lawley and Tompkins (2000) have used the Meta-Model questions to explore the Metaphorical Landscapes in our minds. Their Symbolic Modeling approach refers to modeling the internal models in another's mind by asking questions about what an experience is *like,* what else there is, where it is, what came before, what comes after, etc. It's an excellent application of the Meta-Model questions as applied to metaphors and well documented from sources in Cognitive Linguistics, self-organization theory, etc. The weakness in the work is calling these questions 'clean language.' It is not 'clean' in the sense that it doesn't radically influence the speaker. They got that from David Grove (the source of the model) and seem actually to think that such questions will not and do not influence the speaker's mind, but innocently *discover* what's there. As you'll see in the next two chapters on using the Communication Magic Model conversationally, these questions structure, organize, and frame consciousness itself.

All questions influence. In spite of using 'the client's words' inside these questions, they still set frames for the person's response.

"And is there anything else about that? And what else is there ...?"

"And what kind of a thing is that thing?" (Quality frame, Categorizing frame)

"And that kind of a thing is like what?" (Metaphor frame)

"And where is this thing?" (Location frame)

"And whereabouts is this thing?" (Location frame)

"And then what happens?" (Spatial location frame in future time)

"And what happens next?" (Spatial location frame; consequence frame)

"And what happens just before this?" (Prior spatial location frame)

"And were could this come from?" (Source frame)

Then there are the stretching the edge of the map questions (p. 196).

"What's beyond that?"

"What's outside?"

"What's above, over, on top of ... below, under, beneath ... behind?"

As much these authors may want to believe that such questions keep the results 'clean,' they do not. These words invite people to invent all kinds of things that were not there before the question was asked. Yes, focusing on the person's words and symbols does create a focus on a single event, and to some extent explores the person's mental world, yet it also invites creating things by that very focus. The symbolic domain, like all facets of consciousness, *changes* and *transforms* by the very accessing of it. All memories are like that. With every re-accessing of a memory, that memory will change.

All questions invite frames. Even the simple question, "What kind of an X is that X?" invites a person to step out of the content to describe and invent the qualities and nature of the frame. We do that in Meta-States as a way to elicit and flush out the frames we have around an experience. "What is the quality of your anger?" Whatever the person answers tells about his or her higher frames.

Other questions invite pure invention. "What is that X like? It is like what?" This question "prompts the client to convert her everyday narration into symbolism." (p. 69). Yes, indeed!

A location question, "Where is it?" invites the person to embody and to start populating his or her symbolic space. We do that in NLP and Neuro-Semantics all the time: "Where is your past? Your future? Today?" The time questions (What happened before? What happens next?) are the Pre- and Post-framing questions that we'll describe in the *Mind-Lines* model in Chapter 15.

> There are outcome questions: "What would you like to have happen *instead of* X?"
>
> Epistemology questions: "How do you know that this is X?"

Is That It?

Are there other linguistic distinctions that we can add to these? Of course there are.

When I first presented some of the Korzybskian distinctions in London in a training, Denis Bridoux, an NLP Trainer in England, and I began exploring other potential categories. For instance, we played with the category of the *Imposed Performative*. In this category, a person uses the 'you' pronoun and does so in a way that it sounds like he is speaking about another while actually speaking of him or herself, or of general human experience.

> "It's just that when you feel rejected, you wonder about your own worthwhileness, don't you?"

Functionally, this use of 'you' operates mostly as a hypnotic induction since it invites a person to take on the representations in an attempt to make sense of the words. A question we could use to explore and challenge this usage could be:

> "Is that what *you* think?"
>
> "Are you speaking about yourself or me?"

And so the exploration of the magic in language goes on and will go on. And so it should.

Summary

- We have now explored and expanded the Meta-Model with two additional linguistic distinctions. Personalization creates the magic of bringing things into our sense of self—a pretty magical quality. Metaphor-ing speaks of a world-creating and constructing process that touches us with the magic of creativity and modeling.
- These give us additional *linguistic markers* also, markers that we can use to cue us about possible impoverishment of our mental maps, cues about when, where, and how to touch lives with magic.

The Extended Meta-Model

Patterns/ Distinctions	Responses/ Questions	Predictions/ Results
1. Over/Under Defined Terms (O/U)		
"I married him because I thought he would make a good husband."	What behaviors and responses make a "good" husband for you? What reference facts do you have for "husband?"	Recover the extensional facts about the terms used
2. Delusional Verbal Splits (DVS)		
"My mind has nothing to do with this depression."	How can you have "mind" apart from "body" or "body" apart from "mind?"	Recover the split that someone has created verbally in language
3. Either/Or Phrases (E/O)		
"If I don't make this relationship work, it proves my incompetence."	So you have no other alternative except total success or failure? You can't imagine any intermediate steps or stages?	Recover the continuum deleted by the statement. Either/Or structure
4. Multiordinality (M)		
"What do you think of your self?"	What do you mean when you refer to "self?"	Recovers the level of "Self," can have many different meanings, depending on context & usage speaker operates from. Specifies the context
5. Static Words (SW)		
"Science says that ..."	What science specifically? Science according to whose model or theory? Science at what time?	Recovers the deleted details
6. Pseudo-words (PW)		
"And that makes him a failure."	What do you mean by "failure" as a word that modifies	Challenge a map that uses words which have no real referent
7. Identification (Id.)		
"He is a democrat."	How specifically does he identify with "democrat?" In what way?	Recovers the process of Identification.
"She is a jerk."	Upon what basis do you evaluate her using the term "jerk?"	Invites one to create new generalizations
8. Personalizing (Per.)		
"He does that just to irritate me."	How do you know his intentions? How do you know to take these actions personally?	Challenges the process of personalizing
9. Metaphors (Mp)		
"That reminds me of the time when Uncle John ..."	How does this story relate to the point you want to make?	Recover isomorphic relationship between the story and the person's concepts

Chapter 14

Making Magic Conversational

Mind Lines

"Words are the physicians of a mind diseased."
Aeschylus

- Imagine being able to *speak* magic. Would you like that?
- Suppose you could take what you've discovered regarding the *structure* of meaning and magic in the previous chapters and make them part of your *conversational style*?
- Would you like to make your everyday communications magical?

This chapter is all about going beyond the grammar of the language model to using it magically for persuasion. It's about using it hypnotically to influence the mind, emotions, and actions of others (including ourselves).

While learning the Meta-Model may at first involve a slow and laborious task, it does not remain such. While first exposure to the neuro-linguistic communication model may invite us to look afresh at language usage, at such mundane things as nouns, verbs, adjectives, adverts, pronouns, prepositions, etc., it doesn't stay there. Grammar is only the beginning. From there we move to *using* the word magic to perform *verbal magic* with our words.

To this point you have reviewed the structure and syntax of language. Perhaps you have found this reminiscent of school days when you were first asked to make your intuitive use of language and grammar conscious. How did you experience that? Did you find it confusing, boring, stressful, exciting, wonder-filled, or what? Did you know that even at the level of grammar, you were actually exploring how your use of language punctuates the structure of magic?

This is the way it is with every science and art. To enter any field, every field, at first demands that we become detailed technicians. At first we are asked to go methodically through the basic 'lessons.' Whether its art, music, athletics, computer science, archeology, biology, mathematics, journalism, etc., we first have to master the foundational principles and skills. In doing so, we become competent. In the neuro-linguistics of using language for magic inductions, we obtain our degree in magic as we put in the time, energy, and trouble to perform the drills, to learn the 'chops,' and to practice. Eventually the skills become intuitive and unconscious.

When that happens, we move from *unconscious incompetence* to unconscious competence. We move from the place where we didn't even know that there was magic in language or how to work its magic. Our beginning incompetence at a primary level meant we did not even know that we did not know.

Eventually, however, we became aware of our incompetence. That was the hard stage. That was the stage where we struggled. "This is hard! Why do I have to learn this stuff? What do verbs, nouns, nominalizations, unspecified referential indices, and all of this other crap have to do with meaning or magic?" It's at that stage of conscious incompetence that we complain and fuss a lot! Most of us find it painful to become conscious of our incompetence. We don't like that. Of course, those who view it as exciting, as an adventure, and as a daily discovery, have their learning touched with that magic that textures the process in a very special way.

Quickly or slowly (usually slowly) we become increasingly competent. As this happens, we attain higher and higher degrees of competency, skill, understanding, and awareness. We then experience the discipline of the field as actually enjoyable. We begin to have conscious fun meta-modeling ourselves and others. We begin to delight ourselves in the experience of seeing how to play with words in new ways and the power that results.

As this continues, our progress moves us into higher levels of mastery. And with mastery comes an even higher level of *unconsciousness.* Our knowledge and skills drop out of awareness and we do it naturally, intuitively, unconsciously. When this happens we reach a stage of unconscious competence. We then have an in-knowing (or '*in*-tuition') about how to do it. We can now can do it conversationally while engaged in other things even more exciting—like picking up on and modeling various forms of human excellence.

It was at this stage of competence that Bandler and Grinder first encountered Perls, Satir, and Erickson. They performed the magic but really didn't know how they did; they were not even very aware of what they sorted for or why. When they were asked about it, their explanations fell far short of providing useful models. Of course, this is the typical situation with any expert. The expert no longer knows. Generally, it takes the experts a life-time of learnings and experiences to develop such intuitive skills. And it takes a modeler to unpack the strategies and to create a model of them.

Conversational Reframing

Classic NLP, through Robert Dilts, came up with a set of patterns for using the Meta-Model distinctions conversationally. He called this domain, *Sleight of Mouth Patterns.* These patterns provide a way to reframe meanings as we hear them in everyday language. There was a problem with the original model—it lacked any organizing structure.

There was another problem, its name. While the original name played on the idea of 'magic,' or *perceived* magic, it used the analogy of a quick-hand artist who pulls various sleight of hand maneuvers at a circus, county fair, or amusement park. The so-called magic of that occurs by means of mis-directing the attention of observers. The artist misdirects attention in numerous ways. It begins when he or she sets the expectation frame, 'The hand is quicker than the eye.' To this 'come on,' the observers decide to really 'look' and to look faster and harder than ever so that no hand will trick their eye. The rigidity of focus that develops in observers plays into the artist's 'sleight of hand' movements. It allows him or her to make moves at other places, without being noticed.

This principle holds true also for the *'Sleight of Mouth'* patterns. While we seemingly focus our attention on the content of what a person says, at other levels we pull a 'sleight of mind' as we invite a shifting of frames. Typically, people don't notice this. Caught up in the content and focused there, the new frame slides in. This allows them to accept it and buy into it without noticing or questioning. The basic meta-level presupposition describes what results, "Whoever sets the frame governs the subsequent thoughts, feelings, behaviors, and experiences."

The 'Sleight of Mouth' patterns presuppose a masterful competence of the Meta-Model and with the principle of reframing, that is, of putting an idea or representation into another frame of reference. Then, to the ill-formed semantic maps that we hear in the everyday expressions of people, we conversationally respond with some questions and/or statements that in a line or two provide a Meta-Model transformational challenge. To use 'Sleight of Mouth' patterns, we skip the meta-modeling part and fast forward to the bottom line statement, question, story, proverb, etc. that performs the sleight of mind on the limiting or non-enhancing idea. Doing this re-directionalizes the speaker's mind as it simultaneously offers a streamline statement.

While these patterns were powerful linguistic patterns in terms of exercising persuasion influence, they were not easy to understand, let alone master. That's what we (Bob Bodenhamer and I) sought to improve when we first collaborated to rigorously rework the patterns and develop a logical level system for them (using *Meta-States*). We did that first in 1997 (*Mind-Lines: Lines For Changing Minds*) and have continued expanding the model with every reprinting (1998, 2000).

By rigorously exploring the linguistic patterns and finding a way to put them into a logical level system, we discovered that we could specify *7 directions* for directionalizing attention. This lead to identifying 20 (and later, 26) different patterns inside of the 7 directional classes. We titled these patterns *Mind-Lines* as we recognized them as lines to magically change minds when engaged in conversational reframing.

[The following comes directly from Chapter 2 of *Mind-Lines* (2000, 3rd edition).]

Using Language Patterns to Influence

With the Meta-Model as an explanatory model for recognizing how language works in our neurology as we construct our maps of reality, we can easily see how language patterns govern our lives. Actually, language plays an inescapable role in all areas of life. The language we use governs the workings and health of our families, governs our success or failure in business, dictates our level of influence in our churches, schools, and political parties, and even forms and reforms our social environments. In all of these systems, and many more, language creates or destroys, enhances or limits our experiences.

The influential language patterns that we call *Mind-Lines* derive from the Meta-Model and offer us a gold mine of opportunity for enriching our lives. The language patterns also provide a greater depth of understanding about how we affect life in these systems simply by the way we talk and the symbols we use. We also know that simply by using these language patterns intentionally and elegantly, we can expand our maps to experience more power and flexibility. Doing that in turn, expands our skills of persuasion, influence, clarity, etc. This puts the magic of language into our hands in a new and exciting way.

The importance of such languaging is indicated by how our language both describes and reflects our model of the world. Our languaging reflects *how* we have built our current mental maps using the modeling processes described in earlier chapters. Our languaging reflects how we have deleted, generalized, and distorted our neurological representations of sensory referents.

How is this important? How does this affect our powers of engaging in *conversational magic?*

Ultimately, the secret in moving a person in a desired direction involves offering the kind of language to another and in such a way that the language evokes the person to represent things in an appropriate and enticing way. The communication model in NLP gives us two kinds of conversational magic. One involves *moving up* to higher levels of abstraction, the other involves *moving down* to levels of greater precision. The first hypnotizes, the second specifies. The first creates altered states and experiences, the second provides data that allow others to representationally track right from the words to a very similar movie for their minds. The hypnotic model (or Milton Model) articulates the first; the Meta-Model articulates the second.

The Language of Specificity Magic For Precision and Clarity

Remember what we did with the sensory-based illustration earlier, the rebuke that I imagined a mother might say to a child?

> "Would you turn around (K) and look (V) at the dirt on the carpet? Do you see (V) the dirt that forms the shape of your footprints? Now what do you have to say (A) about that?"

How *clearly* did those words communicate? Go with that description for a moment. Follow the words as if they were instructions. Begin with the words, "Turn around" and "look," etc. You may not have carpet under your feet, so you may have to pretend what that would look, sound, and feel like. You may not be standing, but you can imagine yourself standing. You may not be standing inside a room, but again, you can pretend, can you not? For these words to 'influence' you, to signal your brain to run this particular movie which you've done (have you not?), we only needed to provide you *clear, precise, and specific symbols.*

This is the *magic* of communicating with precision!

Similarly, for you to invite another person to move their internal representations in a specific direction, you get them to make a movie that corresponds to the one in your head by simply *describing* to that person (loved one, client, customer) what you see, hear, sense, and say inside your head.

Sounds simple, doesn't it? Well, it's not really that simple.

And, why, pray tell, not?

Because most people don't know how to talk in sensory-based terms. Instead, we do what humans all over the planet do all too well and too quickly, we *go meta* and head to the ozone into higher levels of abstraction. Then, from those heights of abstraction we talk using lots of evaluative terms. As we do, we talk in non-sensory based terms that seem clear to us while providing no precise sensory instructions to another.

> "You are so rude to come into my clean house and make a filthy mess. I get so angry at your irresponsibility!"

Ah, a different kind of confrontation from the former one, don't you think?

By the way, this illustrates an extremely powerful technology. If we need to say something unpleasant or 'confrontative' (another nominalization), *we can say almost anything to anybody if we use sensory-based descriptive language.* And, we can say almost nothing to anybody if we use evaluative, non-sensory based language. Don't take my word for this, try it out for yourself.

When we abstract from *sensory based words* (first level of linguistic languaging) and move up to greater and greater levels of *non-sensory based language,* we move into increasingly higher levels where 'thought' becomes abstract. As language becomes more abstract, we delete more of the specific sensory information as we generalize. This describes how we create models of reality.

Read the following Orwell passage and the biblical referent that follows. Which makes more sense? Which do you find easier to understand?

> "Objective consideration of contemporary phenomena compels the conclusion that success or failure in competitive activities

> exhibits no tendency to be commensurate with innate capacity, but that a considerable element of the unpredictable must invariably be taken into account."

Did you like that? Thank George Orwell for that one (1950, *Shooting an Elephant and Other Essays*). Sounds abstract, right? Sounds 'intellectual,' right? And did you go "What in the world does he mean with all of that?" Ah, the danger of abstractions. Too many nominalizations (as in that sentence) and the deletions, generalizations, and distortions (the three modeling processes) leave us so high up the scale of abstraction that we can get lost in the ozone.

Would you like to see the original piece from which Orwell made that 'intellectual' abstraction? Here it goes.

> "I returned and saw under the sun that the race is not to the swift, nor the battle to the strong, neither yet bread to men of understanding, nor yet favor to men of skill; but time and chance happeneth to them all." (Ecclesiastes 9:11)

While we have some nominalizations in that one (especially "time"), it basically presents a sensory-based description of events that we can easily see-hear-and-feel, and so representationally track to our mental screen. It offers us symbols that we can easily use to representationally track to our mental screen. We can easily make a movie out of those words.

The point? When we make a meta-move to a higher logical level of symbolization and use more abstract words (nominalizations, class words, etc.), we use a different kind of *representational system,* a non-sensory based one. We use the abstraction language system. And because we can continue the process of saying more words about those words, we can create ever more abstract words and language forms.

Notice all of the sensory-based language referents in the original text and contrast those with the abstractions and generalizations in the 'modern' translation. Though the modern 'translation' sounds more intellectual, it also lacks the power of precision and clarity.

We truly enrich our language and communication skills when we use more and more specific visual, auditory, kinesthetic, and sensory-based language components about the movie that we have constructed in our head. When we want to communicate with more clarity and precision, *we go descriptive.* The words will flow out of our mouth as we *describe* what we actually experience and represent, and what we wish for the person with whom we are communicating.

Actually, without the ability to distinguish between *descriptive* and *evaluative* language, we will never become truly professional or elegant in our use of language. We begin by learning the power and simplicity of see-hear-feel language. Sensory language provides the *magic wand* of clarity and precision. This is a language that also contains the deframing magic—the pulling apart of old constructions or frames.

The Language of Evaluation Magic
For Constructing 'Realities'
Casting Spells, Setting New Frames
Reframing and Outframing

"Should we therefore *never* use abstract or non-sensory based language?"

Of course not.

Such represents our uniqueness and glory as human beings. We only need to do so with more *mindfulness* and thoughtfulness or, as Korzybski put it, develop "consciousness of abstracting."

Here, the NLP Model truly provides a most wonderful paradigm and tool (technology) for guiding our understanding of what we do with words, and the effect that our languaging has on ourselves and others.

Many times, instead of getting a person to accurately and specifically represent information with certain sensory signals, we need to move them to a higher level. From there we can offer new and different ways of abstracting and conceptualizing. Doing that enables the other person to *set a whole new frame of reference,* frames that transform everything. Using such language enables us to *construct* new 'realities,' create new meanings, establish new reference systems, call new worlds into existence.

Sometimes this moves a person from one position at a meta-level to another level.

For instance, suppose a father sees his teenage son lying on the couch watching TV. At this point, we only have a sensory-based set of representations, right? Or have you already drawn a conclusion and evaluated it? Suppose the father sees such and immediately jumps a logical level to classify that behavior as a member of the class that we call 'laziness.' He sets *laziness* as his frame. He looks at the specific behaviors and no longer sees them as mere sensory-based pieces of information anymore. He looks and sees *Laziness* with a capital L. Right?

Of course, 'laziness,' as a nominalization, does *not* exist in the world, but only in the mind. What exists in the world are the see-hear-feel facts: lying on a couch, watching TV. The *meanings* that we give to those sensory signals depend upon our *frames* (e.g., beliefs, values, understandings, abstractions, paradigms, etc.) If they depend on our frames, what are our references? Some parents may look at the same signals, and using *other* frames may say,

> "I'm so glad John can relax and enjoy the good things of life, unlike my traumatic childhood, and I'm so thrilled that I can provide for him all the things I never got."

It could happen!

Meaning (semantics) exists only, and exclusively, in the 'mind.' It exists as *a form of evaluation and appraisal.* It emerges as we bring *frames-of-reference* to our see-hear-feel movies.

This makes *meaning* a higher logical level abstraction *about* the information. 'Meaning' operates as information-about-information at a higher level. It involves meta-level 'thoughts' *about* lower level 'thoughts.' We call the states of these levels *neuro-semantic* states in contradistinction to our primary level *neuro-linguistic* states. Though arbitrary, it usefully distinguishes between the associations at primary and meta levels. It distinguishes consciousness *going out* to the world and consciousness *reflecting back onto itself.* In *reframing,* we essentially do a horizontal shift at the meta-level to set a new frame.

Figure 14.1: The Reframing Model Diagram

"John isn't being lazy, he simply really knows how to relax and enjoy himself."
"Jill isn't rude, she just forgot to wipe her feet."
"Jerry isn't ugly and hateful, he has just gotten into a very unresourceful state and feels really threatened."
"Terri isn't trying to put you down, she just feels overwhelmed and has become emotionally preoccupied with three little ones and the recent death of her mother."

Figure 14.2: Reframing a Statement

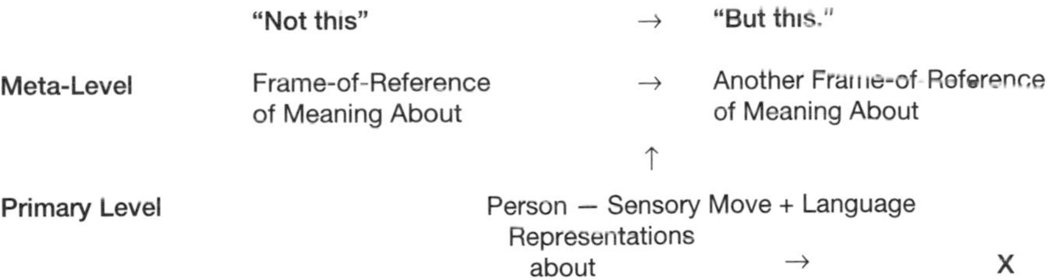

In the language patterns (mind-lines) that follow, this model offers numerous ways to reframe meanings using the horizontal shifting pattern. In this way, we reframe to transform meaning. These linguistic mind-lines give us all sorts of resourceful ways to *put the best frame-of-reference on things so that we can operate more effectively.*

The model also allows us to take control of the meaning-making powers at our disposal. It points the way to how we can order and re-order any meaning that creates limiting beliefs, toxic ideas, and unenhancing ideas. It gives clue to the secrets of magic that are at our command ... if only we notice.

"This doesn't mean this → it means this."
"Not X, but Y."

The Language of Evaluation-of-Evaluation Magic
For Casting Higher Spells
For Outframing All Meanings
For Transforming Everything in One Fell Swoop

The ultimate form of reframing occurs when we make a *vertical move* and go up the abstraction level. When we do that, we leave the first level frame-of-reference and move to a higher level. From that higher level, we can *outframe* the whole context. We then create a new context for the context itself. 'Outframe' refers to setting up a frame-of-reference *over* everything that lies beneath it.

Consider a boy who has encoded his brain with memories of severe spankings as a child. He signals his brain with see-hear-feel and linguistic representations now, as he remembers the abuse he received when he was beaten with a stick. He continues to play out the old movie as if it were occurring now. At the time, he was only acting and thinking like a kid, being silly and his dad flew into a rage and beat him.

Within his mental movie screen, the images, sounds, and sensations played over and over along with the words of insult, "You stupid brat, you'll never succeed in life with that attitude!"

Not very pretty, huh?

Now suppose the kid (let's call him Wayne) grows up and makes several beliefs from those experiences. Suppose Wayne reaches the following conclusions:

> "I'll never amount to anything."
>
> "Something's wrong with me. I must be defective because I have this 'attitude' that provokes dad so much."

> "I don't feel very loved or loveable, therefore I must not be loveable."

With such *evaluative meanings* we can easily guess the kind of neuro-semantic states Wayne will continually create for himself as he grows up. We certainly would not call them resourceful ones. These states will likely only reinforce and deepen his sense of distress. They will provide him 'proof' about the validity and accuracy of those limiting beliefs.

As Wayne grows and receives more of the same, he will draw another and even higher meta-level frame of reference,

> "I'll never change. This is the way life is going to be. No need to get my hopes up that things will turn around. I'm just a loser and always will be."

That neuro-semantic state, as a state-about-a-state, will then *multiply* his psychological pain and create even more of a self-fulfilling prophecy. This will operate as a form of *black magic* in his mind-body system. It will set a high level frame-of-reference typically *outside* of consciousness which will govern his perceptions, behaviors, communications, expectations, etc. in such a way that it actually seeks out and invites more of the same.

Further, with that *belief* working at an even higher meta-level, reframing Wayne at the first meta-level will not have much effect, or at least, no long-term effect. It doesn't get to the highest of executive frame. Suppose we offer the following powerful reframe:

> "It's not that you won't amount to anything, actually you can decide to become anything that you want to if you just put the past behind you."

That reframe will probably not work. At best, it will have little effect because a higher frame will govern his thinking and feeling and so discount the reframe.

> "No kidding I started with a handicap. But as we all know, 'You can't teach an old dog new tricks.' So don't give me any of your psychobabble crap!"

We need to *outframe* Wayne's frames. We need to find the highest frame, go *above* it, and set a whole new frame of mind. We need to step back and comment *on* the previous frames.

> "So those are the ideas and beliefs you built as an eight-year-old boy. Then on top of that, at 17, you built that stuck-and-can't-change belief." ["Yeah, so?"]
>
> "So now, here you are at 30, living out these old beliefs. How well do you like those beliefs? Do they serve you very well?" ["No, not at all."]
>
> "So the conclusions you drew at 8 and 17 don't work very well. Well, that's probably the best kind of thinking that younger you could do when it created those ideas. Yet they do reflect the thinking of a child, not a grown man who can look back on all that and recognize them as misbeliefs and erroneous conclusions. Because children tend to self-blame rather than recognize that their parents didn't take 'Parenting 101' and never learned how to affirm or validate ..."

Figure 14.3: Frames Within Frames

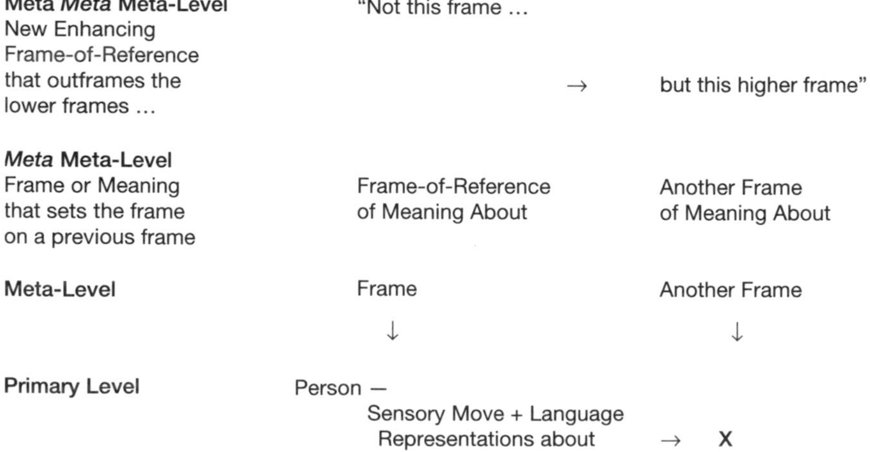

Neuro-Linguistic Magic— The Framing of Meaning

The *Mind-Lines Model* (derived from the Meta-Model and enhanced by Meta-States) essentially uses the process of *framing and reframing* to alter 'reality,' whether our own or someone else's. When we do, we transform the external expressions like emotions, behaviors, speech, skill, relationships, etc. to a trigger. It changes the *'logical fate'* within our *psycho-logics* (or neuro-semantics). All beliefs and ideas have consequences, so when we change an executive frame of reference, it changes our whole future.

If you believe that you 'won't amount to anything,' that you 'can't do anything right,' that you 'don't have the right to succeed'—the *logical fate* of those psycho-logics within those statements will show up in how you present yourself, talk, walk, act, think, feel, etc. As you digest those words, the ideas will be metabolized in your neurology.

Via *mind-lines,* we utilize the neuro-linguistic magic in our use of language to set and to play around with new frames. We can do so until we find those that result in desirable 'logical fates' for ourselves and others. *Frames* refer to the *references* that we use as we relate to people, things, events, words, etc. Such references may be real and historical, personal or impersonal, conceptual like beliefs, imaginary like expectations, realistic or unrealistic, etc.

Neuro-linguistic and neuro-semantic reality begin with our thoughts *about* the world. Apart from our associations, *nothing means anything.* Apart from our thoughts, *events occur* and things happen. Sights, sounds, sensations, etc. stimulate our sense receptors. But they mean nothing. They hold no mental or emotional association, they occur within no mental framework or classification.

Then the magic begins. We see, hear, and feel such and so *represent* it and *connect* (or associate) it with other sights, sounds, and sensations. Later, we connect to it even higher level abstractions.

Giving or attributing meaning to something (to anything) involves an associative process. First we *link* an external event, person, action, or behavior up with some internal representation (or thought). Sounds simple enough, right?

Not!

This seemingly simple and obvious linkage begins the creation of associative 'meaning.' By it we link things together. Our linkage of these things may or may not be reasonable, rational, productive, useful, or valid. But once linked, that's what a thing 'means' because the first thought takes you to the second thought.

We ask, "What does anything mean anyway?"

To identify the meaning we have to find the associations.

What does 'fire' *mean?* It all depends upon what a given individual (or animal) has connected, linked, or associated with it. This sends us back to our referent *experiences.*

Have we seen and experienced fire only as campfires during a weekend camping trip? Have we associated fire with food, marshmallows, companionship, songs, fun, etc.? Then the *external behavior* (EB) of 'fire' *means* (relates to, causes, connects up with, etc.) the *internal state* of fun, delight, joy, togetherness, attraction, excitement, etc.

Consider how very, very different this is for the person whose referent experience of 'fire' relates to getting burned, feeling physical pain, seeing a home destroyed, etc. What does 'fire' mean to that person? Again, it all depends on what that person—conceptually and mentally—has connected to, and associated with, 'fire.' For that person, 'fire' probably *means* hurt, pain, loss, grief, aversion, etc.

Well, what does 'fire' *really* mean?

The surprise is that it 'means' *nothing*. Fire only exists as a certain event of change in the external world. Alone and unconnected by and to consciousness, *it has no meaning*. Nothing has any 'meaning.'

Meaning only and exclusively arises when a consciousness comes along and connects a thing to an internal reference. That creates a frame. That gives us a *frame-of-reference.* We might have 'fire' seen, heard, felt, and languaged from the frame of a campfire or from a home burning down. In both cases—

> *The frame completely and absolutely controls or governs the meaning.*

In fact, we cannot even understand the *External Behavior* (EB) or event apart from the *frame.* Apart from the frame, we don't know anything about its meaning to another person. Apart from knowing another person's frame, we all typically use our own frames-of-references. In that way we impose our 'meanings' upon them.

So when it comes to the *structure of meaning,* what do we have?

We have two major factors, one external, the other internal. The external component involves the *events* of the world. The internal component involves the human nervous system taking cognizance of the event. We cognize the event via our sensory systems and our language system.

These two phenomena occur at different levels and in different dimensions. Yet when we connect them, we suddenly have a neuro-linguistic meaning, a meaning which operates as magic in our experience. Putting this into the format of a formula, we have:

Figure 14.4: The Reframing Equation

External Behavior → **Internal State**
=

This meaning structure gives us the basic *frame-of-reference* which we all use in attributing meaning to things. It explains not only how we humans make meaning, but how animals can also experience and develop associative learning and understandings.

The secret?

Things get connected to things. Things of the outside world (i.e., events, behaviors, people) get associated with internal feelings, moods, states, ideas, understandings, values, etc. When this happens, we typically develop another meta-level phenomenon, a *'belief.'*

Once we have a *frame* (as in the above formula: (EB→/=IS), we don't stop there. Animals generally do, but not us humans. No way.

We have a special kind of consciousness that *reflects back onto itself* (our self-reflexive consciousness). Whenever we have a thought, we never leave it at that.

> "I like fire; it makes me feel warm and loved."
>
> "I hate fire. Fire is scary; it makes me shudder just to think about it."

We have to complicate matters (wouldn't you know it?). We do so by *having a thought about that thought.* This creates a meta-frame.

> "I hate it that I fear fire so much."
>
> "I feel proud of myself for feeling so good about fire, not getting scared of it like some people I know, but enjoying it and appreciating it for its positive values."

Nor do we leave it alone at that level, we bring even more thoughts to bear on the thoughts, etc.

> "*Why* do I let fire frighten me so much? I *should* get over this thing. *What's wrong* with me anyway that I can't be more reasonable? Well, I guess *I'm stuck* for life. Once you've had a traumatic experience like that, it seals your fate."

Of course, this initiates a *real neuro-semantic muddle,* does it not? To the original relations and connections that the person made with fire, the person has layered on more and more abstract ideas onto it. This creates not only beliefs, but belief *systems,* then belief systems about belief systems, etc. Or, to use the metaphor of a frame, the thoughts that we bring to bear on our earlier thoughts, set up a frame-of-reference around a frame, and then a frame around that frame, etc.

More Neuro-Linguistic Magic
Frames-Of-Frames

Once we have a basic frame established (EB→/=IS), then we can set a frame *above* that frame (a meta-frame or an outframe). Or we could set a frame-of-reference about it *prior* to it. Parents do this for kids regarding experiences (events) yet to come, "Now don't *fall into the fire*—that would be terrible!" In this model, this is *Pre-Framing*.

In addition to pre-framing, we can frame events and behaviors afterwards, and that gives us *Post-Framing*. "Yep, sonny, if you burned yourself in a fire once, you are likely to do it again and again!" How do you like that post-frame as a way of thinking? Pretty shoddy and muddled thinking, right? This also will typically operate as a 'post hypnotic suggestion.'

By the way, because all 'beliefs' or frames exist only 'in the mind,' they are forms of hypnosis. Typically, most people don't hallucinate cats, or elephants, or aliens. Instead we hallucinate *concepts*, beliefs, ideas, memories, imaginations, etc. We hallucinate concepts like 'rudeness,' 'fairness,' 'responsibility,' 'blame,' 'ownership,' etc. Sometimes we call this 'thinking.' It's a higher level of thinking—the thinking that occurs at meta-levels.

When we undermine the EB→/=IS formula, we engage in *De-Framing*. Whenever we ask specific questions about either the EB or the IS, our questions tend to have this effect. They pull apart the thought-construction, that is, the belief or meaning equation.

> "When did you get burned?"
>
> "In what circumstances?"
>
> "What did you learn from that?"

> "Have you used that learning to not repeat that experience?"

We can even do some fancy kind of mental gymnastics with our equation that summarizes the *structure of meaning*. For example, we can *Counter-Frame*. We can ask about or suggest experiences that counter the EB→/=IS formula equation.

> "Have you ever been around a campfire and enjoyed cooking a hotdog over the fire?" "How fearful and worried do you get when you strike a match and light candles on a birthday cake?"

These frames-of-frames provide additional ways to reframe. We not only do *not* have to stay inside our *magical meaning box,* we can step outside that box and send our consciousness (or someone else's) in one or more directions. We can go *way down* deep inside the box and ask specific questions of the qualities of our modality representations (and the 'submodality' qualities of those). Again, this *Deframes.*

Figure 14.5: The Directions of Meaning

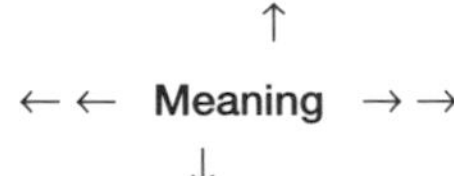

Or, we can *reframe* by going in one of two horizontal directions. We can go over to the left to a time *prior* to the frame-of-reference (the EB→/=IS formula) and *Preframe* the subsequent response. Or, we can go over to the right to a time later to the basic first level meaning, and *Postframe* it as meaning or suggesting something new and different.

Or, we can move up and *Outframe* as we set up a whole new frame-of-reference with a thought-about-that-thought. This steps outside of the frame or context and generates a whole new context, a context-of-a-context. With that move, we can embed the idea as a belief into all kinds of higher ideas.

Learning to make these conceptual and magical shifts gives us the ability to use various *mind-lines* to alter neuro-linguistic and neuro-semantic realities. As we do, we expand our sense of choice. We get an enlarged sense that we have many options about our *meaning attributions.* It develops and expands our sense of flexibility (of mind, emotion, and language). This training in language-patterning skills will enrich your communication skills, making you more effective and professional, more elegant in persuasion, and more influential. (Oh yes, if you didn't notice, this preframes you for what follows about Mind-Lines.)

Summary

- Meaning has structure. We have explored that structure in many chapters now and have summarized it in this chapter in terms of primary and meta-levels.
- To make meaning we begin with a reference. We then frame that reference, then connect it to states, and so the meaning-making process goes on.
- Since meaning does not exist 'out there' in a real and concrete way but within the neuro-linguistic system of a meaning-maker, meaning arises as an emergent property. Meaning occurs as a phenomenon of mind in relationship to the world. Therefore it is only as solid as our thinking, evaluating, and framing.

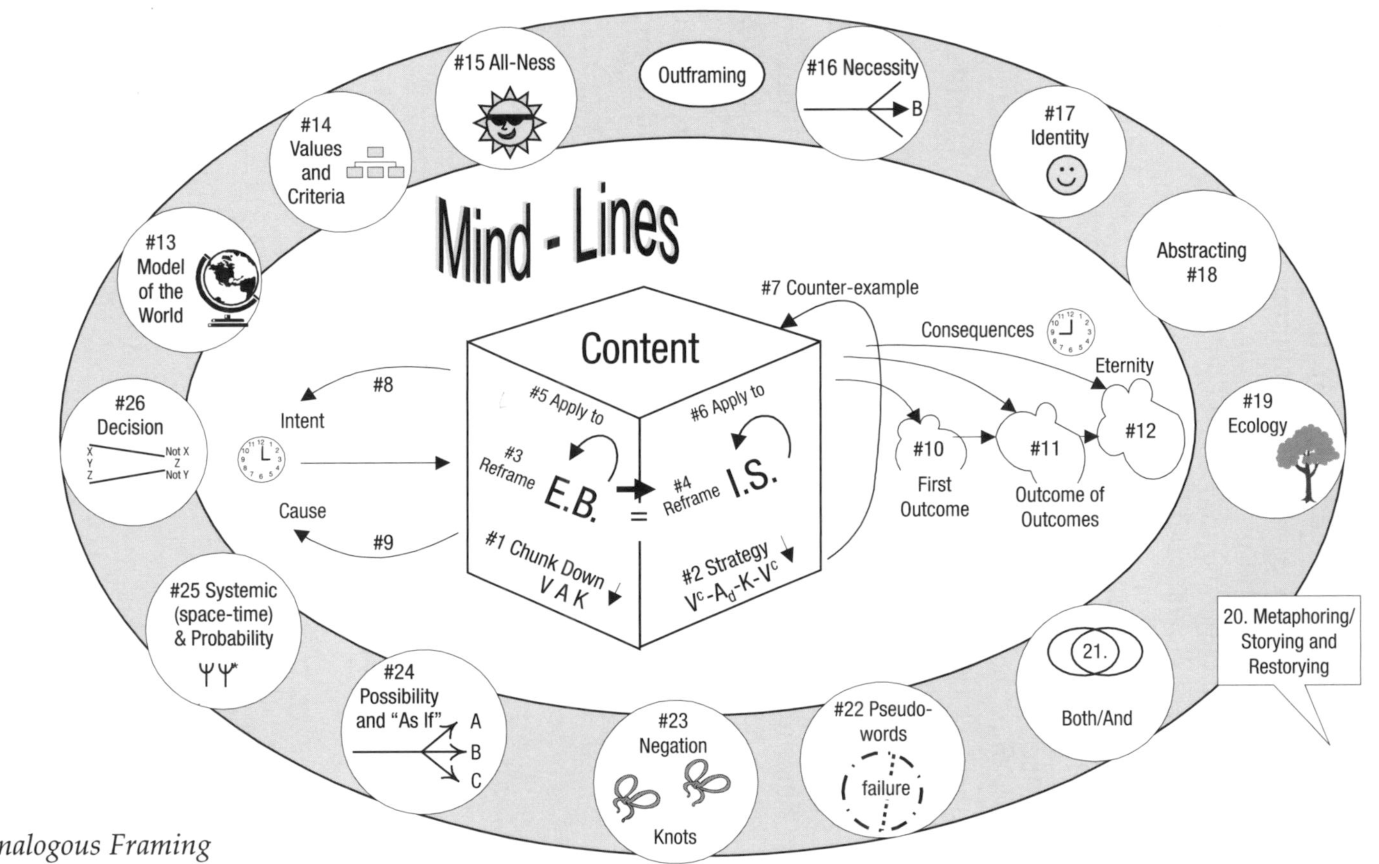

Analogous Framing

Chapter 15

Seven Directions to Send a Brain

The Mind-Lines Model

Lines for Changing Minds

Directionalizing and re-directionalizing consciousness, sending it out in new and different ways as we construct new and different meanings describes the dynamic heart of this model. We construct empowering meanings to frame things so that we become more resourceful, insightful, wise, thoughtful, etc. This is the neuro-semantic process that comes from the Communication Magic Model.

Previously this model was known as the '*Sleight of Mouth*' *Pattern*. I have changed that name primarily because it typically evokes negative connotations for many people. 'Sleight of Mouth' frequently raises thoughts of manipulation, control, pulling something over on someone, etc. To avoid that, while still exulting in the neuro-semantic magic of NLP and Neuro-Semantics, I will use the term Mind-Lines.

Mind-Lines refers to the *lines* or linguistic expressions that we connect and associate to things that create meaning formulas (EB→/=IS). These *mental constructs* carry tremendous neurological effects. As we change the lines that we use in our minds (and those we offer others), we change, alter, and transform our map and sense of reality. This gives us a mechanism for transforming neuro-semantic reality. By the changing of meaning, our emotions change, as do our behaviors, habits, moods, attitudes, skills, health, etc. and our life.

The chart at the end of this chapter overviews and summarizes the *seven basic mind-shifting directions and the twenty different mind-line patterns for reframing reality.* This chart represents our latest thinking about this magical neuro-linguistic art.

The Tool for Mind-Lining

The 'mental,' cognitive, and conceptual shifting of meaning that we've described can take seven basic directions. Each direction (backward, forward, down, up, counter, etc.) provides us a different way to *directionalize consciousness*. By sending (or swishing) someone's 'mind-and-emotion' in one of these different directions, we open up space for them (or ourselves) to experience new *frames-of-references* that can empower and facilitate greater resourcefulness, health, joy, love, etc.

The following briefly summarizes the seven directions that we have more fully described in *Mind-Lines: Lines for Changing Minds* (2000).

As self-exploration, notice the frames you have used in the last few moments as you have read this? What mental frames did you access and use?

> Did you use a "This is overwhelming!" frame?
>
> Did you default to a "Too many big words!" frame?
>
> Perhaps an "Oh this is complicated!" frame?
>
> An "Oh boy, mind-lines to empower me in moving through life!" frame.
>
> An "I find this very interesting and wonder about the exciting ways to use this!" frame.
>
> A "One page and pattern at a time and I'll learn this thoroughly" frame.

Which one of those frames would work best for you? What frame would you like to use? (Do you recognize these questions as *mind-lines*?)

Seven Ways to Change a Brain

1) Deframing

We first go down. We move downward into the specifics of the meaning, indexing, and fragmenting. In chunking-down the *meaning equation* we pull apart the component pieces of the VAK and the language structures that make up the *belief* format. The chunking-down movement involves deductive thinking and reasoning. In Deframing, we invite a person to 'Undermine your mind constructions by fragmenting it like this.' This shift helps us to de-think (our belief thoughts) as we analyze the magic and see it evaporate. Asking about the specific elements that make up a thought sorts the idea out and unglues it. This loosens it. Any indexing question can deframe.

#1 Chunking Down, The Specificity Move
#2 Detailing the Sequence of the Strategy

2) Content Reframing

Reframing lies at the center of the chart where we have the heart and structure of meaning—inside the box of meaning. Here we do a horizontal switch. Here we use the Complex Equivalences and Cause—Effect statements. These *meaning equations and attributions* define the heart of neuro-semantic reality and magic. Here we shift the meaning associations, 'It doesn't mean this, it means this.' This entails various facets of *content reframing*. In content reframing, we say, "Don't think that about this thing, event, act, etc. in that old way, think about it in this new way." "Don't call it X (laziness), call it Y (relaxation)."

#3 Reframe EB
#4 Reframe IS

3) Counter Reframing

Next comes the fancy footwork of offering a reframe that *counters the content*. Here we let our consciousness reflect back onto its own content (the ideas within the meaning box) and as we do, we apply the meaning equation to the other side of the equation to see if it coheres, or if that breaks it up into a thousand pieces. If it does, it deframes.

This reframing move involves reflexivity or self-reflexive consciousness as 'mind' thinks about its own thoughts. In *Counter Reframing,* we ask, "What happens to your ideas when you apply this way of thinking or belief to yourself?" "What do you think of the belief when you apply it to those cases, times, and events, where it does not fit?"

#5 Reflexively Apply EB to Self/Listener
#6 Reflexively Apply IS to Self/Listener
#7 Counter-Example

4) & 5) Pre-Framing and Post-Framing

In these conceptual moves we reframe by moving to a prior or post state to the idea (in our minds, of course). We view the meaning construction (the formula in the box) from the standpoint of what brought it about. Actually this is an Outframing move. We bring two concepts, *causation* and *intention,* to bear upon the idea and ask questions that presuppose a positive external causation and/or a positive internal motive. In post-framing, we 'run with the logic' to see if the meaning equation will continue to make sense when we view it from a larger time frame. We then ask, "Does the magic still work?" Here we bring *consequential thinking and outcomes* to bear upon the original belief.

This reframing move introduces various '*time*' concepts into the process and reframes by playing around with the 'time' frames that we can put around the *meaning box*. Here we bring various 'time' conceptualizations (or thoughts) and apply them to our belief-thoughts in the meaning box.

In Pre-Framing, we say, "When you put this thought in the back of your mind, how does it affect the belief?" In Post-Framing, we say, "When you put this thought in the front of your mind about that belief, how does it play out into your future?" Again, this challenges the magic in the box.

Before Time:
#8 Positive Prior Framing (Intention)
#9 Positive Prior Cause

After Time:
#10 First Outcome
#11 Outcomes of Outcome
#12 Eternity Framing

6) Outframing

In all of the outframing moves, we step aside from the structure of meaning (as coded in the equation) and bring various ideas to bear upon it. By moving up from the meaning construction to higher conceptual levels, we can bring many new and different facets to our neuro-semantic construction. These all directly *meta-state* the belief and offer a wide range of choices. These upward moves involve inductive thinking and reasoning. We now say, "Look at that formula from this point of view and notice how this transforms that."

By Outframing we put a particular conceptual spotlight on the formula. In this way we color and filter the formula with various meta-level frames. "When you wrap your mind around the belief and view it from this perspective, or in terms of this idea, how does it affect things?" These moves not only challenge the old magic, but also bring higher or meta-magic to bear on the belief.

#13 Model of the World Framing
#14 Criteria and Value Framing
#15 Allness Framing
#16 Have-To Framing
#17 Identity Framing
#18 All other Abstractions Framing
#19 Ecology Framing

7) Analogous Framing

In this reframing move, we shift from inductive and deductive thinking as well as horizontal and counter thinking as we move to analogous thinking (or "abduction," Bateson, 1972). We do this by shifting to storytelling, metaphor, and narrative. In this abducting type of framing, we essentially say, "Forget all of that, and let me tell you a story ..." Or, "What if you thought about that formula from this point of view?"

#20 Metaphoring/Storying and Restorying Framing

Overwhelmed With Magic?

"Wow! That's a lot to remember. How can a person ever learn all of that?"

"Ah, the Overwhelm Frame."

If you would like a quick and easy way to hurry your learnings on in this domain, use the following *Mind-Line Statements and Questions.* Think of these as semantic environments and prompters which you can easily memorize. After you learn them, you can use them to elicit your own alternative meanings that you can use to reframe a statement or objection. This will expand your flexibility in communicating, as well as your elegance.

Detecting and Identifying the 'Magic' of the Belief

#1 Chunk Down to deframe the EB or IS:
"What are the specific parts of this?"
"What component sensory pieces make up this?"

#2 Reality Strategy Chunk Down:
"In what order or sequence do these parts occur?"

#3 Reframe EB:
"What really this EB is ..."
"What else would qualify as this EB?"

#4 Reframe IS:
"This isn't IS^1, it is IS^2."
"What other IS could we just as well attribute to this EB?"

Immediate Concept about Concept, Reflexive Applying

#5 Reflexively Apply EB to Self/Listener:

"What an X statement!"

#6 Reflexively Apply IS to Self/Listener:

"So you're doing X to me?"

Reversal of Reflexive Applying to Self—Not-Applying Concept

#7 Counter-Example:

"Do you remember a time when the opposite occurred?"

"When does this Formula *not* apply?"

Run the Reverse of #5 and #6—*not* apply.

Time—Past

#8 Positive Prior Framing (Intention):

"You did that because of ..." (positive intention).

"Weren't you attempting to accomplish X positive purpose?"

#9 Positive Prior Cause:

"Didn't X contribute to bring about ...?" (positive cause)

Time—Future

#10 First Outcome:

"If you follow this belief, it will lead to ..."

#11 Outcomes of Outcome:

"If you experience that outcome, it will then lead to ..."

#12 Eternity Framing:

"Ultimately, this belief will lead to ... how do you like that?"

Recognition of a Map as a Map

#13 Model of the World Framing:

Frame as merely one Model of the world, one worldview.

"Who taught you to think or feel this way?"

"When you think of this as a mental map, how does that change things?"

"So you have mapped it that way, when did you do that?"

Values, Criteria, Standards

#14 Criteria and Value Framing:

"What do you find more important than this?"
"How does X (some other value) affect this?"
"Is this really important?"

Allness, Universal Quantifier

#15 Allness Framing:

Exaggerate the universal quantifier of the statement:
"Always? To everyone?"

Modal Operator of Necessity/Impossibility

#16 Have-To Framing:

Challenge the necessity of the statement:
"What *forces* you to think this way?"
"What would happen if you went ahead and did it?"
"Do you *have to*?"
"What would it be like if you *couldn't?*"

Identity, Self-definitions

#17 Identity Framing:

"What does this say about you as a person?"
"Is this who you are?"

All Other Abstractions

#18 Abstracting the EB or IS:

Create an abstraction or concept about the belief:
"This is a case of ... X, isn't it?"

Ecology, Evaluation of Evaluation

#19 Ecology Framing:

"Does this serve you well? Does it enhance your life?"
"Does this give you the quality of life that you want?"

Meta-phoring—Transferring Over another Domain of Knowledge

#20 Metaphoring/Storying and Restorying Framing:

Literally, 'meta-phrein'—Carry over some other referent and apply to the idea. Look at it in terms of something else.

> "I had a friend who just last month was telling me about ..."
> "If this was a coin, animal, tree, movie, etc., what would that be like?"

The Magic of Directionalizing Brains

From *inside* and from *outside* of the magical conceptual box by which we construct and formulate meanings, we can now flexibly maneuver consciousness in seven directions. As a result, this provides us the chance to magically reframe meaning in a multiple of ways.

Summary

- He who sets the frame *governs the resultant experience* (i.e. emotions, thoughts, and responses).
- Someone (or something, or some idea) always sets a frame. We can't escape from frames, beliefs, presuppositions, paradigms, etc. Since someone will set the frame of the conversation, use *Mind-Lines* to take the initiative in frame setting.
- We take control over the meaning process when we have awareness of it and about it, when we have the mind of a magician. Understanding the structure of mind-lines gives us a mindfulness about meanings in our everyday lives in business and relationships.
- Language's effects give us incantations for success, health, and resourcefulness. Do you have some great incantations for yourself and others?
- These linguistic patterns give us a way to conversationally frame and reframe meanings—a pathway to engage in conversational magic.
- As neuro-linguistic creatures, magic lies in the language that we use. It lies in the very structure of language. The incantations that we create and use, on ourselves and others, operate according to neuro-linguistic principles. May you use the magic to bless all you encounter.
- Lines can change minds. Lines can shift the meaning frames we give to experiences and ideas and can influence us in

powerful ways. Lines can persuade us to think about things in ways that truly support our ongoing empowerment. Now that you know *how* neuro-linguistic magic works and *how* to become a *master magician,* word magic lies at your command. Use it with grace, respect, and honor.

Figure 15.1: 26 Ways to Reframe 'Failure'

Consider the toxic ideas in this statement:

"Whenever I don't succeed, it really bothers me. It makes me feel like a failure. Not reaching my goals is such a bummer. I get depressed. No wonder I put things off and hesitate about other things. I just hate being a failure."

1) **Chunking Down**
So you think you 'are' a 'failure,' do you? As you think about something for which you feel like a failure, and define yourself as such, *how* do you know to do this? If you lost a job once, are you a failure? Twice? Three times? What standard are you using to make this judgment? How do you know to use *that* standard? When, where, and with whom did this occur? How do you represent this generalization of being a 'failure?' What pictures, sounds, feelings, and words do you use to create this meaning? If I were to get a sneak peak into the mental theater of your mind, what would I see? How would I know to give it the same name that you have, 'failure?' How do you represent the action of failing at one thing as 'making' you a failure?

2) **Reality Strategy Chunk Down**
So up until now, you have accepted the idea of viewing and defining yourself as a 'failure.' Well, help me understand this. *How specifically* do you know that failing at one thing on a particular day makes you a 'failure?' What do you see first, then what do you say about that, and so on as you think about this? If I were someone from the Temporary Job Agency and I would take your place so that you could have a vacation from this, teach me *how to do this the way you do*. What would I have to think, see, hear, etc.?

3) **Reframe the EB**
This doesn't mean 'failure,' it means feedback. *Not* reaching some important goals really means that you now have some crucial information about how *not* to get there. So, with that in mind, you can feel free to explore new possible avenues, can you not?

4) **Reframe the IS**
How interesting that you say that. What I really find as a failure, and I mean Failure with a big "F," is someone doesn't reach a goal, and then just sits down in the dirt and quits. The person rolls over in the mud and won't learn or try again. I'd call that a 'failure.'

5) **Reflexively Apply To Self**
Does that mean if you don't reach your goal in presenting this limiting and painful belief to me, that just talking to me will turn you into an even bigger failure? You have to succeed at this communicate or it means that, and *that* only?

6) **Reflexively Apply to Listener**
So with that way of thinking about things, if I don't succeed in coming up with a good way of responding and helping you with this limiting belief, I will also become a big failure? In other words, my success or failure as a human being depends on succeeding in this conversation in just the right way? There's no room for experimenting or feedback or dialogue?

7) **Counter-Example Framing**
When you think about some of your successes, and how good and resourceful you feel about them, you mean if you mispronounced a word, or failed in any aspect of any goal surrounding that, that such would turn you into a failure? 'Success' is that fragile and 'failure' is that solid?

8) **Positive Prior Intentional Framing**
Reaching the goals that you set for yourself must mean a lot to you. I can imagine that you take that view in order to protect yourself from messing things up and to push yourself to higher levels. And since you want that, perhaps some other attitudes about failure might help you to really succeed in your goals.

9) **Positive Prior Causation Framing**
It strikes me that it's important for you to set and reach goals. So you probably have taken on this limiting belief because you have had some painful experiences in the past and you now want to protect yourself against more pain. I wonder what other beliefs you could build that you would find even more effective than this one?

10) **First Outcome**
What results for you when you move through life defining experiences and yourself as 'failures' just because you don't reach a goal as you want to? Do these serve you well in setting and reaching goals or in feeling successful? Do you like those negative unresourceful feelings?

11) **Outcome of Outcome**
Imagine going out, say five or even ten years from now, after you have defined every unsuccessful attempt at reaching a goal as turning you into a 'failure,' and then living from *that 'failure' identity* and feeling unresourceful—what will come out of that? Will you take on many risks? What other outcomes emerge when you feel like a 'failure' and take that into your future?

12) **Eternity Framing**
When I think about this, I wonder what you will think when you look back on this belief about failure when you step over into eternity, and I wonder how you will think and feel about this limiting belief that you used as you moved through life?

13) Model of the World Framing

What an interesting way to think about events that so overloads them with meaning! Do you know where you got this way of mapping about 'one unsuccess equaling failing?' Do you know that most people don't use that map to torture themselves?

14) Criteria/Value Framing

When you think about your values of enjoying life, appreciating people, doing your best, experimenting, learning, etc., do you not think of those values as more important than making 'success / failure' judgments about your actions?

15) Allness Framing

So since everybody has failed at something at some time in life, that must make everybody on this planet a 'failure,' a complete and absolute 'failure.'

16) Have-To Framing

So you *have* to frame your attempts at reaching a goal in this way? What would it feel like for you if you did not evaluate events in terms of success or failure? What would happen if you didn't do that? Suppose you got to frame attempts as experiments, feedback, or playing around?

17) Identity Framing

What an interesting belief about your self-identity—so totally dependent on your behaviors. Do you always *identify* people with their behaviors? Do you really consider that people 'are' their behaviors?

18) Ecology Framing

How enhancing do you find this belief when learning a new skill, trying a new sport, taking a risk and practicing a new social behavior? Would you recommend this belief as a way for others to succeed with greater ease and positive feelings? Does it empower or limit your endeavors?

19) Other Abstractions

So as you think about not reaching a goal and labeling it as making you a 'failure,' I take it that you do this a lot? You take a specific instance and over-generalize it into a whole category? And you do this so successfully, don't you? Would you like to fail at this success?

20) Metaphoring/Storying and Restorying Framing

So the day that you brushed your hair but did not get every single hair on your head in just the way that you wanted, that also made you a failure?

When my daughter Jessica turned nine months, she began the process of learning to walk, but she couldn't walk upon the first attempt—nor upon the first hundred attempts. She constantly fell down. And she would sometimes cry. But most of the time she would just get up and try again. As she did, she learned more and she developed more strength in her legs, and more balance and movement, so that eventually she got the hang of it, and had a lot of fun in the process. And I wonder if this says anything that you can *take and apply to yourself now.*

21) Both/And Framing
It sounds like so much of life is *either success or failure* and that there's hardly anything that you notice in-between. It seems like the boundary between what you call 'success' and 'failure' has hardly any distance so that you can step from one to the other in a moment. How useful would you find it to be able to measure the *degree* of these states? Or, perhaps, even better, to recognize that they can both occur at the same time?

22) Pseudo-Word Framing
So you're using this term 'failure' with a lot of abandon and yet we haven't been able to actually point to any specific reference, either in the world or even in concept. This suggests that it's actually a pseudo-word and that you've been tricked by the linguistic fraud of the label itself? And since it refers to nothing *real* or *tangible*, but only to a mapped construct in your mind, do you really need to use this non-referencing term?

23) Negation Framing
I know this isn't possible, but I'm just wondering what would it be like for you if you couldn't compute the meaning of 'failure.' As you think about 'failure' as a non-existing concept, as an experience you cannot experience, because you always get information and feedback, and discover how not to do something, I'm curious about how much more resourceful that would be.

24) Possibility and 'As If' Framing
Since the state and experience of 'failure' has been so unproductive and painful, take a moment to imagine the possibility of living in a world where being a 'failure' could not occur, because you were so focused on always gathering more data about how to refine your actions ... now just pretend that you are there fully and completely and as you do, show me the face of that state, and the posture, and the breathing, good ...

25) Systemic and Probability Framing
What's the probability that when you start this new project that you will totally and absolutely fail at it to 100% like someone who knew nothing at all about it? To what extent do you think you'll fail at it within the first 15 minutes? The first day? What about the first month? What are some of the other factors and contributing influences that could improve your odds at making this successful?

26) Decision Framing
So now that you have entertained several new ideas about this whole realm of succeeding and failing, what have you actually decided serves you best? What frame would empower you to get on with life, bounce with the ups and downs, and forever put yourself in a learning orientation? Have you decided to feed and nurture your mind on that idea? What one thing will you do today to begin this new way of moving through the world?

Figure 15.2: The Mind-Lines Model

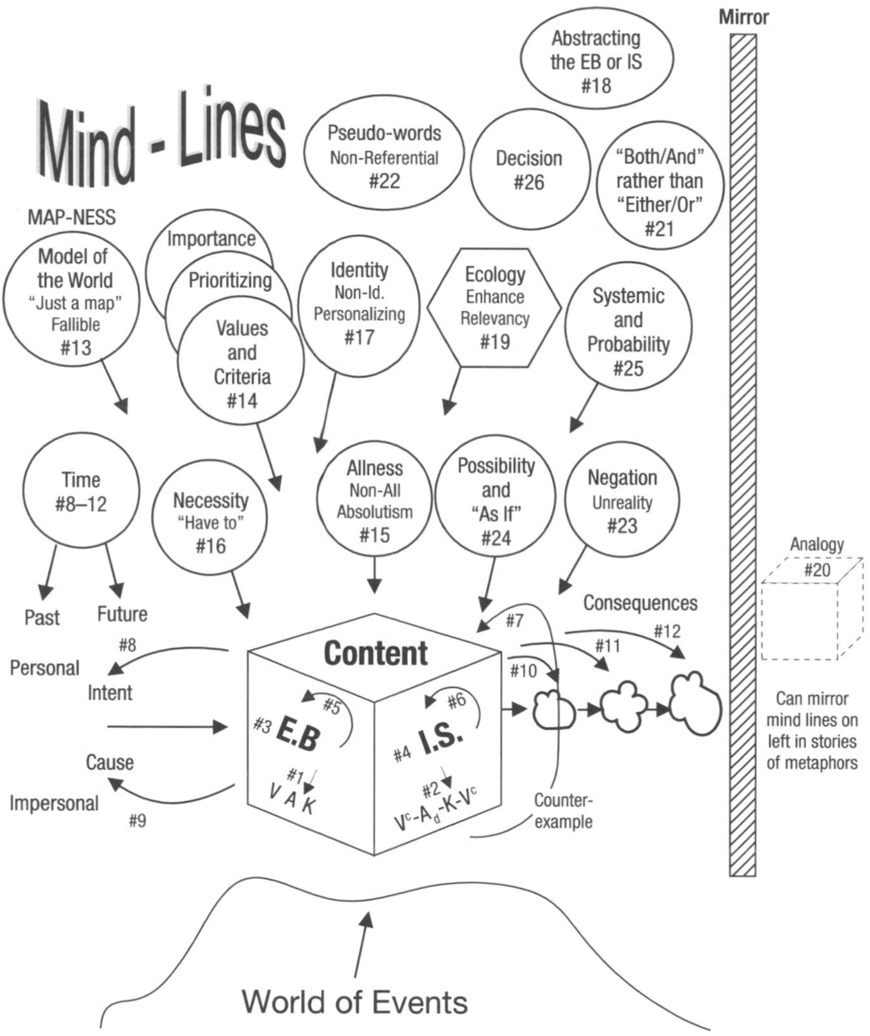

Chapter 16

Sensory and Systemic Magic

Magic beyond words

Does neuro-linguistic *magic* only occur *in* words and *with* words? Given that we have mostly focused on *language* in this book, you could get that impression. Throughout the previous chapters, I have focused primarily on the structure of magic occurring in *language,* that is, in the meta-representation systems. Yet the structure of magic involves more, it also relates equally to *non-linguistic systems.*

In both NLP and Neuro-Semantics, we focus on the magic wand of linguistic patterns. After all, our linguistic maps give us our main entrance into the effective use of language when we communicate. And true enough, *The Structure of Magic* (1975) focused almost exclusively on the language dimension.

Yet it did not stop there.

The following year, Bandler and Grinder published the second volume of *The Structure of Magic* (1976). As they identified additional formats for performing magic, they essentially forecasted many of the key features that would make up the field of NLP. They explored other sensory representational systems that give us the 'languages' of the primary states. In Volume II, they also described two other mapping features: the presence of multiple maps and synesthesia mapping.

They began with *representational systems* as 'other maps for the same territory' in examining the human modeling processes. These neurological maps of the sensory systems precede the linguistic maps, and so occur 'before words.'

They next looked at the experience of incongruity. This phenomenon arises from attempting to operate from *multiple models* of the world that conflict with each other. One facet (or part) of these models operates from one map while another part has abstracted another map. When we attempt to use both at the same time, we become incongruent—and so does our communication. This can even habituate so that we don't notice.

They also turned to the domain of "Fuzzy Functions"—the 'cross-over circuits' between the senses. Technically, these are *synesthesias.* In terms of our mental mapping, when we have circuits or functions that cross over, our multiple maps interface and sometimes interfere with each other. This describes how we might receive input from one channel as a particular sensory map but we code and represent it in another sensory system. For instance, we 'see' blood and 'feel' panicky. We 'see' the leaves of a tree blowing in the wind and 'feel' relaxed. We 'hear' a harsh tonality and 'feel' threatened. The way maps interface in these fuzzy functions describes certain kinds of 'magic' or subjective experiences—some heavens and living hells.

Bandler and Grinder also addressed the domain of multiple maps arising in groups and families. As a systemic process, how do different models of the world interface within a family or between a couple?

To highlight these mapping processes, I will focus on the NLP technologies of 'magic' which transcend our communications in words: the representational systems, anchoring, non-verbal pacing and leading, and 'going meta' to operate at meta-levels using other symbols than words. For a more extensive description of the basic NLP model, see *The User's Manual for the Brain* or *The Sourcebook of Magic.*

The Magical 'Language' of the Senses

One of the most surprising and profound developments in NLP arose from an area of the most sublime simplicity—the *sensory based awareness* that we experience and represent via our senses. Anthropologist Gregory Bateson noted this in his *Introduction* to *The Structure of Magic.*

> "We did not see that these various ways of coding—visual, auditory, etc.—are so far apart, so mutually different even in neurophysiological representation, that no material in one mode can ever be the same logical level in any material in any other mode. This discovery seems obvious when the argument starts from linguistics ..." (pp. x–xi)

To more fully describe this domain, the second volume of *The Structure of Magic* begins with a chapter dedicated to this subject. It is entitled, *"Representational Systems: Other Maps For The Same Territory."* Here the authors introduced their exposition about words *working* in the human nervous system by evoking sensory-based representations and that each of the senses operates as a *language system.* This means that the mapping processes (deletion, generalization, and distortion) which play such a crucial role in the Meta-Model of propositional language similarly play as crucial a role in the sensory 'languages.' Just as we delete, generalize, and distort linguistically, we do so also with the sensory information of seeing, hearing, feeling, smelling, tasting, etc.

Underneath the language system then, we have other 'language' systems. We have the more primitive and basic sensory systems. They function as 'languages' in that they operate as *symbols* of the world. We *map* the world into our awareness by using these systems.

- *Visual System:* sights, images, pictures, diagrams, cartoons, movies, etc.
- *Auditory System:* sounds, music, noise, tones, volumes, etc.
- *Kinesthetic System:* sensations, feelings, movements, pressure, temperature, etc.
- *Olfactory System:* smells.
- *Gustatory System:* tastes.

Bandler and Grinder (1976) wrote,

> "Human beings live in a 'real world.' We do not, however, operate directly or immediately upon that world, but, rather, we operate within that world using a map or a series of maps of that world to guide our behavior within it. These maps, or representational systems, necessarily differ from the territory that they model by the

> three universal processes of human modeling: *Generalization, Deletion,* and *Distortion.* When people come to us in therapy expressing pain and dissatisfaction, the limitations which they experience are, typically, in their *representation* of the world and not in the world itself." (p. 3)

These *neurological maps* of the world arise from our use of our senses and sense receptors. The energy manifestations of the world (in the forms of waves, particles, vibrations, etc.) activate the sense receptors in our neurology. At that point our eyes, ears, skin, etc. transform and transduce this 'information' or 'data' from those forms to neuro-electrical forms as the 'information' moves from neuron to neuron to the brain where it becomes transformed into bio-chemical expressions, i.e., neuro-transmitters.

Then, in the brain, we receive an *impression* of sights, sounds, sensations, smells, tastes, balance, etc. Yet this phenomenological impression of the interaction of our eyes, ears, and skin with the world only exists as a facsimile or representation of the world—it is not the world itself. Our cortical 'mapping' of the world does *not literally* have images, sounds, sensations, etc. There is no movie theater, screen, sound system, etc. in the brain. It just *seems* that way to us. It's our *re-presenting* at the phenomenological level of awareness.

Truly, we do not operate on the world directly, but only indirectly via our maps and maps of maps.

Recognizing these dynamics as *mappings* makes all the difference in the world. In the NLP model, the original co-founders identified how our *neurological maps* and *linguistic maps* interplay to create the structure of our sensed internal subjective experiences. What did they discover? How did they formulate the neuro-linguistic model? The highlights of their discoveries include the following:

- Most people seem to have and use a *favorite representational system* as they represent and code information. Some prefer the visual system and so easily make pictures in their mind; others prefer sounds, yet others prefer sensations (kinesthetics). This leads to different learning preferences and operating on different information systems.

- We have both lead *input* channels and *representational* channels in our processing of information and map-making. Oftentimes these differ. We may use the visual system to *input* information, but only have conscious awareness of the kinesthetic system. We may *input* kinesthetically and *represent* auditorially.
- When we input information using one language system and code it in another, we create a 'fuzzy function' in our nervous system/ brain. This generates a cross-over circuit so that we might see-feel (V-K), or feel-hear (K-A), or hear-see (A-V), etc. Synesthesias can work in magic-like ways to enhance our lives or to impoverish our experiences, it all depends upon context, use, and flexibility with the processes.
- We can so under-use a representation system that we pay very little attention to the input from that channel and have little to no conscious awareness of it (e.g., few images, sounds, sensations). Typically this will impoverish our maps, our map making skills, and we will lack the critical information about such distinctions.
- In the process of inputting in one system and encoding in another, we will sometimes seemingly have no awareness of the sights, sounds, sensations, etc. of the input. The visual cortex may be working inputting all kinds of images, but we will not be *aware* of it. Similarly, our auditory cortex, associative cortex, motor cortex, etc. also may be working without our awareness.
- We can put any of the representation systems in a meta-position to any other system. Obviously we can say words *about* our images. We can also see pictures *about* our words, sounds, sensations. We can entertain a feeling *about* a sound, a picture, a word, etc. This means that as information in every system functions as a *para-message,* no system is more 'real' or important than any other. Words are not more important or less important than images; images are not more or less important than sounds, etc. The sensory systems are not more or less important than the linguistic systems.
- When, however, we use one system to *comment on* another system, the first becomes a *meta-message*. A sigh can comment on a statement, then another statement can comment on the sigh. When we speak or use a symbol *about* another symbolic system, we establish a meta-communication system.

- Learning to hear someone's favorite representation system gives us a way to 'speak that person's language.' Doing this hastens and increases the person's sense of connectedness and rapport. By so *pacing* a person we build a bridge for 'trust.'
- Much misunderstanding and miscommunication results from warring representation systems. People simply use different input and output channels and so do not connect with each other. It's as if they are speaking different languages, which, in a way, they are. They don't match or pace each other's representation systems.
- Switching representation systems gives us the ability to speak another's language; it also enriches both persons' models of the world. This process offers a magical way to enrich communication and touch each person's life with magic.
- *Mapping over* from one representation system to another offers a direct and powerful way to enrich our maps. This enrichment results in us having more choices and skills. It gives us a richer map for understanding things.
- When we use an inappropriate representation system in a particular area or skill, we typically will create problems, difficulties, and limitations for ourselves. Trying to spell without visualizing makes spelling much more difficult. Trying to improve our singing voice without 'hearing our voice on the outside' cuts off informative feedback.
- By learning to match representation systems to skills and re-mapping (re-coding) according to the representation system appropriateness, we can suddenly make skills and abilities possible (e.g., using the visual system for spelling, the auditory-tonal channel for music appreciation and skill, the kinesthetic language system for archery, etc.). In instances where people have tried and tried to do something without success, this can suddenly allow a skill to emerge like magic.
- By identifying inappropriate synesthesias, we can then break them up and use the sensory language systems more appropriately (e.g. a nurse see-seeing blood rather than see-feeling; hear-hearing tones and volumes rather than hear-feeling). This can break up limiting semantic relationships and dispel old spells.

All of these insights and procedures arise from several basic assumptions about human neuro-linguistics. The first is the simple yet profound recognition of the map-territory distinction. If Korzybski's aphorism, *"the map is not the territory"* holds true for words, it also holds true for the sensory representations. Yet the system of neurological 'language' (i.e., the sensory systems) occurs at a level prior to language. Language occurs *above* the primary level of the sensory systems. It is a meta-level representation system. This is one of the reasons that we may at times feel tempted to believe in our senses more than in our words. Yet both senses and words are constructions, representations, symbols. Neither 'is' real. Nor is one more real than the other.

> "The statement by Korzybski that 'the map is not the territory' is true in two major ways. First, we, as humans, create models of our world which we use as a guide for our behavior. Second, we have a number of different maps available to represent our experiences—kinesthetic, visual, auditory, natural language, etc. These maps of our experience do not necessarily represent *only* information from the direct input channels of the senses to associated representational systems." (1976, p. 25)

The second basic assumption is that we create maps at multiple levels. Prior to awareness, we are mapping the world at the neurological level via our sense receptors. Eventually we map that data into sensory-based representations, and from there we map the sights, sounds and sensations into linguistic-based representations, and then those into abstract concepts, etc. All are constructions and abstractions of our nervous system. Each one occurs sequentially, one after the other.

This gives us many different 'languages' at different levels to meta-model. We can question and explore our mapping at all these levels to enrich our mental maps. As we do, we have multiple channels by which to do magical things. Sometimes a whole new world suddenly comes into existence by simply adding an underused representational system. Sometimes a new strategy and skill arises from learning to use the most appropriate representation system. Sometimes lapping over from one to another empowers us in new and exciting ways as it gives us the ability to see and hear new things and to experience a higher level of flexibility. Sometimes setting a higher frame over previous frames totally outframes and transforms things.

When Maps Multiply

Prior to NLP there was little thought about the sensory systems as 'languages,' much less the very *languages of the mind.* So when we include the neurological maps of seeing-hearing-feeling to our meta-representation system of language, we discover that we have a multiple number of language systems by which to input, process, and code the territory. And, given the varying strengths and weaknesses of our sensory systems, how we favor some systems over others, etc., we can now more fully understand how we can so easily end up with different models of the world.

Sometimes this leads to conflicts, misunderstandings, confrontations, the lack of rapport, etc. What indicates that our maps are jarring and warring inside of us?

Incongruity.

When messages carried by the various output channels do not fit together or coalesce to create a singular meaning or focus, then we probably have maps that conflict. The guiding paradigms of our lives may themselves jar and jolt against each other. This is where recognizing all of our maps and messages as *para-messages* becomes a valuable resource.

In fact, Bandler and Grinder (1976) took issue with Bateson on this point. They developed their model based upon this very assumption:

> "... we accept each message as an equally valid representation of that person's experience. In our model, no one of these paramessages can be said to be more valid—or truer, or more representative of the client—than any other. No one of a set of paramessages can be said to be meta to any other member of its set. Rather, our understanding of a set of paramessages is that each of these messages represents a portion of the client's model of the world. When the client is communicating congruently, each of the paramessages matches, fits with, is congruent with each of the others. This tells us that all of the models which the client is using to guide his behavior at that point in time are consistent ... When the client is communicating incongruently, we know that the models of the

world which he is using to guide his behavior are inconsistent." (p. 38)

There are no *inherent* meta-messages. No message, by its very nature, stands in a meta relationship to another. Meta speaks of relationship. Yet we can use any message or representational system to make a comment about another. Imagine the flexibility this endows a neuro-linguistic system with the combinatorial power. That which makes a message *meta to* another is *our use of it*. When we use a system or symbol to comment on or *about* another message, we create a meta-structure.

A word or sentence that *comments on* a gesture, facial expression, pointing of a finger, tone of voice, etc. operates *meta* to those non-verbal messages. If we point our finger in reference to a word as a comment on that word, then the finger gesture plays a meta-role to the word in that particular sequence of events. For us to label message A as *meta to* message B, then "A is a message about B" (equivalently, A has B in its scope—the Bateson/Russell condition) (1976, p. 41).

The meta-experience of conflicting maps shows up emotionally, behaviorally, and somatically in our faces and bodies as incongruity. How then do we effectively respond to such?

Bandler and Grinder suggested that we first *identify* and *sort* out the incongruencies. Later, we can *integrate* them. Identifying incongruities necessitates that we develop greater sensory acuity to the visual, auditory, and kinesthetic channels, listen for such linguistic cues such as 'but,' or 'an implied but' that expresses a statement with a slight rise in intonation at the end of the sentence (pp. 55–57). Another indicator occurs when the right and left sides of a person's body look (or operate) out of sync (p. 58).

To integrate incongruities, we have to 'go meta,' that is, take a meta-position so that we can then meta-comment or meta-question, regarding the conflicting maps. In this way we can set new and higher frames that engulf and embrace both sides of the incongruities.

"How do you feel *about* feeling angry?"

> "What does your drive for both work and recreation have in common?"

> "How well balanced are your skills at asserting your point of view and listening attentively to those of others?"

> "What value embraces both sides of this conflict for making lots of money and remaining a down-to-earth kind of guy?"

Assisting someone in achieving a meta-position to his or her polarities enables that person to make contact with the polarities in the system and simultaneously to transcend them. There's magic in this kind of integrating of conflicting parts or polarities. Virginia Satir accomplished this in her famous 'parts parties.' Others have used psychodrama and various enactment techniques to bring out the differences and find a way to integrate them. Early NLP developed the magical pattern of the Visual Squash Pattern (pp. 86–88) to generate a new neuro-linguistic integration. Yet ultimately, we integrate the conflicting parts by finding a higher frame that unites the differences at a higher logical level. In negotiating we use the Agreement Frame to achieve this.

When Maps Intersect

Multiple maps do not always conflict. Sometimes they merge and interface in a smooth way so that they create more power. When that happens, we experience the *power of congruency.*

Generally, however, the more maps we have, the more possibilities arise for potential conflicts. These multiple mappings also invite maps to *intersect* in such a way that we switch from one to the other without awareness. A person who speaks two or more languages may frequently experience this phenomenon of switching from English to German or Russian or Hebrew or whatever. This *cross-over circuit*—going from one map suddenly to another—often beautifully enriches description, choices, and skills.

Years of backpacking the high country in Colorado has taught me the advantage of using several kinds of maps—a highway road map to get to the location where I find the trail head. From there I shift and begin using a topographical map to navigate the mountains. When in a National Forest, however, I may prefer using a Forest Rangers map in order to find camping areas, restrooms, etc.

A similar operation occurs when we bring information in via the visual system, encode it kinesthetically, and output it linguistically. Such *synesthesias* serve as the neurological foundations for what the Meta-Model designated as 'semantic ill-formedness.' We create ill-formed meaning maps when we use inadequate forms of Cause—Effect, Mind-Reading, Complex Equivalences, Identifications, etc. Consider what this means for a statement like the following:

"You make me angry."

When we say that this statement is semantically ill-formed, what do we mean?

The sentence probably has arisen when the speaker, seeing or hearing a disliked stimulus (e.g., a tone, facial gesture, etc.), linked it with a negative feeling. The speaker has automatically and unconsciously evaluated the stimulus in a negative way. At the sensory level, the speaker sees → feels or hears → feels. The *cross-over wiring* or synesthesia from seeing (V) to feeling (K) occurs so quickly, automatically, and unconsciously, that the person truly experiences the *stimulus as causing/triggering the felt response.*

Immediately the person maps this linguistically and so it comes out: "You [stimulus person] *make me* [causative verb] *feel* this emotion." Yet in assigning the cause of this relationship to something outside the person's nervous system, and therefore outside his or her control, we thereby construct an ill-formed map.

At the neurological foundations of the statement we have a *synesthesia.* The cross circuit (see → feel) serves as the experience from which we map things using Mind-Reading, Cause—Effect, and Complex Equivalence statements. In this case, rather than making distinctions, our sensations merge together leaving us with an ill-formed sensory map and an ill-formed linguistic map.

Synesthesias are not necessarily bad. They occur throughout our lives in many experiences. We may hear tones → and see different colors. We may see numbers → and hear various tones. We may see a beautiful painting → and feel certain internal kinesthetic sensations.

Child psychologists have noted the lack of differentiation in infants and young children. They have noted that the skill of differentiating between oneself and the external stimuli which strike the sense organs involves a learning and individuation process. Apparently we are born without such differentiations. At first we all represent stimuli (i.e., noises, sights, smells, images, etc.) as kinesthetic sensations.

> "In traditional psychophysics, this term, *fuzzy function,* is most closely translated by the term *synesthesia*. ... fuzzy functions are not bad, crazy or evil, and the outcome of what we consider effective therapy is not the elimination of these functions, but rather the realization that these functions can be the basis for much creative activity ..." (p. 101)

In Mind-Reading, we typically activate feel → see or feel → hear circuits. In doing this, we begin with a feeling of some sort and then use sights and sounds upon which we *project* our feelings.

> "... in the case of Mind Reading ... the client takes body sensations—his kinesthetic representation—and distorts the information arriving visually and auditorially from outside him in such a way that it conforms to his body sensations." (p. 102)

This kind of sensory mapping then shows up in such linguistic expressions as:

> "When you look at me that way, and roll your eyes, I feel discounted and disliked; you're saying I'm worthless."
>
> "When you use that tone of voice, I feel scared."
>
> "When you cut me off that way in a conversation, I feel enraged."

In Cause—Effect statements, we see → hear, see → feel, hear → feel, etc. Here we see, hear, or even feel a stimulus and as we then selectively focus on it, we do so in such a way as to map out that the stimulus itself *causes, makes, forces,* etc. us to experience certain feelings, or to behave in certain ways. This sensory experience is then languaged as:

> "You make me so depressed when you talk in that tone."
>
> "You make me sick with your negativity."
>
> "You make me angry slurping like that."
>
> "You know how to make me fall in love with you."
>
> "You make me so happy!"

We can even identify merged, intersected maps by listening to the unique arrangement of predicates that they produce.

> "You look (V) so warm (K) in that outfit."
>
> "The judge appeared (V) to be a really cold man (K)."
>
> "From what you've said (A), I can't see (V) how to get a hold of this concept (K)."
>
> "Clearly (V), this experience has been hard on you (K)."
>
> "I feel (K) your despair, it rings clear as a bell to me (A)."

Touches of both impoverishing and empowering magic arise from synesthesias, from our cross-circuit maps. From this Bandler and Grinder postulated several possibilities with regard to the structure of various experiences. They suggested that:

> *Asthma* results from see → feel and hear → feel representations of another's aggression toward them and storing such in their bodies (especially their neck and throat).
>
> *Sadism* involves see → feel circuits in which visual input of another's pain gets represented as kinesthetic pleasure (p. 117).

> *Violence* results from visual input represented kinesthetically (see → feel) so that seeing a dis-value in another person for whom we feel responsible may activate the motor responses (pp. 107–109).

Multiple Intersecting (or Conflicting) Maps Within a Human System

In these descriptions of experiences and communications, we begin with a single 'system,' that of an single individual. In the neuro-linguistic system of a single individual we have multiple levels of models of the world which can intersect in multiple ways as visual map interfaces with auditory map which interfaces with kinesthetic map which interlaces with the linguistic map which intersperses with the visual map, etc. If we have that much complexity with a single person, how much more do multiple maps explode when we consider several other people coming together to communicate, relate, engage in business, etc.?

NLP began as a social and *systemic* model inasmuch as it modelled Virginia Satir's *Family Systems* as well as the Non-Aristotelian *system* approach from Korzybski. In *The Structure of Magic, Volume II* Bandler and Grinder offered descriptions of what happens when we have multiple maps operating within a *system* of individuals. They took their cue from Virginia Satir and her *Family Systems Therapy.* This allowed them to consider what happens when two or more people interact and become a system (e.g., a family, a couple, a business, company, group):

> "To accept the family as the system unit for therapy is to use an overall strategy to work with the family as if it were one living organism, each member being an essential part and resource ..." (1976, p. 126)

The *system* of a family, in fact, operates not only as 'one living organism' itself, but also provides one of the most important *contexts* to which we adapt ourselves and learn the patterns that we do. First we meta-model the persons in the system to discover their individual maps and to get a sense of the system as a whole—the 'rules' and generalizations that have developed inside a system which the people use for coping and interacting. Meta-modeling 'the system' means learning to see what emerges from all of the interacting patterns. We begin detecting and identifying the system in terms of its beliefs, rules, processes, permissions, taboos, etc. Central to modeling a system is modeling the Cause—Effect frames that govern the way the system operates. What leads to what? What contributes or influences what? What do the individuals in the system *believe* cause various responses?

> "In our experience, in every family or couple we have encountered, we have identified the particular form of semantic-ill-formedness called Cause—Effect semantic ill-formedness—the situation in which one member of the family is represented as causing another family member to experience some feeling or emotion." (ibid., p. 128)

The magic of transformation here begins when we meta-model the specific representations of the present state of the system of interactions and the desired state that each person longs for. Next, we begin exploring how the individual maps intersect with each other and where the system prevents the persons from accessing needed resources. As we do that, our questioning begins to open up more communication channels which, in turn, allows the system to know itself and to use feedback to evolve itself.

By the magic of meta-modeling the parts of the system (e.g., what each member wants, how each member views the situation, what resources each person needs, etc.), a consultant begins to see and hear the current maps of its members, the system's maps, and the emergent properties that arise from it all. This then allows an exploration of what prevents the individuals from fully experiencing their desired maps and what the individuals would need to think, feel, know, believe, etc. to have those resources.

As with individuals, groups, businesses, companies, families, teams, etc. typically get into pain due to the impoverished maps which they use to navigate their world. These usually involve maps that prevent the members from openly and flexibly receiving current feedback. A system with rules against seeing, hearing, feeling, and speaking to each other and/or a system that has become calibrated to each other so that now they only react, already assuming that they know what the other means, has become a closed and rigid system.

Much of the magic of the Meta-Model occurs in simply exploring how the current reality works. This brings insight and understanding, it shifts to a meta-level of acceptance and appreciation, it deframes ill-formed maps, and it maps new resources and possibilities into existence.

Summary

- The magic for changing our neuro-semantic reality does not depend upon words only. We have other 'language' systems in our repertoire for creating representations or maps than just words. We have numerous sensory-based systems: the visual, auditory, kinesthetic, olfactory, and gustatory systems.
- We do not move through life with just one model of the world, we have numerous models, numerous levels of models, etc. These multiple models operate in awareness and outside of awareness.
- Our multiple maps can create problems. They can conflict with each other and put us at odds with ourselves. This inevitably reduces our personal power, congruency, and integrity.
- Conflicting internal maps can create warring 'parts' or facets of ourselves which then need integration, resolution, and/or healing.
- Meta-communicating about conflicting parts or maps can enable us to create higher-level agreement frames that bring integration and congruency.
- When we input in one system and process in another we create cross-circuit synesthesias. Mapping things in this way can create the highest expressions of creativity, genius, and power *and* some of our worst demons.
- Recognition of this mapping gives us the power to choose our magic and to construct enhancing frames.
- Putting together the many multiple maps of many people invites a new level of complexity, the complexity of relational systems. We can also use the Meta-Model here to do magical things interpersonally as we communicate and relate more effectively.

Epilogue

And the Magic Continues ...

"Magic is hidden in the language we speak. The webs
that you can tie and untie are at your command if only you pay
attention to what you already have (language) and
the structure of the incantations for growth ..."
The Structure of Magic, p. 19

A long time ago Sigmund Freud (1915–1917) noted that "Words were originally magic and to this day words have retained much of their ancient magical power." (p. 17). He noted how with words we make each other blissfully happy and/or can drive each other into the depths of despair. He made these notations about *words* in the context of therapy having noted that nothing happens in treatment "but an exchange of words."

Today we extend our definition of *'language'* itself to include gestures, facial expressions, tones, pitches, volumes, silences, and all of the other things that we do in signaling and cuing ourselves and others. *Language,* as involving numerous symbol systems, includes much more than just words. It includes non-verbal expressions and multiple non-propositional language forms.

This book has updated the original 'Magic' model (the Meta-Model) to expand its use and structure. The original genius of John Grinder and Richard Bandler bequeathed us numerous keys for beginning to understand the *structure of magic* and to use the *secrets of neuro-linguistic magic*. Their Meta-Model enlightened us about the inner structure of magic and pointed us in the direction for how to tap into it and how to use it for enhancing our lives. With the extensions of magic here and with the secrets of magic more explicitly articulated, we can now go further and build even more *incantations of growth, excellence, and genius.* After all, even magic gets to evolve!

Magic is indeed hidden in the language that we speak. It lies in the self-languaging that we engage in as we think, dream, imagine, rehearse, question, etc. It lies in how we language our descriptions of the world, how we language difficulties and problems, and even in how we language our relationships. It lies in how we language others. By such languaging, we weave our incantational webs.

May you now *take command* of your languaging as you utter numerous incantations for yourself and others today. May you find yourself *paying attention* in new and useful ways to the 'magic' of your words so that you begin to feel yourself tuning up your linguistic ears to the *music of the magic* all around you! May you become a *Neuro-Linguistic Magician* so that you become a blessing to all those whom you touch—and may you touch people with such magic that it significantly enriches the world!

I often end trainings on *Conversational Magic* with the following piece as a benediction to conclude the workshop. It seems equally appropriate to offer it here as a benediction to this book.

Magic lies hidden in the language we speak.
In the world of ongoing and ever-changing events
where nothing inherently means anything
apart from an enchanting mind,
magic is always ready to occur.
It only takes an engaging mind to create the magic.
In this the magic lies—in the meaning.
Though nothing inherently means anything,
everything can mean something.
By the words which lie at our command,
we cast spells as we weave our webs.
With the Mind and Eyes of a Magician,
we link events in the world with internal states
and call forth *neuro-semantic* magic.
With the Heart of a Magician
we embed spells in higher contexts and frames,
meanings within meanings
and those meanings embedded in yet higher meanings.
The spells we cast then lie at our command
if only we pay attention
to our wand of symbolism
and its secrets about the structure of meaning.
And now may you touch many lives, minds, and hearts
with the magic that now lies at your command.
Rise up, ye Magician of the Heart!

Appendix A
The Field of Linguistics and the Meta-Model

From the beginning of this work, I noted that while the Meta-Model was derived from the field of Transformational Grammar (TG), it was *not* dependent on it. In fact, the TG model that Grinder knew and based the Meta-Model on was pretty much abandoned by Noam Chomsky at the same time.

Does this de-value or undermine the Meta-Model? Not in the least. As a model describing *how words work to create meaning in human neurology,* the Meta-Model truly does not depend on Transformational Grammar. This is one of the major differences in *Communication Magic* from the original volumes of *The Structure of Magic.* Those books depended upon, and grounded themselves in, TG. This one does not.

Grinder and Bandler first tied the Meta-Model to the 'Aspects' model of Noam Chomsky. In its original development, the Meta-Model depended heavily upon Chomsky's TG model. Yet, the year after they first published the Meta-Model, the original form of TG became outdated. Its adherents had showed the model inadequate as an explanatory model in the field of Linguistics. Gross (1979) attempted to construct a transformational generative grammar of French, but failed. He noted that the project became "much more complex than expected" and ultimately turned out "to be entirely taxonomic. This result calls into question the validity of the so-called theory of generative grammar." (p. 859)

In the years that passed, the *Aspects* model (1956) that Chomsky developed and championed continued to undergo changes and developments. Harris (1993) charted most of this change in his insightful book, *The Linguistic Wars.* He detailed the in-house conflicts that arose between Chomsky and his students many years prior to 1975. Even before the publication of *The Structure of Magic, Generative Semantics* had split off from Chomsky's model under the visionary leadership of Lakoff, McCawley, Ross, and others. Bandler and Grinder wrote one brief note about this in *The Structure of Magic* (see Note #6 after Chapter Four on Generative Semantics p. 109).

Generative Semantics took the idea of the deep structure (DS), that eventually lead them to the domain of 'meaning' (semantics) and they ran with it. They ran with it much further than Chomsky could personally endure. As a result, Chomsky backed away from his deep structure (D-structure) hypothesis and began to posit that transformations occurred also at the surface structures (SS).

Eventually, TG gave way to new linguistic models: Chomsky's Generative Grammar and then EST (Extended Standard Theory) and Lakoff's Generative Semantics. Yet these models also could not provide a completely satisfactory description or explanation of linguistic phenomena. During the 1980s and 1990s ever newer models continued to arise.

A great many of the former linguists of the TG school have followed Lakoff and others into cognitive grammar. Langacker produced two massive two-volume books, *Foundations of Cognitive Grammar* (1987/1991) and *Concept, Image, and Symbol* (1991) which comes much closer to the representational model of NLP.

The original '*Aspects*' of Chomsky has, in the passing years, become more and more dated as various cognitive linguistic models have taken its place. Chomsky and colleagues helped to bring this about as they pushed the transformational grammar model and thereby increasingly discovered more and more irregularities and inadequacies of the paradigm. These inadequacies of transformational grammar and especially 'deep structure' explain why this model eventually collapsed.

What does this do to the Meta-Model?

To what extent does the Meta-Model depend upon TG? Do inadequacies in TG undermine the Meta-Model?

Bandler and Grinder's Meta-Model clearly began within the context of the transformational grammar and certainly grounded much of their model upon its formulations. Without doubt, they depended upon, and used, the terminology which they received from TG. They also depended upon the general distinction between the DS and SS which played such a crucial role in Chomsky's model in the 1960s and 1970s.

Yet, while admitting that much reliance, overall *the Meta-Model does* not *depend upon transformational grammar* at all. After all, TG addresses an entirely different question, and a very different domain from the focus of the Meta-Model. As a linguistic theory, TG (as does any linguistic model) sought to provide an explanatory model and the necessary and sufficient mechanisms for the syntactical structure of language, language acquisition, the relation between sound and meaning, phonology, morphology, etc.

NLP, and especially the Meta-Model, does *not* address or speak to this domain at all. It does not exist or operate as a strictly *linguistic model*. After all, we do *not* use it to describe or explain linguistic phenomena. Our focus lies *not* in theorizing about the interrelationships between grammar, symbolism, syntax, or meaning. We rather use it as a *neuro-linguistic* model. We use it to explain the *effect* of language in human neurology and experience in creating human 'reality.'

How the transformations occur, or what transformational rules sufficiently explain the processes, do not concern the functioning of the Meta-Model. Most NLP practitioners know very little about the transformational rules or functioning. Such has nothing to do with using the model and it plays no role whatever in understanding the *structure of magic* which occurs in human neurology regarding some experience of excellence.

Rather than delving to the depths required in a linguistic theory about the cognitive mechanisms that govern language, the Meta-Model focuses on the *phenomenological level of nervous system* and upon psychological abstracting. It focuses on neuro-semantic issues. Although Bandler and Grinder devoted a lot of attention to TG, and even provided an introductory appendix about TG (Appendix A, p. 183), the model does *not* depend on it.

The Meta-Model actually correlates to a greater extent to the *General-Semantics* model of Alfred Korzybski than to TG. Korzybski coined the terms *neuro-linguistics* and *neuro-semantics* to focus more on *neurological semantics* than on linguistic mechanisms. He described General Semantics as "a new extensional discipline which explains and trains us how to use our nervous systems most efficiently" (1933, p. xxvi). NLP speaks about this as how to 'run your own brain.'

Obviously, the Meta-Model begins with our *surface expressions* which formulate understandings and representations. Here we encounter our most conscious expression of our cognitive maps. The Meta-Model assumes and posits that below, behind, or above (depending upon your choice of metaphor) we inevitably have a richer and fuller phenomenological map. The terminology of *deep structure and surface structure* served the NLP developers well and provided them with a basic *logical level format* of human mapping. We see a similar concept in Cognitive Grammar in that *above* any word or term we have various cognitive domains (categories) and then matrixes of categories—contexts and contexts-of-contexts that set the frame and govern meaning.

Bandler and Grinder adopted the cognitive presupposition that people operate via some kind of cognitive map of the world, others, and themselves. Yet because the human nervous system always and inevitably 'leaves characteristics out' (Korzybski), 'deletes' significant information (Bandler and Grinder), and functions as a 'reducing valve' (Huxley), the *process of inquiring* about that cognitive map helps the person to expand and enrich it. Yet this formulation does not belong exclusively to TG. It reflects a basic cognitive or constructivist frame. By facilitating someone to 'go back inside' to earlier reference maps, we can enable one to remap and create more accurate and useful maps from which to operate. This updates the limiting and impoverishing parts as well as corrects erroneous facets.

The bottom line of this discussion about linguistic models is this: The Meta-Model only depends upon the *phenomenological constructivism* implied (and supplied) by TG. We can just as adequately build the Meta-Model upon the Structural Differential model of Korzybski and his Levels of Abstractions. We can just as adequately build the Meta-Model upon the Levels of Thought in the Meta-States model. We can do that because the Meta-Model only posits that consciousness operates at various levels of abstracting (1975, pp. 158–159).

Korzybski's General Semantics epistemological model actually provides a much fuller and more accurate paradigm for the Meta-Model. After all, it first and foremost relates to *neurology*—to how our nervous system (including our brain and physiology) *abstracts* from the world of energy manifestations and makes various *transforms* along the way as it codes and recodes the 'information' in the nervous system. Korzybski's *structural differential* model designates levels and orders from various deeper structures to increasingly higher structures. This keeps the general format of the 'deep structure' of neuro-linguistic and neuro semantic representation and higher structures without needing to bring over wholesale everything in the transformational grammar model.

Further, this emphasis on human 'abstracting' (abstractions) fits very well into the more recent work of Lakoff (1987) who puts similar emphasis on human 'cognition' in the following terms:

- **Embodied.** Our conceptual systems grow out of bodily experience and make sense in terms of our bodies and somatic experiences. "The core of our conceptual systems is directly grounded in perception, body movement, and experience of a physical and social character" (p. xiv). This embodiment of 'thought' means that thought and reason do not exist as 'the mechanical manipulation of abstract symbols.'
- **Imaginative.** Cognitive concepts go beyond literal mirroring or representations of external reality and partake of imaginative features involving metaphors, metonymies, and images based on experience and bodily experience. Langacker (1991) goes even further, describing "grammar as image." In his works, he focuses on the dimensions of imagery using figure/ground, profile/base, scanning operations, etc.
- **Gestalt properties.** Rather than being 'atomistic,' concepts take on systemic features—features which *emerge* to create an overall configuration that exists as so much more than the sum of the parts.

- **Experientialism**. Lakoff labels this "experiential realism" and defines it as saying that yes, there is a real world out there—a reality that places constraints on us, but that what we experience as 'real' depends also in part upon how we conceive, conceptualize, and construct that reality.
- **Categorizing.** Lakoff has popularized the work of Eleanor Rosch who developed *prototype theory* of categories. Langacker has brought much of this work into *Cognitive Grammar* and used it to construct new formulations for the 'categorizing relationships' that explain language. Prototype theory differs significantly from the classical Aristotelian presentation of categories.

Even though the field of linguistics have moved on beyond TG, there are some who continue in that tradition. In the past two decades Ray Jackendoff, a former student of Chomsky, has become one of the few scholars to continue the Tranformational Grammar (TG) tradition. In *Patterns in the Mind: Language and Human Nature* (1994), he has presented the following definition that simplifies it along with some qualifications of misunderstandings about 'Deep Structure.'

> "This is one of the foundational ideas behind Chomsky's theory of *transformational grammar*: a sentence in the mind has an 'underlying structure' or 'deep structure' that is different from its surface form, and various principles of mental grammar can transform the sentence by moving certain parts such as wh-words around." (p. 77)

> "Deep structure (now often termed 'D-structure') has always been understood simply as an aspect of syntactic structure that expresses certain structural regularities. These regularities, since they include word order, have to be syntactic (i.e. distinct from meaning) and have to express variation among languages (i.e. they are not universal). However, because of the way deep structure was characterized at a certain stage of development of the theory during the mid and late 1960s, many commentators erroneously identified it with either meaning or Universal Grammar or both. However, this was never the intent of the term, except in certain circles for a certain brief time." (p. 77)

Linguistics vs. Neuro-*Linguistics*

While the Meta-Model was originally formulated on the theories, postulates, practices, and language that came from the field of linguistics, the model does *not* function as a *linguistic* model. The goals and purposes differ radically from those of formal and theoretical linguistics. Various linguistic models, from Transformational Grammar, Generative Semantics, Space Grammar, to Cognitive Grammar seek primarily to understand and identify *theoretically* how language works. Such endeavors aim to model the processes of language, linguistic phenomena, language acquisition, etc. As such, they offer no evaluation about the value or usefulness of nominalizations, universals, modals, tree structures, derivations, etc. in human functioning.

The Structural Differential (General Semantics) and the Meta-Model do *not* address such linguistic concerns. They focus on *neuro*-linguistic *experience* in the *psycho-logical* life of the human being. Korzybski especially emphasized that while the older 'semantics' focused primarily on theories of *verbal* meanings, his General (meta) Semantics did not. He rather sought to deal only with *neuro*-semantic and *neuro*-linguistic living reactions of individuals.

Similarly with the Meta-Model—it focuses primarily on identifying poor mapping (ill-formedness) that prevents full and resourceful living. In this it transcends grammar and grammatical, syntactical, morphological, etc. problems and issues. As a *neuro-linguistic model,* it seeks only to identify expressions that mark out problem areas in mapping (in one's schema or model of the world) that affect psychological functioning (how we think, feel, speak, behave, relate, etc.).

We also use this model in a very different way from how we would use a linguistic model. We use this model to identify and address the cognitive mapping distortions that create difficulties for how we live, feel, and think. We do this in order to develop more enhancing phenomenological models of the world for ourselves and others. The 'linguistic distinctions' of the Meta-Model operate as markers of places where we might find neuro-linguistic mapping problems. Then, as we ask questions and offer challenges, we perform the *transformational magic* of facilitating a new and enhancing mapping.

Cognitive Grammar

In studying the latest developments in Cognitive Grammar, I have been pleasantly surprised to find that many of these newer developments in linguistics offer a much more encouraging and exciting theoretical foundation for the Meta-Model.

In fact, in some ways, Cognitive Linguistics provides even better and more thorough support. Langacker (1991), for instance, has completely rejected and moved on from the Chomsky TG model. He has equated *meaning* with *conceptualization* and has built a system of linguistic semantics based upon providing structural analysis and explicit description of abstract entities like 'thoughts' and 'concepts.' This sends him to *cognitive processing itself.*

> "Because conceptualization resides in cognitive processing, our ultimate objective must be to characterize the types of cognitive events whose occurrence constitutes a given mental experience." (p. 2)

Langacker broadly interprets 'conceptualization' as encompassing "novel conceptions as well as fixed concepts; sensory, kinesthetic, and emotive experience." He begins with the sensory-based level of representation. He also includes recognition of 'contexts' (social, physical, linguistic, etc.). This brings in the abstract representations at higher logical levels. He then adds other qualifications: *entrenchment* to refer to the habitual and solidified concepts that have become fixed in a community, *cognitive salience* to refer to differing degrees of importance, *semantic structures* or domains that a conceptualizer uses, *extensions and elaborations* to refer to new and novel uses of concepts, and *network* to identify that we experience thoughts within matrixes and hierarchies of concepts.

This use of Cognitive Grammar utilizes the work of Rosch and Lakoff in distinguishing traditional categories from prototype category theory. As a result, we are enabled to 'think' in degrees of prototype and use a highest-level schema or a schema that does not fit the prototype. Thinking utilizes various cognitive domains in order to 'make sense of' something as it creates meaning. Such domains can refer to any sort of conceptualization: a perceptual experience, a concept, a conceptual complex, an elaborate knowledge system, etc. As we use such domains, we generate various 'cognitive routines' for ourselves and by these we construct our models of the world.

These newer Cognitive linguistic models highlight the *representational value* of concepts in a way that the old transformational grammar did not. In these models, our grammatical expressions reflect our cognitive processing—the entities and processes that we imagine and symbolize, how we profile figures up against various backgrounds, what stands out saliently for us, the trajectors in our language that move through this 'grammar space' to various landmarks, etc.

They also provide a construct of logical levels as they posit hierarchies of conceptual complexity. We used to use 'deep structure' to conceptually posit an underlying level of neuro-linguistic mapping. Now the new cognitive grammars posit cognitive domains and network of domains arranged in hierarchies. A person goes to these over-arching contexts (domains) to 'get' their fuller model of the world that only shows up in abbreviated form in their everyday expressions.

Appendix B

The 'Is' Biz

Originally I wrote *The Secrets of Magic* in E-Prime. Lots of people didn't like that. I wrote four other books using the extensional device of *E-Prime,* even more people did not like that. Why? Without question, part of it was due to my inexperience in writing *English* without using the 'to be' verbs. Such writing made many sentences jarring, unclean, and contrived. Yet some of it was also do to the awkwardness of language without the 'is' verbs.

I described E-prime briefly under 'Identifications,' in Chapter 12. This refers to English-*primed* of the 'to be' verb family of passive verbs (is, am, are, was, were, be, being, been). Invented by D. David Bourland, Jr. and popularized by Bourland and Paul Dennithorne Johnston in *To Be or Not: An E-Prime Anthology* (now three volumes), E-Prime and E-Choice empowers people not to fall into the 'is' traps of language.

The 'is' traps? Yes, Alfred Korzybski (1941/1994) warned that the *'is' of identity* and the *'is' of predication* present two dangerous linguistic and semantic constructions that map false-to-fact conclusions. The first has to do with identity—how we identify a thing or what we identify ourselves with and the second with attribution, how we frequently project our 'stuff' onto others or onto things without realizing it.

Identity as 'sameness in all respects,' does not even exist. It can't. At the sub-microscopic level, everything involves a 'dance of electrons' always moving, changing, and becoming. So no thing can ever 'stay the same' even with itself. So nothing 'is' in any static, permanent, unchanging way. Since everything continually changes, nothing 'is.' So to speak and use 'is' mis-speaks, mis-evaluates, and mis-maps reality. To say, "She is lazy," "That is a stupid statement," falsely maps reality. Korzybski argued that unsanity and insanity ultimately lie in *identifications.*

Predication refers to 'asserting' something. So to say, "This is good," "That flower is red," "He is really stupid!" creates a language structure which implies that something 'out there' contains these qualities of 'goodness,' 'redness,' and 'stupidity.' The 'is' suggests that such things exist *independent of the speaker's experience*. Not so. Our descriptions speak primarily about our internal experience indicating our judgments and values. More accurately we could have said, "I evaluate as good this or that," "I see that flower as red," "I think of him as suffering from stupidity!"

Making 'Is' statements falsely distracts, confuses logical levels, and subtly leads us to think that such value judgments exist outside our skin in the world 'objectively.' Wrong again. The evaluations (good, red, stupid) function as definitions and interpretations in the speaker's mind.

The 'to be' verbs dangerously presuppose that 'things' (actually events or processes) stay the same. This is not so! These verbs invite us to create mental representations of fixedness so that we begin to set the world in concrete and to live in 'a frozen universe.' These verbs code the dynamic nature of processes statically. "Life is tough." "I am no good at math."

Do these statements not sound definitive? Absolute? "That's just the way it is!" Bourland calls 'is,' 'am,' and 'are,' etc., *'the deity mode.'* "The fact is that this work is no good!" Such words carry a sense of completeness, finality, and time-independence. Yet discerning the difference between the map and the territory tells us these phenomena exist on different logical levels. Using E-Prime (or E-Choice) reduces slipping in groundless authoritarian statements which only closes minds or invites arguments.

If we confuse the language we use in describing reality (our map) with reality (the territory), then we *identify* differing things. And that makes for unsanity. *There 'is' no is.* 'Is' non-references. It points to nothing in reality. It operates entirely as an irrational construction of the human mind. Its use leads to semantic misevaluations.

Conversely, writing, thinking, and speaking in E-Prime contributes to *'consciousness of abstracting'* (conscious awareness) that we make maps of the world which inherently differ from the world. E-Prime enables us to think and speak with more clarity and precision as it forces us to take first-person. This reduces the passive verb tense ("It was done." "Mistakes were made."). It restores speakers to statements, thereby contextualizing statements. E-Prime, by raising consciousness of abstracting, thereby enables us to index language. Now I realize that the person I met last week, $\text{Person}_{\text{last week}}$, 'is' not equal in all respects to the person that now stands before me, $\text{Person}_{\text{this week}}$. This assists me in making critical and valuable distinctions.

E-Choice differs from E-Prime. It does not take such a radical view. Thus, it allows one to use the *'is' of existence* (e.g. "Where is your office?" "It is on 7th Street at Orchard Avenue."), the *auxiliary 'is'* (e.g. "He is coming next week.") and the *'is' of name,* (e.g. "What is your name?" "It is Michael." "My name is Bob.").

Appendix C

Meta-Model Exercises

Use the following exercises to train your intuitions about the Meta-Model distinctions and questions.

Meta-Model Practice

1) Ask one person to think about an area of life wherein you experience a limitation of some sort and describe it.

2) Designate one person as *recorder* to keep track.

3) After the first person shares for 3 minutes, the others *meta-model* the statements *only* using Meta-Model questions. Especially inquire about nominalizations, cause—effect statements, and complex equivalences.

4) Afterwards use the *record* to check the distinctions identified, the questions used, the resulting response, and the effect.

Beginning Meta-modeling

1) Make a list of 6 to 12 examples of each of the following: deletions, comparative deletions, unspecified nouns, unspecified verbs, and nominalizations.

2) When ready, take turns delivering the ill-formed statements to the others letting the group practice *meta-modeling*.

3) Debrief after each speaker about what questions seemed most effective in gathering the highest quality information and effecting positive change.

More Advanced Meta-modeling

1) Make a list of 6 to 12 examples of mind-reading, complex equivalences, modal operators, cause—effect statements, and nominalizations.

2) When ready, take turns delivering the ill-formed statements to the others letting the group practice *meta-modeling* these statements.

3) Debrief after each speaker to determine what questions seemed most effective.

Finding and Exposing Psychological 'Can'ts.'

1) Complete the following *sentence stems* with a list of 6 to 12 responses:

   "I can't stand ..."

   "What really gets me and rattles my cage is ..."

   "I feel most unresourceful when ..."

2) Take turns reading the responses. For example, "I can't stand it when someone talks to me with a harsh tonality."

3) Invite group members to respond with appropriate *meta-modeling challenges*. For example, "What stops you from standing the other person's harsh tonality?" "What would happen if you did 'stand' that person's unpleasant tonality?"

Playing with Modals

1) Take turns thinking about some area in life in which you tell yourself that you 'have to' or 'must' do something. What do you specifically say? Or how do you use these words when communicating to someone else?

2) After presenting the information, let the group members take turns *meta-modeling* the person by shifting to other modal operators. For example, "And what would it feel like (seem like, be like) for you if you said, 'and I *get to*?'"

3) After you have playfully shifted the *modal operators*, reflect on how playing with them shifted your sense of your *modus operandi* in the world if you used them.

Playing with Causation

1) Construct a list of *causation words* and fit them into a hierarchy that moves from "0" causation (chance, chaos, random) up the scale to more and more direct causation so that at "100" you have such conceptual terminology as "determines," "makes," "causes," etc. Use a sheet of paper with a Vertical Line so that the bottom represents "0" and the top represents "100."

2) Take turns, inviting each other to make a cause—effect statement that creates a limitation. For example, "When my wife asks me to do some chore around the house, I feel manipulated."

3) First *reformulate* the statement so that it has a cause—effect format. For example, "So her asking *makes* you feel manipulated?"

4) Respond with *meta-modeling* questions to challenge the speaker to try on more or less intense causation words. For example, "How would it feel to you if her asking *invited* you to feel that way—knowing that you can always accept or reject the invitation?" "How would it feel if her asking *suggested* manipulation?"

5) Continue experiencing different levels of causation terms as each person takes a turn. Then reflect on what worked best and what had the least impact.

Meta-modeling Complex Equivalence

1) Present some complex equivalence that doesn't serve you well in life. For example, "When I think about someone talking to me and pointing at me with their index finger, I feel put down or scolded."

2) First confirm the complex equivalence. For example, "So, for you, a pointing index finger equals the internal state of feeling put down or scolded?"

3) Present the statement to each member to let each *meta-model* it and present an alternative meaning (a reframe). For example, "How would you like it (how would you feel) if you thought about the pointing finger meaning that the other has an unconscious 'schoolmarm anchor'?"

4) Play around with alternative meanings until the person finds one that he or she finds resourceful and useful.

Meta-modeling Complex Equivalence (Part II)

1) Present some complex equivalence that doesn't serve you well in life. For example, "When I think about someone talking to me and pointing at me with their index finger, I feel put down or scolded."

2) First confirm the complex equivalence. For example, "So, for you, a pointing index finger equals the internal state of feeling put down or scolded?"

3) Invite the speaker to teach the group *how to do this constructive skill.* "If I took your place for a day so that you get a day off from this, how would I do this? What pictures, sounds, words, etc. would I use—their quality, nature, order, etc. so that I could 'run my brain' in this way?"

4) De-construct the *strategy* of the complex equivalence until all feel satisfied that they have all the necessary ingredients for it.

Then, taking turns, offer shifts and alterations in the strategy that will disrupt it.

Meta-modeling Empowering States

1) Describe a resource and/or resourceful state that you would like to have or to have more of (e.g. confidence, pose, self-affirmation, enthusiasm, love, energy, etc.). Then describe this resource fully.

2) As the person offers their map of the resource, meta-model him or her to invite a richer and fuller map of the experience. Continue until the person confirms that richer map.

3) As one of the members kinesthetically *anchors* this resourceful state, ask for an *auditory digital term* that summarizes it—"Confidence," "joy," "calmness," etc. Anchor repeatedly saying the term at the peak of the experience until just the word anchors it.

Running the Operational Levels on the Meta-Model

1) Read the following list of statements to your group and brainstorm to explore the Meta-Model violations that you find in it. List them.

2) Identify the highest level Meta-Model distinction that provides the most useful information or that provides the most leverage for change.

You always talk as though you're mad.
It's impossible for me to trust people.
My brother thinks our parents were abusive.
Everybody knows that you can't change a bureaucracy.
Communication is really hard for me.
Running away doesn't help.
I laughed at the irritating man.
Why do you always bring up such stupid examples?
Self-righteous people just burn me up.
The over-whelming price of food disturbs me.

Distinguishing Cause—Effect and Complex Equivalences

1) Work through the following list together as a group, determining which of the following statements you would classify as a C—E or as a Ceq.

   I know he loves me when he touches me.
   It makes me angry when my husband looks at me like that.
   If you really loved me, you'd call when you're going to be late.
   I know you understand me when you talk to me.
   You don't appreciate me anymore. You don't kiss me when you leave for work.
   Turning in your reports on time will let me know that you're truly a responsible person.
   My partner's pessimistic attitude has caused our recent financial slump.
   I want to stay here longer, but I know you'll get angry at me if I do.
   My depression came upon me because my husband constantly criticized my body.
   Your nagging has given me another headache.

Visiting the Land of Nominalizations

1) Identify the nominalizations that you find in the following statements.

   People always push me around.
   Nobody pays any attention to anything I say.
   I like friendly dogs.
   I heard my mother in law yesterday gossiping about the neighbors.
   One should always respect the feelings of others.
   It's painful for us to see her like this, you know.
   Let's not get bogged down in details.
   There's a certain feeling in the room.
   Everybody feels that way sometimes.

Finding Behavioral Complex Equivalences

1) Decide on two or three Complex Equivalences that you want to play with, and find the *behavioral equivalents*. This will enable you to practice eliciting and feeding back distinctions around the Meta-Model distinction of Complex Equivalences. For example: love, trust, respect, confidence, ferociousness, etc.

2) Work with each person asking, "How do you know when you *trust* someone? What does *trusting* mean for you in terms of see-hear-feel terms? How do you recognize *trust*?"

3) As each person presents his or her *behavioral equivalents* of trust, let another member adopt and run this behavior and feed it back until the person feels satisfied with the behavioral equivalents. "Yes, that looks like, sounds like, and feels like *trust*."

Fuzzification and Meta-modeling Battling

1) In groups of 3 or 4, create the most convoluted set of sentences that contains *all* of the Meta-Model violations. Robert McCrory prepared the following one, published in *Anchor Point* many years ago: "People[1] are always[2] surprised[3] by learning[4] their efforts[9] equal the best[5] that others[6] believe must[7] be achieved[8] by experimentation[9, 10]."

   [1] Lack of Referential Index: Who or which people?
   [2] Universal Quantifier: Always?
   [3] Deletion: How specifically are they surprised?
   [4] Cause—Effect: How specifically does learning surprise people?
   [5] Comparative Deletion. Best as compared to what?
   [6] Mind-reading: How do you know what others believe?
   [7] Modal Operator of Necessity: What if achieved by another method?
   [8] Unspecified verb: How specifically achieved?
   [9] Nominalization: experimentation achieves?
   [10] Lost Performative: Entire sentence; according to whom?

2) Once you have a list of 5 to 10 really good convoluted super-fluffy statements, each group may enter into the Battle of the Meta-Modelers: presenting a line and recording the amount of time it takes for the second team to identify all of the violations. After so many rounds (e.g. 5 each), the team with the lowest 'time' wins.

Extended Meta-Model Exercises

Identification Exposure Exercise: "Who Are You—Apart from Are."

1. Introduce yourselves to each other for 3 to 4 minutes—presenting the kind of information you typically present as you disclose yourself. The only constraint: *the others will not allow you to use any of the 'is' verbs.*

2. Observing persons should listen for any of the 'to be' verbs:

   is, am, are, be, being, been, was, were, and contractions

3. 'Beep' the speaker each time he or she uses an 'is' verb. Totally disallow the *'is' of identity* and the *'is' of predication*—while permitting the auxiliary 'is' or the 'is' of existence.

4. Switch so each person gets a 4-minute presentation.

Identity Statements in Complex Equivalences

1. Experiencer presents a complex equivalence statement about self that he or she has found limiting and unenhancing.

   Examples: "I am a failure." "I'm just not a math student."

2. Responders take turns offering meta-modeling challenges (Ceq., Id., C—E., etc.) to loosen up the belief statement

3. After each round, invite the experiencer to offer a new self-statement that more empoweringly provides a better map.

Continue until the experiencer feels satisfied with the new mapping.

Finding the Multiordinal Words of Life

1. Each person takes turns describing a very positive experience of learning, growth, insight, personal development.

2. Listeners write down as many nominalizations as they can hear and identify.

3. Afterwards compare lists and run the tests for multiordinality:

   At what level or in what context does this term apply?
   Can we apply this term to itself?

4. Share with each other the level of specificity or ambiguousness that you experienced with the term.

Static Word Identification—Recovering 'Process'

1. Relate to the others a negative emotional experience that you have experienced at some time in your life—or that you could experience. Describe what it meant to you, how you felt, etc. Do so for 4 minutes.

2. Listeners write down as many nominalizations as possible.

3. Debrief by comparing lists and running the tests for multiordinality

   At what level or in what context does this term apply?
   Can we apply this term to itself?

4. Explore together which multiordinal word may have been turned into a *static word (sw)* thereby stopping the process world and creating a frozen universe of pain. Offer responses for inviting the person to remap with more process in his or her model of the world.

The Unsanity Showdown

1. Brainstorm together to generate a list of 10 examples of the following patterns that create limitations and problems:

   a) Identity statements
   b) Either/or statements
   c) Personalizing
   d) Metaphoring

2. Two groups of 3 join together so that Group A match off with Group B, etc. Spokesman for the first group presents the statements to the second group—inviting the second group to (1) identify the Meta-Model distinction and (2) to meta-model it with an appropriate response.

Value Elicitation Exercise

1. Each person makes a list of responses to the following statement.

   I hold X valuable and significant in personal relationships.

   X: ______________________________

   ____

   I hold X valuable and significant in work and career.

   X: ______________________________

   ____

   I hold X valuable and significant in parenting.

   X: ______________________________

   ____

   I hold X valuable and significant in communication.

   X: ______________________________

   ____

2. With one experiencer in the group, explore and fully identify the *behavioral equivalences* of his or her values. Translate back down into extensional language—*What specifically would you see, hear, feel, etc. that would convey to you this X?*

3. Pace the person's values back to him or her as you communicate the following message:

   As you learn these Meta-Model distinctions and responses and practice them over the next few weeks and months, it will give you more X in your personal relationships, career, parenting, etc.

Appendix D

The Meta-Levels of the Meta-Model

Person A	Person B
Structure	**Challenging the Assumptive Structure**
Metaphor Presuppositions (Ps) Multiordinality (M) Identification (Id)	The Assumptive Frames Map-Territory Confusions
Distortion	**Challenging Distortions**
Mind-Reading Complex Equivalences Nominalizations Cause—Effect Lost Performatives Delusional Verbal Splits Pseudo-Words Personalizing Static Words	Specifying the knowledge source Specifying logical level confusions Specifying equations Specifying causation, syntax, order Specifying referents Hyphenating
Generalization	**Challenging Generalizations**
Universal Quantifiers Model Operators Either/Or Phrases Over/Under Defined Terms	Challenging the Allness Challenging the Rules Challenging One-Valued Structures Challenging Two-Valued Structures Challenging the specificity
Evaluative Based Language **Deletion**	**Indexing Deleted References**
Deletions — Simple Del. Comparative/Superlative Del. Unspecified Relations Unspecified Referential Indices (Unspecified Nouns and Verbs) Unspecified Processes: Adverbs Modifying Verbs Adjectives Modifying Nouns	Specifying the what, when, who, where, how, etc. Representationally Tracking
Sensory-Based Language **Descriptive**	**Sensory-Based Language**
Person A	Person B

Appendix E

The New and Extended Meta-Model

Patterns/ Distinctions	Responses/ Questions	Predictions/ Results
1. Simple Deletions		
"They don't listen to me."	Who specifically doesn't listen to you?	Recover the Deletion
"People push me around."	Who specifically pushes you?	Recover the Ref. Index
2. Comparative & Superlative Deletions (Unspecified Relations)		
"She's a better person."	Better than whom? Better at what? Compared to whom, what? Given what criteria?	Recover the deleted standard, criteria, or belief
3. Unspecified Referential Indices (Unspecified Nouns & Verbs)		
"I am uncomfortable."	Uncomfortable in what way? Uncomfortable when?	Recover specific Qualities of the verb
"They don't listen to me."	Who specifically doesn't listen to you?	Recover the nouns
"He said that she was mean."	Who specifically said that? Whom did he say that you call mean? What did he mean by 'mean'?	Recover the individual meaning of the term
"People push me around."	Who specifically pushes you	Add details to the map
"I felt really manipulated."	Manipulated in what way and how?	
4. Unspecified Processes—Adverbs Modifying Verbs		
"Surprisingly, my father lied about his drinking."	How did you feel surprised about that? What surprised you about that?	Recover the process of the person's emotional state
"She slowly started to cry."	What indicated to you that her starting to cry occurred in a slow manner?	Enrich with details of the person's referent
5. Unspecified Processes—Adjectives Modifying Nouns		
"I don't like unclear people."	Unclear about what and in what way?	Recover the projection of the speaker's sense of feeling unclear
"The unhappy letter surprised me."	How, and in what way, did you feel unhappy?	
6. Universal Quantifiers		
"She never listens to me."	Never? She has never so much as listened you even a little bit?	Recover details to the extent of a process and counter-examples

Patterns/ Distinctions	Responses/ Questions	Predictions/ Results
7. Modal Operators (Operational Modes of Being)		
"I have to take care of her." "I can't tell him the truth."	What would happen if you did? What wouldn't happen if you didn't? "You have to or else what?"	Recover details of the process, also causes, effects, and outcomes.
8. Lost Performatives (Evaluative statement/s with the speaker deleted or unowned)		
"It's bad to be inconsistent."	Who evaluates it as bad? According to what standard? How do you determine this label of "badness?"	Recover the source of idea or belief—the map-maker, standards used
9. Nominalizations (Pseudo-Nouns that hide processes and actions)		
"Let's improve our communication."	Whose communicating do you mean? How would you like to communicate?	Recover the process and the characteristics left out
"What state did you wake up in this morning?"	How specifically did you feel, think, etc.? What behaviors, physiology, and internal representations make up this "state?"	Specify the verb and actions
10. Mind-Reading (Attributing knowledge of another's internal thoughts, feelings, motives)		
"You don't like me..."	How do you know I don't like you? What evidence leads you to that conclusion?	Recovers the source of the information—specifies how a person knows
11. Cause—Effect (Causational statements of relations between events, stimulus-response beliefs)		
"You make me sad."	How does my behavior cause you to respond with sad feelings? Counter Example: Do you always feel sad when I do this? How specifically does this work?	Recovers under standing of how a person views causation, sources, and origins—specifies beliefs about how world works
12. Complex Equivalences (Phenomena that differ which someone equates as the same)		
"She's always yelling at me, she doesn't like me."	How do you equate her yelling as meaning she doesn't like you? Can you recall a time when you yelled at someone that you liked?	Recover how the person equates or associates one thing with another. Ask for
"He's a loser when it comes to business; he just lacks business sense."	How do you know to equate his lack of success in business with his lack of sense about it?	counter-examples to the meaning equation. Could other factors play a role in this?

Patterns/ Distinctions	Responses/ Questions	Predictions/ Results
13. Presuppositions (Silent Assumptions, Unspoken Paradigms).		
"If my husband knew how much I suffered, he would not do that."	How do you suffer? In what way? About what? How do you know that your husband doesn't know this? Why do you assume that his intentions would shift if he knew Does your husband always use your emotional state to determine his responses?	Recover the person's assumptions, beliefs, and values that he or she just doesn't question. Specify processes, nouns, verbs, etc. left out.
14. Over/Under Defined Terms (O/U)		
"I married him because I thought he would make a good husband."	What behaviors and responses would make a "good" husband? What references do you use for the word "husband?	Recover the extensional facts about the terms used.
15. Delusional Verbal Splits (DVS)		
"My mind has nothing to do with this depression."	How can you have "mind" apart from "body" or "body" apart from "mind?"	Recover the split that someone has created verbally in language
16. Either/or Phrases (E-O)		
"If I don't make this relationship work, it proves my incompetence."	So you have no other alternative except total success or failure? You can't imagine any intermediate steps or stages?	Recover the continuum deleted by the E/O
17. Multiordinality (M)		
"What do you think of your self?"	On what level of abstraction do you refer to "self?" "Self" can have many meanings, depending on context & usage How do you mean it?	Recovers the level of different abstraction that the speaker operates from. Specifies the context and order
18. Static Words (SW)		
"Science says that..."	What science specifically? Science according to whose model or theory? Science at what time?	Recover the deleted details
19. Pseudo-words (PW)		
"And that makes him a failure."	What do you mean by "failure" as a word that modifies a person?	Challenge a map that uses words that have no real referent.
20. Identification (Id.)		
"He is a democrat."	How specifically does he identify with the term "democrat?" In what way?	Recovers the process of identification or prediction.
"She is a jerk."	Upon what basis do you evaluate her using the term "jerk?"	Invites one to create new generalizations.

Patterns/ Distinctions	Responses/ Questions	Predictions/ Results
21. Personalizing (Per.) "He does that just to irritate me."	How do you know his intentions? How do you know to take these actions in a personal way?	Challenges the process of personalizing.
22. Metaphors (Met) "That reminds me of the time when Uncle John..."	How does this story relate to the point you want to make?	Recover the isomorphic relationship between the story and the person's concepts.

Bibliography

Bacon, Francis. (1620). *Instauratio Magna. Novum Organum.* London: John Bill Publishing.

Bandler, Richard and John Grinder. (1975). *The Structure of Magic, Volume I: A Book About Language and Therapy.* Palo Alto, CA: Science & Behavior Books.

Bandler, Richard and John Grinder. (1976). *The Structure of Magic, Volume II.* Palo Alto, CA: Science & Behavior Books.

Bandler, Richard and John Grinder. (1979). *Frogs into Princes: Neuro-Linguistic Programming.* Moab, UT: Real People Press.

Bandler, Richard and John Grinder. (1982). *Reframing: Neuro-Linguistic Programming and the Transformation of Meaning.* Moab, UT: Real People Press.

Bandler, Richard. (1985). *Magic in Action.* Moab, UT: Real People Press.

Bandler, Richard. (1985). *Using Your Brain for a Change: Neuro-Linguistic Programming.* Moab, UT: Real People Press.

Bandler, Richard. (1987). *Paranoid Schizophrenia, Parts I & II.* Videotape. Boulder, CO: NLP Comprehensive.

Bartlett, F.C. (1932). *Remembering: An Experimental and Social Study.* Cambridge, England: Cambridge University Press.

Bateson, Gregory. (1972). *Steps to an Ecology of Mind.* New York: Ballantine.

Bateson, Gregory. (1979). *Mind and Nature: A Necessary Unity.* New York: Ballantine.

Beck, A.T. (1976). *Cognitive Therapy and the Emotional Disorders.* New York: International University Press.

Bodenhamer, Bobby G. and L. Michael Hall (1997). *Time-Lining: Patterns For Adventuring In "Time."* Wales, UK: The Anglo American Books Company.

Bourland, Jr., David. D., Paul Dennithorne Johnston and Jeremy Klein. (1994). *More E-Prime: To Be or Not* (II). Concord, CA: International Society for General Semantics.

Carroll, John B. (Ed.) (1956). *Language, Thought, and Reality: Selected Writings of Benjamin Lee Whorf.* New York: Wiley.

Chomsky, Noam. (1957). *Syntactic Structures.* The Hague: Mouton Publishers.

Chomsky, Noam. (1965). *Aspects of the Theory of Syntax.* Cambridge, MA: MIT Press.

Chong, Dennis and Jennifer Chong. (1991). *Don't Ask Why?!: A Book About the Structure of Blame, Bad Communication, Miscommunication.* Oakville, Ontario, Canada: C-Jade Publishing.

Chong, Dennis and Jennifer Chong. (1993). *Power and Elegance in Communication: People, Paradigms, and Paradoxes.* Oakville, Ontario, Canada: C-Jade Publishing.

Chong, Dennis and Jennifer Chong. (1994). *The Knife Without Pain: Communication and Hypnosis.* Oakville, Ontario, Canada: C-Jade Publishing.

de Shazer, Steve. (1988). *Clues: Investigating Solutions in Brief Therapy.* New York: Norton.

de Shazer, Steve. (1991). *Putting Difference to Work.* New York: Norton.

de Shazer, Steve. (1994). *Words were Originally Magic.* New York: Norton.

Dilts, Robert. (1983a). *Applications of Neuro-Linguistic Programming.* Cupertino, CA: Meta Publications.

Dilts, Robert B. (1983b). *Roots of Neuro-Linguistic Programming.* Cupertino, CA: Meta Publications.

Dilts, Robert, John Grinder, Richard Bandler, Judith DeLozier. (1980). *Neuro-Linguistic Programming, Volume I: The Study of the Structure of Subjective Experience.* Cupertino, CA: Meta Publications.

Efran, J.S. Lukens, M.D., and R.J. Lukens. (1990). *Language Structure and Change.* New York: Norton.

Ellis, Albert. (1962). *Reason and Emotion in Psychotherapy.* New York: Lyle Stuart.

Ellis, Albert. (1973). *Humanistic Psychotherapy: The Rational-Emotive Approach.* New York: Julian Press.

Ellis, Albert and Robert A Harper. (1976). *A New Guide to Rational Living.* Englewood Cliffs, NJ: Prentice-Hall, Inc.

Frankl, V.E. (1957/1984). *Man's Search for Meaning: An Introduction to Logotherapy* (3rd ed.). New York: Simon & Schuster.

Freud, Sigmund. (1915–1917). *The Complete Introductory Lectures on Psychoanalysis* (J. Stachey, Ed. & Trans.). *The Standard Edition of the Complete Psychological Works of Sigmund Freud* (Vol. 15 & 16). New York: Norton.

Gilliland, Burl E., Richard K. James, and James T. Bowman. (1989). *Theories and Strategies in Counseling and Psychology* (2nd ed.). NJ: Prentice Hall.

Gordon, David. (1978). *Therapeutic Metaphors: Helping Others Through the Looking Glass.* Cupertino, CA: Meta Publications.

Grinder, John and Judith DeLozier. (1987). *Turtles All the Way Down: Prerequisites to Personal Genius.* Scotts Valley, CA: Grinder & Associates.

Gross, Maurice. (1979). On The Failure of Generative Grammar. *Language, Vol. 55,* No. 4, pp. 859–885. Baltimore: Linguistic Society of America.

Hall, L. Michael (1996). *Becoming a Ferocious Presenter.* Grand Jct. CO: ET Publications.

Hall, L. Michael (1996d). *Languaging: The Linguistics of Psychotherapy.* Grand Jct. CO: ET Publications.

Hall, L. Michael (1996/2000). *The Spirit of NLP: The Process, Meaning, And Criteria For Mastering NLP.* Wales, UK: Crown House Publishing Limited.

Hall, L. Michael. (1997a). *Neuro-Linguistic Programming: Going Meta—Advance Modeling Using Meta-States & Logical Levels.* Grand Jct. CO: ET Publications.

Hall, L. Michael (2000). *Dragon Slaying: Dragons to Princes.* Grand Jct. CO: ET Publications. (2nd ed.).

Hall, L. Michael. (2000). *Frame Games: Persuasion Elegance.* Grand Jct. CO: Neuro-Semantics Publications.

Hall, L. Michael (2000). *Meta-States: Mastering the Higher Levels of Your Mind* (2nd ed.). Grand Junction, CO: Neuro-Semantics Publications.

Hall. L. Michael. (2000). *Secrets of Personal Mastery.* Wales, UK: Crown House Publishing Limited.

Harris, Randy Allen. (1993). *The Linguistic Wars.* NY: Oxford University Press.

Hayakawa, S.I. (1941/1980). *Language in Action.* New York: Harcourt, Brace, & Co.

Huxley, Aldous. (1954). *The Doors of Perception and Heaven and Hell.* NY: Harper & Row.

Jackendoff, Ray. (1994). *Patterns in the Mind: Language and Human Nature.* New York: Basic Books, HarperCollins Publishers.

Jacobson, Sid. (1989). *Meta-Cation. Volume II: New Improved Formulas for Thinking About Thinking.* Cupertino, CA: Meta Publications.

Johnson, Wendell. (1964/1989). *People in Quandaries: The Semantics of Personal Adjustment.* San Francisco, CA: International Society for General Semantics.

Kelly, George A. (1955). *The Psychology of Personal Constructs.* New York: Norton.

Korzybski, Alfred. (1933/1994). *Science and Sanity: An Introduction to Non-Aristotelian Systems and General Semantics* (5th ed.). Lakeville, CN: International Non-Aristotelian Library Publishing Co.

Korzybski, Alfred. (1949). Fate and Freedom. In Irving, J. Lee (Ed.). *The Language of Wisdom and Folly.* New York: Harper & Brothers.

Korzybski, A. (1990). *Collected Writings: 0291-0591.* Kendig, M. and C.S. Read (Eds.). Englewood, NJ: Institute of General Semantics.

Kosko, Bart. (1993). *Fuzzy Thinking: The New Science of Fuzzy Logic.* NY: Flamingo, HarperCollins.

Lakoff, George. (1987). *Women, Fire, and Dangerous Things: What Categories Reveal about the Mind.* Chicago: The University of Chicago Press.

Lakoff, George and Mark Johnson. (1980). *Metaphors We Live By.* Chicago: The University of Chicago Press.

Lakoff, George and Mark Johnson. (1999). *Philosophy in the Flesh: The Embodied Mind and its Challenge to Western Thought.* NY: Basic Books.

Langacker, Ronald. (1987). *Foundations of Cognitive Grammar,* Vol. 1. Stanford, CA: Stanford University Press.

Langacker, Ronald W. (1991). *Concept, Image and Symbol: The Cognitive Basis of Grammar.* New York: Mouton de Gruyter.

Lankton, Stephen R. (1980). *Practical Magic: A Translation of Basic NLP into Clinical Psychotherapy.* Capitola, CA: Meta Publications.

Lawley, James and Penny Thompkins. (2000). *Metaphors in Mind: Transformation through Symbolic Modelling.* London: The Developing Company Press.

Lewis, A. Byron and R. Frank Pucelik. (1982). *Magic Demystified: A Pragmatic Guide to Communication and Change.* Lake Oswego, OR: Metamorphous Press.

Lisnek, Paul M. (1996). *Winning the Mind Game: Negotiating in Business and Life.* Capitola, CA: Meta Publications.

Mandler, George and William Kessen. (1975). *The Language of Psychology.* NY: Robert E. Krieger Publishing Co.

McClendon, Terrence L. (1989). *The Wild Days: NLP 1972 to 1981.* Cupertino, CA: Meta Publications.

McLauchlin, Larry. (1993). *Advanced Language Patterns Mastery.* Calgary, Alberta, Canada: Leading Edge Communications.

McMaster, Michael and John Grinder. (1983/1993). *Precision: A New Approach to Communication—How to Get the Information You Need to Get Results.* Scotts Valley, CA: Grinder, Delozier & Associates.

Miller, George. (1956). "The Magical Number Seven, Plus or Minus Two: Some Limits on our Capacity to Process Information." *Psychological Review, 63,* 81–97.

O'Connor, Joseph and John Seymour. (1990). *Introducing Neuro-Linguistic Programming: The New Psychology of Personal Excellence.* Bodmin, Cornwall, UK: Hartnolls Ltd.

Perls, Fritz. (1973). *The Gestalt Approach and Eye witness to Therapy.* Palo Alto, CA: Science and Behavior Books, Inc.

Pfalzgraf, Rene. (1989). "Meta-Model III." Rapporter. May, 1989. Cottonwood, AZ.

Piaget, J. and B. Inhelder. (1956). *The Child's Conception of Space.* London, UK: Routledge & Kegan Paul.

Robbins, Anthony (1989). *Unlimited Power: The New Science of Personal Achievement.* NY: Simon & Schuster.

Robbins, Anthony (1991). *Awaken the Giant Within: How to Take Immediate Control of your Mental, Emotional, Physical, & Financial destiny!* NY: Simon & Schuster.

Satir, Virginia. (1972). *Peoplemaking.* Palo Alto, CA: Science and Behavior Books, Inc.

Spitzer, Robert S. (1992). "Virginia Satir and Origins of NLP." *Anchor Point Magazine* (July, 1992), pp. 40–44. Franktown, CO: Cahill Mountain Press.

Vaihinger, H. (1924). *The Philosophy of 'As If.' A System of the Theoretical, Practical, and Religious Fictions of Mankind.* (Translated by C.K. Ogden). New York: Harcourt, Brace.

Wilber, Ken. (1983). *Eye to Eye: The Quest for the New Paradigm.* Garden City, New York: Anchor Press/Doubleday.

Yeager, Joseph. (1985). *Thinking about Thinking with NLP.* Cupertino, CA: Meta Publications.

Zink, Nelson and Joseph Munshaw. (1995). "Collapsing Generalizations and the Other Half of NLP." *NLP World* (Vol. 3. No. 1). Switzerland.

The Author

L. Michael Hall, Ph.D.
P.O. Box 9231
Grand Jct. Co. 81501. USA
(970) 523-7877
Michael@neurosemantics.com
NLPMetaStates@OnLineCol.com

L. Michael Hall is an entrepreneur who lives in the Rocky Mountains in Colorado. He worked as a psychologist in private psychotherapeutic practice for two decades, investor in real estate, prolific author, international trainer, and co-developer of the Society of Neuro-Semantics. After studying NLP with Richard Bandler and writing some books for him, Michael began turning out dozens of NLP books.

Dr. Hall's doctorate is in Cognitive-Behavioral Psychology with an emphasis in psycho-linguistics. He wrote his doctoral dissertation on the *languaging* of four psychotherapies (NLP, RET, Reality Therapy, Logotherapy) using the formulations of General Semantics. In 1994, Michael developed the *Meta-States Model* while modeling *resilience* and presenting his findings at the International NLP Conference in Denver. That discovery led to hundreds of articles, more than a dozen books, and international trainings.

Meta-States: Managing the higher states of your mind (Self-Reflexiveness) (2000 2nd edition)

Dragon Slaying: Dragons to Princes (2000, 2nd edition)

The Spirit of NLP: The Process, Meaning & Criteria for Mastering NLP (1996, 2000)

Languaging: The Linguistics of Psychotherapy (1996)

Patterns For "Renewing the Mind" (with Dr. Bodenhamer) (1997)

Time-Lining: Patterns Foe Adventuring in "Time" (with Dr. Bodenhamer) (1997)

NLP: Going Meta—Advanced Modeling using Meta-Levels (1997)

Figuring Out People: Design Engineering With Meta-Programs (with Dr. Bodenhamer) (1997)

The Sourcebook of Magic (formerly, How to Do What When (with B. Belnap) (1999)

Mind Lines: Lines For Changing Minds (with Dr. Bodenhamer) (1997, 2000 3rd edition)

The Secrets of Magic: Communicational Magic for the 21st Century (1998)

Meta-States Journal, Patterns, Volume I, II, III (97, 98, 99)

The Structure of Excellence: Unmasking the Meta-Levels of Submodalities (with Bodenhamer) (1999)

Instant Relaxation (with D. Lederer) (1999)

Secrets of Personal Mastery (2000)

Frame Games: Persuasion Elegance (2000)

The Structure of Personality: Modeling "Personality" Using NLP and Neuro-Semantics (with Bodenhamer, Bolstad and Hamblett) (2001)

Games Business Experts Play (2002)

Games Thin People Play (2001)

Persuasion Games (2001)

Accelerated Motivation: Human Propulsion Systems (2001)

Neuro-Semantics (2002)

The Society of Neuro-Semantics®

The Meta-States model was developed in 1994 and has since given birth to the field of Neuro-Semantics. We have several websites that you can visit that will provide lots of information and free articles, patterns, etc. about the current developments in Meta-States, Frame Games, and much more. There also you will find out about Institutes of Neuro-Semantics around the world.

www.neurosemantics.com
www.learninstitute.com

Index

The Spirit of NLP
Revised Edition
The Process, Meaning And Criteria For Mastering NLP
L. Michael Hall, Ph.D.

This fully revised edition of ***The Spirit of NLP*** represents the core of a brilliant Richard Bandler master training. It also includes significant contributions from other master trainers, including Eric Robbie, Wyatt Woodsmall, Tad James, Christina Hall and the late Will McDonald. Providing a deeper understanding of the true genius of the co-developer of Neuro-Linguistic Programming, it includes mastery of the neurology of NLP, and developmental work associated with sleight of mouth patterns. Systematically tackling the areas of Programming, Linguistics and Neurology, ***The Spirit of NLP*** is ideal for all those wishing to update and expand their understanding of the subject, or wanting a fresh and exciting new perspective on NLP.

PAPER 352 PAGES ISBN: 1899836047

"No other book covers this breadth of NLP Master Practitioner material ... essential reading for all those who want to go beyond Practitioner level."—*Frank Daniels, NLP trainer.*

Secrets of Personal Mastery

Advanced Techniques for Accessing Your Higher Levels of Consciousness

L. Michael Hall, Ph.D.

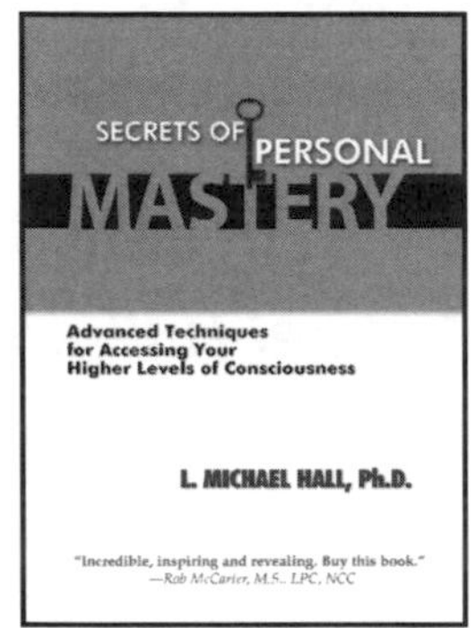

Secrets of Personal Mastery guides you through various Thought Experiments that work upon your 'executive' mind powers. As you partake in these processes you will enter into the higher management of your own mind at all its levels, and that will prepare you for the ultimate development of excellence—accessing your personal genius. In its exploration of 'personal mastery,' this book addresses:

- the mind and emotion
- the excellence of expertise
- the tragedy of complacency
- identity and existence
- madness and genius
- language and semantics
- procedures and magic
- the mind-muscle connection
- personal and interpersonal development.

PAPER 304 PAGES ISBN: 189983656X

"Incredible, inspiring and revealing. Buy this book."
—Rob McCarter MS, LPC, NCC.

Games Business Experts Play

L. Michael Hall, Ph.D.

Games Business Experts Play reveals the games business experts play in order to succeed—and the successful ways to play them. As you read this book you will learn to play games that work for you, and you will understand that successful game-playing involves changing your frame of mind—because it is only when you change your own frame, and replicate the frame of a business expert, that you too will become a consistently, habitually successful business person.

Analyzing the core components of successful game playing, ***Games Business Experts Play*** identifies:

- the name of each game (what is it? how does it work?)
- the rules of each game (who plays it? when is it played?)
- the cues of each game (what questions elicit the game? what are the triggers?)
- the payoff (what are the benefits?).

It then coaches you in games for personal empowerment, teaching you how to win at specific games that address: positioning yourself; making work meaningful and satisfying; handling things; being your own best boss; adding value to the lives of others; resolving conflicts; inventing even better games.

Presenting unique insights into the games business experts play, this revelatory book applies powerful techniques from the sphere of Neuro-Linguistic Programming that will target your behavior and transform you into a brilliant player. An essential guide for all game players seeking inspiration, ***Games Business Experts Play*** delivers all the winning moves.

CLOTH 304 PAGES ISBN: 1899836721

"Read this book. This one will completely revolutionize business literature."
—Sean Kearney, *Executive Director, AT & T Broadband, Learning and Development, Denver, Colorado.*

USA & Canada *orders to:*

American International Distribution Corporation
50 Winter Sport Lane, Williston, VT 05495, USA
www.crownhouse.co.uk

UK & Rest of World *orders to:*

The Anglo American Book Company Ltd.
Crown Buildings, Bancyfelin, Carmarthen, Wales SA33 5ND
Tel: +44 (0)1267 211880/211886, Fax: +44 (0)1267 211882
E-mail: books@anglo-american.co.uk
www.anglo-american.co.uk

Australasia *orders to:*

Footprint Books Pty Ltd
101 McCarrs Creek Road, PO Box 418, Church Point
Sydney NSW 2105, Australia
Tel: +61 2 9997 3973, Fax: +61 2 9997 3185
E-mail: footprintbooks@ozmail.com.au